HORACE PLUNKETT:
CO-OPERATION AND POLITICS,
AN IRISH BIOGRAPHY

HORACE PLUNKETT:
CO-OPERATION AND POLITICS,
AN IRISH BIOGRAPHY

Trevor West

John,

With Every Good Wish

Trevor

1986
COLIN SMYTHE
Gerrards Cross, Bucks.

THE CATHOLIC UNIVERSITY
OF AMERICA PRESS
WASHINGTON, D.C.

First published in 1986 by Colin Smythe Limited,
Gerrards Cross, Buckinghamshire

British Library Cataloguing in Publication Data

West, Trevor
    Horace Plunkett : co-operation and politics,
    an Irish biography.
    1. Plunkett, Horace 2. Agriculture—Ireland—
    Biography
    I. Title
    630'.92'4   S417.P/
    ISBN 0-86140-235-9

First published in the United States of America
by the Catholic University of America Press
Washington DC 20064

Library of Congress Cataloging in Publication Data

West, Trevor.
    Horace Plunkett : co-operation and politics.

    Bibliography: p.
    Includes index.
    1. Plunkett, Horace Curzon, Sir, 1854–1932.
    2. Legislators—Ireland—Biography.
    3. Agriculture, Cooperative—Ireland—Biography.
    4. Ireland—Politics and government—1837–1901.
    5. Ireland—Politics and government—20th
    century. 6. Ireland—Rural conditions.
    I. Title.
    DA965.P6W47 1986   941.5081'092'4   [B]   86-12988
    ISBN 0-8132-0630-8

Typeset by Action Typesetting, Gloucester
Printed in Great Britain by
Billing & Sons Limited, Worcester

A tribute to the idealism of
those who pioneered with Plunkett:
Lord Monteagle, R. A. Anderson,
Father Tom Finlay, AE and Harold Barbour.

CONTENTS

ILLUSTRATIONS

PREFACE

Horace Plunkett's many-sided career, his work for co-operation and rural reform, his attempts to promote understanding between unionists and nationalists, between Ireland and England, and between Europe and America, all attracted considerable comment, both benevolent and critical, during his lifespan from 1854 to 1932.

The first attempt at a biographical study was made by Edward Lysaght (afterwards MacLysaght) in *Horace Plunkett and his Place in the Irish Nation* (1916) but publication was ill-timed for the Easter Rising, which turned so much of Irish history on its head, intervened between the completion of the book and its appearance before the public. Several unsuccessful attempts were made to persuade Plunkett to write his autobiography. The Plunkett Foundation in Oxford contains just a couple of notebooks, compiled at the very end of his career, giving a tantalising glimpse of what that autobiography might have been. The author would surely have shown some more enthusiasm for his task had not the bulk of his papers been incinerated with Kilteragh during the Irish Civil War.

This important work was eventually undertaken by Margaret Digby who joined the Plunkett Foundation in 1927 and achieved a reputation as the leading writer on co-operation. Her fine biography, placing Plunkett firmly in an international context, based on his diaries and letters in the Plunkett Foundation, *Horace Plunkett, an Anglo-American-Irishman* (1949) includes an introduction by W. G. S. Adams (chief statistician in the DATI from 1905 to 1910 and later an influential figure in Lloyd George's cabinet secretariat) as well as an epilogue by Gerald Heard who was associated with Plunkett from 1919 until his death. Miss Digby's book stood alone until Patrick Bolger completed his wide ranging and informative study, *The Irish Co-operative Movement, its History and Development* (1977). Other useful sources for the history of the Irish co-operative movement in its early phase are Smith-Gordon and Staples, *Rural Reconstruction in Ireland, a*

Record of Co-operative Organisation (1917); Smith-Gordon and Cruise O'Brien, *Co-operation in Ireland* (1921); R. A. Anderson, *With Horace Plunkett in Ireland* (1935); C. C. Riddall, *Agricultural Co-operation in Ireland, the Story of a Struggle* (1950); James Johnston, *Agricultural Co-operation in Northern Ireland: a History of the Ulster Agricultural Organisation Society Limited, the First Forty Years* (1965); and, in a more modern vein, Cormac O'Gráda's article, 'The Beginnings of the Irish Creamery System, 1880-1914' (1977).

Other up-to-date assessments of Plunkett's ideals, and of his achievements in Ireland, include Daniel Hoctor's study, *The Department's Story, a History of the Department of Agriculture* (1971); the theses of Michael Clune, 'Horace Plunkett, the Origins and Development of the Department of Agriculture and Technical Instruction and the Political Context, 1895-1902' (1978) and of Carla Keating, 'Sir Horace Plunkett and Rural Reform, 1889-1914' (1984); a six-part centenary tribute by F. S. L. Lyons in the *Irish Times* (October, 1954) and articles by Lieut.-Gen. M. J. Costello, 'Farming Programme for Ireland' (1952); P. J. Meghen, 'Sir Horace Plunkett as an Administrator' (1966); J. J. Byrne, 'AE and Sir Horace Plunkett' in *The Shaping of Modern Ireland* (C. Cruise O'Brien ed., 1970); Paul L. Rempe, 'Sir Horace Plunkett and Irish Politics, 1890-1914' (1978); Cyril Erlich, 'Sir Horace Plunkett and Agricultural Reform' (1981); while Charles W. Holman, 'Sir Horace Plunkett's Co-operative Philosophy and Contribution to American Co-operation' (1937); and Clayton S. Ellsworth, 'Theodore Roosevelt's Country Life Commission' (1960), measure his considerable impact on American life and thought.

ACKNOWLEDGEMENTS

This book would not have been written without the generous encouragement, wise criticism, and unstinting support of many friends. The author particularly acknowledges his indebtedness to:

Mr. Leonard Abrahamson, Miss Elise Bayley, Dr. David Berman, Mr. Patrick Bolger, the late Mr. Michael Clune, Miss Saive Coffey, Prof. Lester Conner, Lieutenant General M. J. Costello, Prof. Gordon Davies, the late Dr. Margaret Digby, Lord and Lady Dunsany, the Countess of Fingall, Dr. Muriel Gahan, Dr. Andrew Gailey, the late Mr. George Gilmore, Prof. Gene Gressley, Prof. David Harkness, Mr. Maurice Henry, Mr. Sarsfield Hogan, Dr. John Kelly, Dr. Liam Kennedy, Prof. Brendan Kennelly, Prof. John Lukacs, Dr. Patrick Lynch, the late Dr. F. S. L. Lyons, Prof. Oliver MacDonagh, Mr. Seamus MacEoin, Dr. R. B. McDowell, Dr. Paul McVeigh, Dr. James Meenan, Mr. James Moloney, Mr. Ulick O'Connor, Mr. Florence O'Donoghue, Mr. Sean O'Luing, Dr. Diarmuid O'Mathúna, Mr. Edgar Parnell, Mr. James Pethica, the late Major George Ponsonby, Mr. William Ross, Prof. Yvette Sencer, Dr. A. T. Q. Stewart, Dr. W. E. Vaughan and Dr. L. Milton Woods; to the members of the Bank of Ireland Centre for Co-operative Studies in University College Cork; and to his colleagues in the Society for Co-operative Studies in Ireland.

The author also wishes to thank the staffs of the libraries and record offices in which he worked: Trinity College Dublin; the Plunkett Foundation, Oxford; the National Library of Ireland; the National Library of Scotland; the National Register of Archives (Scotland); the Irish Public Record Office; the Public Record Office of Northern Ireland; the Irish Department of Agriculture; the Irish Co-operative Organisation Society; the Ulster Agricultural Organisation Society; the Linenhall Library, Belfast; the Linen Industry Research Association, Lambeg; the American Heritage Center of the University of Wyoming; and the Oireachtas Library, Leinster House, Dublin.

Acknowledgements are due to Michael B. Yeats and Anne Yeats for permission to reproduce pictures by John Butler Yeats, and to the National Gallery of Ireland, the Hugh Lane Municipal Gallery of Dublin, and the Ulster Museum for permission to reproduce pictures in their collections. The relevant pictures are indicated by (NGI), (HLMG), and (UM) respectively. Acknowledgements are also due to the Director-General of ICOS for permission to reproduce the portraits of Horace Plunkett, R. A. Anderson and Lord Monteagle by Dermod O'Brien and to photograph the bust of Horace Plunkett in the Plunkett House, and to the Director and Trustees of the Plunkett Foundation for permission to make use of the Plunkett papers in their possession.

CHRONOLOGY

HORACE CURZON PLUNKETT 1854-1932

1854 Born on 24 October, the third son and sixth child of the sixteenth Baron Dunsany at Sherborne, Gloucestershire.

1858 Mother died.

1860 Family moved to Dunsany, Co. Meath.

1868-72 School at Eton.

1873-78 University at Oxford.

1878 Formed Dunsany Co-operative Society.

1879-89 Ranched in Wyoming during the spring and summer, spending the winters in Ireland.

1883 Randal, his eldest brother, died of tuberculosis. Lord Fingall, his cousin, married Elizabeth (Daisy) Burke of Galway.

1884 His brother-in-law, Chambré Ponsonby, died leaving him guardian of his four children.

1888 Published his first co-operative article *Co-operative Stores for Ireland*.

1889 Father died. Attended his first Annual Co-operative Congress at Ipswich. Launched his co-operative campaign in Ireland in September. Started a co-operative store in Doneraile, Co. Cork. The CWS established the first Irish co-operative creamery at Drumcollogher, Co. Limerick.

1890 R.A. Anderson and Father Finlay recruited.

1891 Founded his first co-operative creamery at Ballyhahill, Co. Limerick. RDS refused to support co-operative dairying. CDB established with Plunkett a member.

1892 Elected to represent South Dublin in July.

1893 Second Gladstone home rule bill defeated.

1894 IAOS formed on 18 April. 33 co-operative societies affiliated to IAOS, total turnover £150,000.

1895 *Irish Homestead* commenced publication in March. Re-elected for South Dublin in May. Recess Committee launched in August.

1896 Recess Committee reported in August.

1897 First Irish agriculture and industries bill withdrawn in favour of Irish local government bill. AE recruited. Sworn to Irish Privy Council. IAWS founded.

1898 *Daily Express* purchased. 243 co-operative societies affiliated to IAOS, total turnover £675,000.

1899 DATI bill passed and DATI established with Plunkett as vice-president.

1900 *Daily Express* sold to Lord Ardilaun in January. Defeated in South Dublin election in October. 477 co-operative societies affiliated to IAOS, total turnover £1 million.

1901 Defeated in Galway by-election in November.

1902 Fellowship of the Royal Society.

1903 Knighted.

1904 *Ireland in the New Century* published. 778 co-operative societies affiliated to IAOS, total turnover £1.5 million.

1905 Wyndham forced to resign as chief secretary for Ireland. Sinn Féin founded.

1906 Kilteragh completed. Honorary degree from Oxford.

1907 Forced to resign as vice-president of DATI. Digby committee of enquiry into the modus operandi of the DATI reported. 913 co-operative societies affiliated to IAOS, total turnover £2 million.

1908 *Noblesse Oblige* published. Honorary degree from Dublin. Publication of Rolleston letter. Withdrawal of DATI subvention to IAOS. Presented with the Plunkett House.

1909 Country Life Commission reported in USA. Roosevelt letter published. Honorary Fellowship of University College, Oxford.

1910 *The Rural Life Problem of the USA* published. The United Irishwomen founded.

1911 Erskine Childers published *The Framework of Home Rule*.

1913 IAOS obtains obtains annual grant from the Development Commissioners.

1914 Asquith-Redmond home rule bill passed. *A Better Way: an Appeal to Ulster not to Desert Ireland* published. War declared in August. Established link with Col. House. 1023 co-operative societies affilliated to IAOS, total turnover £3.7 million.

1916 Easter Rising in April. X-ray burns received in London in June.

1917 America declared war on 2 April. Elected chairman of the Irish Convention in July.

1918 Redmond died in March. Convention reported in April. *Home Rule and Conscription* published. Confidential report on Irish Convention concluded. Sinn Féin obliterates Nationalist Party in general election. Resigned from CDB in December.

1919 Commencement of hostilites in Anglo-Irish conflict. Irish Dominion League launched. First *Irish Statesman* commenced publication in June. Horace Plunkett Foundation endowed.

1920 Creameries attacked by military. *England's Irish Policy before and after the War* published. Home rule act passed and Northern Ireland government established. First *Irish Statesman* ceased publication in June.

1921 Compulsory closing of creameries by military. Anglo-Irish truce declared on 8 July. Anglo-Irish treaty signed on 7 December.

1922 Treaty ratified by Dáil in January.Civil war commenced with destruction of Four Courts in July. Erskine Childers executed in November. Plunkett nominated to the Irish Senate. UAOS established. IAOS obtains annual grant from Free State administration.

1923 Kilteragh mined and then burned at the end of January. Resigned Senate seat. *Irish Homestead* combined with the second *Irish Statesman* which commenced publication in September. The Crest House purchased in Weybridge.

1924 Lennox Robinson forced to resign as Carnegie Librarian. Co-operative Reference Library moved to Horace Plunkett Foundation, London.

1929 Learned to fly at 75 years of age.

1930 Second *Irish Statesman* ceased publication in April. Last visit to Ireland in August.

1932 Died in Weybridge on 26 March.

Abbreviations

APL	Anti-Partition League
CDB	Congested Districts Board
CWS	Co-operative Wholesale Society
DATI	Department of Agriculture and Technical Instruction
IAOS	Irish Agricultural Organisation Society
IAWS	Irish Agricultural Wholesale Society
IDL	Irish Dominion League
IRA	Irish Republican Army
RDS	Royal Dublin Society
UAOS	Ulster Agricultural Organisation Society
ULUA	Ulster Liberal Unionist Association

I

Meath and Wyoming

In May of 1881, a young Irish aristocrat making his way across America in search of health and fortune checked into a hotel in Omaha, Nebraska, registering simply as H. C. Plunkett, Ireland.[1] Just one year before, Charles Stewart Parnell, the 'uncrowned king' of nationalist Ireland had made his triumphal tour of North America telling of the work of the Land League and of English misgovernment of Ireland.

The League, founded by Michael Davitt in 1879, intertwined a great agrarian movement with the strands of Irish nationalism, campaigning on behalf of the tenants to wrest possession of their farms from the landlords. The League's activities were much publicised in the United States; Irish-American enthusiasm was channelled into support for the League; Land League committees were established in every state and considerable sums of money crossed the Atlantic in support of its campaign. Michael Davitt had spoken in Omaha some six months previously.[2] Now an alert reporter from the *Omaha Daily Bee*, recognizing Plunkett as springing from one of Ireland's great landed families and scenting a story, gave the young man his first political interview.

Appositely entitled 'A Son of Lord Dunsany on his Way to the West',[3] the article described Plunkett as 'about five feet, ten inches in height and well built, with a ruddy complexion, light hair and what might be called a spring crop of closely trimmed whiskers on his cheeks', going on to record that he possessed the 'deportment of a gentleman', an 'unprejudiced judgement' and a 'ready knowledge of Irish affairs'. He was reported as saying that landlords in the west of Ireland had been unjust to their tenants, that the Land League was supported by the majority of the people, that Parnell was the 'mastermind of the movement' and a man of 'invincible strength of character'. Acting as agent on his family estate, Plunkett had had no trouble in collecting rents from tenants all of whom were

1

members of the League but, he felt, a coercion act was
necessary as agitation had gone too far. Gladstone had just
introduced his second land bill giving tenants fair rent, fixed
tenure and free sale. This measure, he reckoned, would ruin
many landlords, driving capital and intelligence from the
country and, in the circumstances, it would be wise for those
affected to look out for opportunities in America.

The *Bee* report failed to please the young aristocrat,[4] for he
was neither a disciple of Parnell nor a supporter of the League.
But, bearing in mind the journalist's desire to please his editor,
the admission by a landlord of a link between the plight of
small farmers and the system of land tenure was revealing in
its frankness; constructive remarks on the subject of Parnell
went against Plunkett's ascendancy grain; while the interview
made it clear that his family were numbered among those
gentry who, as landlords, earned and deserved, the respect of
their tenants, and who, as men of learning, wealth and
experience, provided guidance and leadership for the
community.

Plunkett's social conscience had been stirred before he set out
for America. Then ten hectic years as a ranchman in Wyoming
opened up new horizons besides reinforcing his idealism; thus,
on his return home in 1889, he dedicated himself to raising
economic standards among the farmers besides improving the
quality of life in rural Ireland. But constitutional and agrarian
issues had been linked together by Davitt and Parnell, so he set
to work to untie the knot. Parnell's party had attacked the
problem of landownership but had few constructive suggestions to offer as to the proper use of the land once that issue
had been settled. Plunkett took the opposite view. Irishmen
could and should unite to deal with social and economic
problems; then having established a bridgehead from which
further progress was possible, political differences would
appear in their true perspective and constitutional issues would
be easier to resolve.

Tempering his lofty idealism with a shrewd business sense,[5]
Plunkett established a co-operative movement among Irish
farmers, supported by protestants and catholics, by unionists
and nationalists, by north and south. It is for this achievement
that he is chiefly remembered, but his aims lay deeper. The
restoration of a proper balance between town and country,

between the patterns of urban and of rural life has been put forward as the primary task confronting modern man.[6] Plunkett tackled this problem in an Irish countryside, once grossly overpopulated, then devastated by famine and subsequently bled by emigration. A practical social philosopher as well as a co-operative enthusiast, he designed and put into effect a comprehensive scheme for the regeneration of country life based upon the twin pillars of co-operation and education; his three-pronged aim of introducing the scientific method to Irish agriculture, of re-organising rural commerce along co-operative lines, and of restoring a sense of dignity, a spirit of self-reliance and an air of optimism to the Irish countryside neatly encapsulated in his famous slogan: Better Farming, Better Business, Better Living.

His reforms were designed to appeal to Irishmen irrespective of class, creed or religious affiliation. They perfectly fitted the mood of the closing years of the nineteenth century — one of those rare periods in Irish history when the constitutional question remained in abeyance and an accommodation between opposing political forces could not be entirely ruled out. This mood was reflected in his own political development for Plunkett was one of the few, but influential members of the protestant landowning aristocracy to come to terms with Ireland's uncertain but inevitable progress towards independence; moving from a belief in progressive unionism to become a staunch proponent of dominion home rule. Along the way he encountered the turbulence which bedevils Anglo-Irish relations: but, in an era of polarisation and of increasing violence, the qualities which stood him in such good stead as a social reformer were insufficient to compensate for his defects as a politician.

En route to the conclusion that the strained relationship between the two islands needed to be given a new constitutional framework, ('When will our rulers realise,' he asked, 'that Ireland is Ireland?') Plunkett jettisoned his connections with unionism, with anglicanism, and with the landlords, but even this was not enough to protect him from the maelstrom that was to come. A leading advocate of the need for economic reconstruction after independence, his house was destroyed by republicans in the ensuing civil war. And though his last decade was darkened by rejection and exile, he never abandoned a constructive vision of his country's future, remaining an Irishman without rancour, an aristocrat with the desire to serve.

*   *   *

Horace Curzon Plunkett was born in the home of his maternal grandparents at Sherborne, Gloucestershire on 24 October 1854. He was the third son and the sixth child of the sixteenth Baron Dunsany. The Plunketts, originally Danish, but increasingly part of the Norman-Gaelic hegemony, had settled in Co. Meath in the twelfth century.

Dunsany Castle, surrounded by rich pastureland, stands about twenty miles from Dublin in the shadow of the Hill of Tara. It was built by Hugo de Lacy and originally inhabited by Cusacks. The Plunketts lived nearby and married the Cusack heiress in 1401; they were, and still are, among the biggest landowners in Ireland. In pride of place in the dining hall hangs a portrait of the thirteenth baron who opposed the Act of Union in 1800, refusing to be bribed by the offer of an English peerage. Without a seat in the Lords they built a parliamentary tradition in the House of Commons which Horace was to follow from 1892 to 1900.

The family who, for seven hundred years have lived chiefly in the eastern counties of Dublin, Meath and Louth, bear a distinguished Irish surname. From the year 1316, when Thomas Plunkett of Louth was chief justice of the common pleas, down to the present day, there has scarcely been a generation in which one, or more, have not been prominent in the life of the country, either in the church, the law, in politics or in literature. Irish families of this vintage frequently possess both protestant and catholic branches. The Plunketts are heirs to the three peerages of Fingall, Louth and Dunsany. During the penal days the lords of Louth and Fingall remained catholic while the Dunsanys, in order to retain the family lands, became protestant. When the necessity had passed the lands were returned to their catholic kinsmen but the religious distinction remained. The Dunsanys, members of the Church of Ireland, are proud of their connection with the catholic martyr, Oliver Plunkett, who was consecrated archbishop of Armagh in 1669. Tireless in his efforts on behalf of his flock in the face of persecution and tyranny, he was hanged, drawn and quartered at Tyburn in 1681 and, three hundred years later, was canonised. In an article entitled 'The Plunkett Ascendant', Shane Leslie writes of the family:

It has come through history with three old unpurchased Anglo-Irish peerages in its lap, with a record of catholic and protestant archbishops. It has contributed brilliantly to the modern Irish stage and the ancient Irish faith. It has given Ireland martyrs both ecclesiastical and political. [7]

Survivors of the vicissitudes of both English politics and Irish settlement, the Plunketts were leading members of the Anglo-Irish, as descendants of the English had come to be called. A certain duality is evident in the way in which this remarkable group of Irishmen regarded themselves; while mainly unionist their class had produced most of the leading nationalists; while generally protestant it had some distinguished catholic adherents; while often eccentric it included some of the great writers (Swift, Goldsmith, Yeats, Shaw), leading contributors to history (Lecky, Bury), philosophy (Berkeley) and science (Boyle, Parsons, Hamilton) and had been responsible for the architectural triumph of eighteenth century Dublin.

The Anglo-Irish referred to themselves as Irishmen but valued their connection with the crown; they shared neither the myopic view of England as the source of all of Ireland's woes, nor the English disinclination to acknowledge Ireland's distinctive nationality; they had opposed the Act of Union prior to 1800 and, in the following century, gave outstanding service to the British empire. A privileged minority, their control of Irish government had been weakened by the Union (which induced a garrison mentality increasing their dependence on the British connection) and then successfully challenged by O'Connell and Parnell. Whatever its fate, Gladstone's first home rule bill of 1886 was a signal that an era was coming to an end.

The Dunsanys belonged to the upper strata of Anglo-Irish society consisting of the major Irish landlords most of whom owned houses in London and often estates in England. They frequently intermarried with their English counterparts and lived as much in one country as the other. Next came the minor gentry, more firmly wedded to Ireland by possessions and by family ties, generally landlords whose fate was bound up with the fortunes of their tenants and whose wealth depended almost entirely upon their Irish estates. Many of Plunkett's closest supporters were to emerge from this second group. Below them in the social scale, of more importance economically, as well as being the mainspring of Ireland's intellectual life, was a professional class of lawyers, clergy, doctors, civil servants and businessmen, graduates of Trinity

College Dublin, possessing an influence out of all proportion to
their numbers.

To a banquet in his honour given by Irishmen of all persuasions in 1901, Horace offered this pleasant, if idiosyncratic
account of his background:

I was reared in one of those two castles of the Pale, almost under the
shadow of the Hill of Tara, where the Plunkett family for nigh seven
centuries have managed to cling to the same house. There I suppose
we came under the spell which the spirit of the Celt used to weave
round the offspring of the sternest of Irish invaders, making them more
Irish than the Irish themselves. Of course in the good old days we
fought for what we considered our rights, which were to treat the
inhabitants of our adopted country as mere Irish, and to avail ourselves
of their long-horned cattle without payment. I never planted a new
creamery without a sense of restitution for those little irregularities. [8]

Educated at a private school in England and then in the
classical mould at Eton; he graduated from Oxford (where he
captained the university chess team) with a second class degree
in history in 1878. He had entered university at a time when the
moral ardour of some of its teachers was stirring the social
conscience of the more serious students. Thirty years before,
John Stuart Mill in his *Principles of Political Economy* had stressed
the need for reform of the Irish system of land tenure as well as
underlining the importance of the co-operative movement in
ameliorating the lot of the working class. The teaching of
economics, under his humane influence, was growing out of its
past narrow dogmatism. The brash individualism which had
sought to justify itself by economic dogma was withering under
the denunciation of John Ruskin. T.H. Green was shaking the
hold of utilitarianism in ethics. Arnold Toynbee, historian of the
industrial revolution, was compelling thoughtful minds to
reflect on the cost of the material progress of the previous
century in terms of human life and suffering. And though, in
later years, he constantly bemoaned his failure to make the most
of his educational opportunities, some of this social thinking
must have rubbed off on the young Plunkett, for, having come
down from Oxford, he opened a co-operative store for his
father's tenants.

Business was conducted in one of the three houses in the
'town' of Dunsany. The store was organised not as a true co-
operative but as a limited liability company whose shareholders
were tenant farmers and labourers, the steward and Plunkett

himself. He took turns in the shop before they could afford a manager; as he wrote, 'the co-operation between rich and poor which I advocate entails hard, and for a long while, thankless work'.[9] It was just a small store selling groceries and offering a local market for butter and eggs, but, thanks to Plunkett's determination it survived to provide a 'small beginning in that community of interest between classes, which if it ever existed in Ireland, has disappeared'.[10]

In Ireland, Horace dwelt in Dunsany Castle, looked after his father's estate and hunted during the season three or four times a week. There was a regular routine of Sunday worship (in the Church of Ireland at Kilmessan), the theatre in Dublin, hunt balls and the Punchestown races, interspersed with regular trips to England to see friends, to visit relatives and to supervise the family business interests on the other side of the Irish Sea. A generous host, he delighted in the company of active and intelligent people but the social life centred around Dublin Castle he found pointless and boring and strove to avoid it without giving offence.[11]

Horace's maternal grandfather, Lord Sherborne belonged to a county family from the west of England, connected to Coke of Norfolk, a pioneer of agricultural science and modern farming and with the Curzons, from whom he derived his middle name. His mother bore seven children, four boys and three girls. She was a stern evangelical woman who died from tuberculosis when he was four years old, a brother and sister succumbing to the dread disease in childhood. His second brother, John had married and was settled in England while his sister Mary was married to a Ponsonby of Kilcooley Abbey in Co. Tipperary. Horace and Randal, the heir, also threatened with the tuberculosis then endemic in Ireland, were advised to move from the lowlands of Meath to a drier and more bracing climate. Randal headed for southern Africa but the disease had got a foothold and he died on the return journey.

Horace's diaries survive from 1881 thus it can only be surmised that his decision to settle in the western United States was influenced by acquaintances who preceded him, as much as by the fantastic tales of fortunes being made in cattle and gold. Reaching Denver in the autumn of 1879, he pressed northward via Cheyene four hundred miles along the old Bozeman trail to Johnson County, eventually establishing the EK ranch in the valley of the Powder River. Wyoming was not then a state of the Union, incorporation did not take place until 1890 and the

Territory was administered by federal officials with the help of a mini-legislature of local men. Railroads were, at the time, cutting swathes across the interior of the continent, driving before them the buffalo and the Indian, clearing the way for the miners, the speculators and the cattlemen. From Cheyenne in the south to the Platte River had been settled since the 1860s. North of the Platte was Indian country. General Custer had been routed by the Cheyenne Indians in the Black Hills to the east in 1876 but, on account of the treaty with the Plains Tribes of 1868 coupled with the virtual extinction of the buffalo (their main source of provender and clothing), Plunkett encountered little or no hostility from the Indians in his neighbourhood.

The Big Horn Mountains at the eastern extremity of the Rockies run north-south through Wyoming, richly supplied with grasslands often 6,000 feet above sea-level. Gently undulating plains, covered with bunch grass and sage brush, roll away to the east, watered by the plains rivers winding towards the Missouri through broad sandy beds fringed with cottonwoods. Fronting the mountains is a smaller sandstone ridge, coloured, wherever the rock shows through, a rich brick red. Up against the Red Wall nestles the Powder River Valley, fertile, sheltered and amply supplied with timber. To the settler from the east no contrast could have been more striking but Wyoming, in the eighties, was a land of contrasts.

Cattle had been moving into southern Wyoming since the 1860s; coal and oil had been discovered by the 1880s (Plunkett noted a 36 foot coal seam in the bank of the Powder River in 1885);[12] the state is now renowned for enormous reserves of coal, oil and natural gas. Cheyenne, the 'Magic City of the Plains', whose importance stemmed from its position on the railroad*, had acquired a veneer of civilisation; and Plunkett, the wealthy Irish aristocrat, made a welcome recruit to the headquarters of Wyoming's professional and business community — the Cheyenne Club.

From 1879 to 1888 he wintered in Ireland, crossing the Atlantic in the early spring. After a hectic stopover in New York came a few days relaxation in the westbound train running via Chicago and Omaha to Cheyenne. (Although as Plunkett discovered, having collided with a freight train travelling in the opposite direction, even this method of travel was not without its excitements. 'All a bit shaken', he wrote, 'conductor rather

---

*The magnificent Union Pacific Station was built in 1886.

broken, engines smashed up!').[13] The final leg of the journey, by horse-drawn conveyance, was an altogether different matter.

Started 6 a.m. on the dreaded journey north. Cold, miserable weather. Snowed, sleeted, hailed and rained on us. Blew strong and cold. We found the canyon full of torrents and had great difficulty getting across. Reached Point of Rocks, however, at 7 p.m. Left 8 p.m. and got alright to Staymakers, where we got stuck and all had to lend a hand to get the coach out. This happened twice shortly after. Then we got into a long stretch of mud and walked till daylight, arriving at the Laporelle 5.30 a.m. This stream was an impassable torrent. There was a rope stretching across the stream and a wooden box tied to it by a pulley. On this contrivance we all got across and then got the mails and baggage over ... I had to go outside the whole night and was half frozen. After breakfast they started us off in a common 'Peter Schuttle' wagon with two horses! These soon played out and we had to walk ... eight miles. Then we got fresh horses which also played out ... we had to walk another eight miles ... I got lame and weary plodding through the deep mud. At Brown Springs I got some supper, 12 midnight, having had nothing to eat except a biscuit for 15 hours. the stage then took us ... to Powder River without adventure, but with much suffering from cold and fatigue, at 8 p.m.[14]

'Nothing gained by fighting the weather in this country',[15] he ruefully recorded. Climatic changes were swift and sometimes violent. The vast expanses of sky which, in fair conditions enhance Western scenery, make the onrushing storm appear all the more ominous. Hail, in a freak storm of 1888, bounced six feet into the air, killed chickens on the EK ranch, a calf and a colt in the Crazy Woman Canyon and would certainly, Plunkett believed, have proved fatal to children.[16] Winters were severe but snow storms were normally followed by a wind which cleared the range sufficiently to enable cattle to graze and to survive.

Away from the railroads travelling was hard and sometimes hazardous. After a storm in May 1884 'the upper bridge had done what it had threatened to do for three years and gone downstream.'[17] Lengthy journeys took several days, involving stopovers at ranches en route or accommodation at the local hotel. Western hotels provided a variety of entertainment for their tired guests; they had been immortalised by Oscar Wilde's discovery of the slogan, in one such establishment, 'Don't shoot the pianist, he's doing his best!' The Occidental Hotel at Buffalo, fifty miles north of the EK ranch, held no appeal for the abstemious Plunkett. It was 'a regular gambling hell; Monte, Pharo, Keno and other iniquitous games occupy the large hall ... while whiskey and music make the nights hideous for those who don't drink, gamble or swear.[18]

He was in Wyoming for the beef boom, (prices reached their peak in 1882) and for the collapse which followed the drought of 1886; the subsequent severe winter (there had been a crisis in Johnson County two years earlier) sending many of the big cattle companies into bankruptcy. It was a period of intense speculation by investors in the home countries and in the east, the majority of whom had no knowledge of the conditions and little possibility of checking the size of their herds. Plunkett suggested establishing a stock exchange in Cheyenne; 'it would have the grand effect of bringing enterprises which are blindly valued on distant exchanges to their proper level'.[19] Fortune making, in theory, was simple. Range land was federally owned so the big cattlemen operated a free-range system with round-ups twice yearly. Capital was required only for purchasing stock, for paying hired hands (itinerant cowboys who were required for round-ups) and for setting up the base ranch. If, as Moreton Frewen suggested to his backers in London, herd size doubled every four years, then the initial investment could be quickly paid off and everything that remained would be surplus.

Round-ups were communal affairs at which cowboys from every ranch in the neighbourhood would congregate at some prearranged spot until the cattle were brought in. Calves branded in the spring, in the fall the herd was culled prior to sending the beeves to market. On paper the scheme was perfect, in practice the free-range system led to overstocking. A rancher's life was demanding, there were long hours in the saddle, round up work was tough ('hair, dust and corruption' the cowboys called it) but Plunkett's horsemanship stood him in good stead.

We had to cross a rough 'bad land country' for about 30 miles. At last we struck the trail of horses and cattle and knew we were near the Round-Up. We had to swim Nowood, which was flooded into a good size river about 25 yards across. My horse, not recovered from his narrow escape in Tensleep, refused to swim and only struggled and rolled over and over in midstream. I had to swim ashore and leave him to drown. Sykes* saved the saddle and my two coats (containing

*A trapper Plunkett had hired to guide him to the round-up.

important papers) and I had to swim the stream, having got out on the wrong side ... At last found the encampment I had sought for 7 days. Food in abundance and a good bed, the cheery welcome of the country and for a change a fine evening.[20]

After the round-up came the trek to the nearest railhead followed by a journey to Chicago (where it was the slaughtermens' boast that every portion of the beast was utilised except the breath which left its nostrils!).

We get off by nightfall and travel all night in the way car. No sleep, as the cattle have to be looked after everytime the train stops. They travel 20 in a truck, and one has to prod them with a long goad everytime they get [lie] down, as they are liable to suffocation. It is tiring work perpetually rushing along the track in the dark with the lantern, and then, if the train starts having to climb on top of it [over the cattle cars] and climb down the last car into the 'way' car or 'caboose'.[21]

In spite of its discomforts Plunkett enjoyed the life; long hours out of doors in the champagne air benefited his health; but, as early as 1881, he was aware that the free range system was a recipe for disaster. 'As far as I can prophesy the time will come when the fruits of overcrowding will be heavy winter losses and only those who can lower the number of their herds will have the necessary safety valve.'[22]

The Wyoming Stock Growers' Association had been formed in 1872 to introduce some order to the cattle business. Stock detectives were appointed to prevent thieving and to check cattle numbers at the railhead.

Our cattle used to roam at large, the only way of identifying them being certain marks made by the branding iron and the knife ... The Stock Association, with its 'round-ups' and its occasional resort to the supreme court of Judge Lynch ... [was] an adequate substitute for the title deeds to the lands, and for fences horse-high, bull-strong and hog-tight.[23]

All the big cattlemen, including Plunkett, were members of the Association, though he rarely attended its meetings which were held in Cheyenne. The Stock Growers' Association did useful work but it failed in its primary duty of preventing overstocking. Johnson County could comfortably accomodate 50,000 cattle; in 1884 there were three times that number. Small ranchers who were attempting a modest but more orthodox system of farming formed another interest group. The intro-

duction of barbed wire helped to secure territories which they
had irrigated and this led, inevitably, to friction with the cattle
companies. Hideouts for rustlers abounded in the mountainous
terrain and, in 1892, tension finally erupted into a cattle war
with frequent lynchings. Eventually the federal troops were
called in after three 'rustlers' had been killed in a shootout with
the cattlemen.

Accompanied by Alexis and Edmund Roche (brothers of Lord
Fermoy) Plunkett had arrived in Wyoming able to call upon a
considerable inheritance. Willing to speculate with the best, he
soon became involved in an intricate series of business deals
including the purchase of 135,000 acres of land from the Union
Pacific Railroad*, a large scale irrigation project and an
electricity generating scheme besides his membership of a
number of cattle companies. At once he set himself the task of
learning to keep the books, triumphantly recording in August,
1881, 'Got accounts into shape so that I can account for every
penny from 15 October 1879 to the present day'. [25]

Other distinguished residents of the Powder River Valley
included George Parker and Harry Longabaugh (better known
to posterity as Butch Cassidy and the Sundance Kid) who
operated with their colleagues in the 'Hole-in-the-Wall-Gang'
from a gap in the sandstone ridge. They came after Plunkett at
the end of the century. The Frewen brothers Moreton and
Richard were his direct contemporaries. From a landed Sussex
family with Irish connections, they set up ranch not far from the
EK. Moreton, an aristocratic adventurer (three Jerome sisters
from New York married Frewen, Randolph Churchill and John
Leslie) was later to earn the nickname 'mortal ruin' for the
unscrupulous way in which he disposed of other people's
fortunes. Plunkett, who was not always a reliable judge of
character, was initially impressed. But Frewen's recklessness
soon began to show through causing Plunkett to comment
drily:

the English visitors cost us a lot of money, make themselves and us
unpopular in the country by their incapability to adapt themselves to
the people and interfere much with business. [26]

The severe winters of 1884/5 and 1886/7 spelt trouble for the
graziers. Prices had plummetted and Plunkett returning from
his winter sojourns in Ireland found the herds much depleted.

---

*At a price of one dollar per acre payable over 10 years at 6% interest. [24]

The London based directors of Frewen's Powder River Cattle Company decided to dispense with the services of their founder and offered the managership to Plunkett. He seemed to feel an obligation to Frewen's backers, he may have been acquainted with some of them, there was by now ample evidence of Frewen's duplicity and Plunkett, prone to rush in where angels feared to tread, foolishly accepted the offer. He soon had to take unpopular measures, foremen were sacked, the cowboys threatened to shoot him for reducing their wages, even Alexis Roche had to be discharged, on account of his business incapacity, from the EK partnership. The Powder River Co. was eventually sold off to its major creditors with a loss of £200,000 but not before Frewen had done all in his power to blacken Plunkett's name before the board. Frewen had constructed a huge packing station at Sherman. In the fall of 1887 just before he left for home Plunkett valued it for lumber and, a few days later, Frewen's Folly was no more.[27]

Wyoming's struggle for statehood reached its climax during this period (for Plunkett this experience would be repeated in Ireland in the new century); significantly he found himself ready to accept the challenges which statehood posed. In a low poll on 5 November 1889 residents of Wyoming Territory voted three to one to accept a state constitution drawn up by a convention in Cheyenne. The preparation of the constitution had led to considerable controversy; those opposed to statehood, including some of the wealthier residents, arguing that it would entail an exorbitant increase in taxation. On the morning of the poll Plunkett pointed out, in a letter to the *Cheyenne Leader*, that this had been his reaction when the idea had first been mooted; but a careful study of the proposals had convinced him that

the framers of the constitution have, with an ability which I admire and a boldness which I admire far more, provided us with a form of government that is so much purer than the system with which our politics has been disgraced that the advantages of statehood wholly outweigh the risks and render them insignificant.[28]

Additional family responsibilities in the wake of his father's failing health put an end to his spell as a cowboy. Early on he had realised the need to diversify and, although the cattle industry had suffered severely, Plunkett, through honest dealing and business acumen had established the basis of a fortune in America. The Cheyenne Club gave him a farewell dinner:

Many speeches testified to my high honour in business and, what I didn't expect, to my readiness to help others in the pursuit of the dollar.[29]

There was a real hint of nostalgia as he prepared to leave for Ireland.

Spent the day packing up ... I don't think my ten years in the West wholly wasted ... I have gained much experience of men and affairs — more valued is my understanding of the vast sprawling energy, the idealism, the crudity and generosity of a country like America![30]

The challenge of Wyoming lay in the fact that the a priori advantages of class and social standing counted for little in the Powder River Valley where he was simply a man among men. Later he was to recall that 'my nearest approach to practical agriculture was a decade of cattle ranching in the western states of America. There I learnt more about men than about cattle'.[31] American business methods, the competition which American exports would provide for European farmers and the American habit of translating thoughts so quickly into deeds all made an indelible impression on the young Plunkett. He never entirely lost the pioneering spirit of those early days on the ranch and his sojourn among the cattlemen he often recalled with feeling. The striking obituary tribute paid to him in the *Boston Sunday Globe* (included in the appendix) describing a story telling contest between Plunkett and the old Indian scout Jim Bridger, in which Bridger's tales of the Yellowstone were voted bigger lies than Plunkett's retailing of Baron Munchausen by a bunch of cowboys around a camp fire, captures the flavour of Wyoming in the 1880s in the unmistakable tones of the West.

* * *

In 1883, after a whirlwind courtship, Plunkett's cousin the Earl of Fingall from the neighbouring castle at Killeen, married seventeen years old Elizabeth Burke from Galway. Daisy Fingall, as she then became, was as lively as her husband was somnolent. The Countess longed for travel and society; the Earl confined himself to horses and the great hunting county of Meath; their marriage can hardly have been an idyllic one.

During the winters of his Wyoming days and for sometime

thereafter Plunkett lived a carefree, batchelor existence in Dunsany Castle. Reid, the treasure of his domestic staff, a jack-of-all-trades, referred to expressively as an 'up-with-the-kettle, round-with-the-car, man', was a northern protestant who cursed the papists but lived with them in perfect amity. He used to wait at dinner with ends of his trousers tucked into his boots, and when he felt that the guests had stayed too long, would thrust his head around the door asking, 'Does any of yez want your yokes?' There was no mistaking that hint![32] Quite oblivious to the unorthodox nature of his domestic arrange-ments, Horace regularly entertained his many friends. If there were ladies in the party, Daisy would come over from Killeen to make the castle habitable. With beauty, wit and charm, and a ready, if not a deep, intelligence, she was eager for company and conversation and Horace, with his strange ideals, fascinated her. For his part, although fond of children he had shown no sign of settling down. Soon the fascination was reciprocated. In April 1891 he was 'getting dangerously fond of her'.[33] 'I must be careful', he wrote two months later, 'The strange relations with Fingall make it all the more duty to fight against the big temptation'.[34] But scrupulously respecting the position of his cousin, the Earl, he never allowed his emotions to get the better of him and at the end of 1892 recorded in his diary:

I am still unmarried and likely to be so till my dying day. The year has decided this. I can say no more out of justice to my memory. To write all would be hard on a friend. To write less would be cruel to others who respected me.[35]

It was a strange relationship which was to last throughout his life without ever rupturing the friendship with his cousin. 'Go away little woman!' he would brusquely exclaim if ever his affection for Daisy looked like interfering with his work. Plunkett remained a batchelor for the sake of Lady Fingall and was unquestionably in love with her, Bernard Shaw remarked many years later, 'yet I never felt convinced that he quite liked her'.[36]

Lord Dunsany died in 1889 having been predeceased by his heir Randal in 1883. His second son John, a talented eccentric and now an MP, was married and living in England but in danger of addiction to drugs and alcohol, thus the responsibility for the family estate, plus the guardianship of some nieces and nephews (his sister Mary had been widowed in 1884) all fell upon Horace's shoulders. Besides Dunsany and some land in Wales this included coal mines at Pelton on Tyneside, a fleet of coal boats, and a boat yard at Romsey in Hampshire. His father had left him considerably more than a younger son's inheritance so his fortune was assured whatever the fate of his American investments.

Many young Anglo-Irishmen of a similar background shared the ideal of service whose fulfilment would be sought in the British army or in colonial administration. Plunkett's ambitions were different for early on he had conceived the ideal of serving Ireland. The American interlude had given him a unique view of the tangled relationship between Ireland and her next door neighbour. 'Anglo-Irish history', he loved to repeat, 'is for Englishmen to remember but for Irishmen to forget'. The amazing progress of Britain in the nineteenth century made a stark contrast to stagnation, famine and emigration in Ireland: 'If ever there was a case where President Kruger's* "moral and intellectual damages" might fairly be claimed by an injured nation, it is to be found in the industrial and commercial history of Ireland during the building up of England's commercial supremacy'.[37]

Restrictions on trade and the land system of the past stood out from the long list of Irish grievances as those for which the victims were least responsible. It was essential, for a correct estimation of Irish agricultural and industrial possibilities, that note should be taken of the true bearings of these historic grievances upon existing conditions.

The English mind, he believed, had quite failed, until the end of the nineteenth century, to grasp the situation which had thus been created in Ireland. The industrial revolution found the Irish people fettered by an industrial past for which they themselves were not largely responsible. They needed exceptional treatment of a kind which was not conceded. They were, instead, still further handicapped, towards the middle of the century, by the adoption of free trade which was imposed when they were not only unable to take advantage of its benefits, but were so situated as to suffer to the utmost from its inconveniences. England, he felt, was largely responsible for his country's industrial defects and must not hesitate to face up to the consequences of that responsibility.

Land holding in Ireland remained based on the tribal system of open fields and common tillage for nearly eight hundred years

*Leader of the Boers.

after collective ownership in England had begun to pass away. The sudden imposition upon the Irish, early in the seventeenth century, of a land system which was no part of the natural development of the country, ignored, though it could not destroy, the old feeling of communal ownership. This sudden change in the system of land holding was followed by a century of reprisals and confiscation, and what war began the law continued. The Gaelic race, impoverished in mind and estate by the penal laws, became rooted to the soil, for they had, on account of the repression of their industries, no alternative occupation. Upon the productivity of their labour the landlord depended for his revenue, but he did little to develop that productivity, and the system did everything to lessen it. An enlightened system of land tenure might have brought prosperity and contentment. What was chiefly required for agrarian peace was a recognition of that sense of partnership in the land which went back to tribal days. But like most English concessions it was granted too late, and then in the wrong way. When, at last, the recognition of partnership was enacted, it became, Plunkett believed, a lever for the demand of complete ownership. But by then Ireland had suffered the devastation of the famine and 'upon the England that sowed the wind there was visited a whirlwind of hostility from the Irish race scattered throughout the globe'.[38]

These views he recorded at the zenith of his career in the first chapter of his controversial book *Ireland in the New Century*. The celebrated historian Lecky, to whose memory the book is dedicated, had a important influence on Plunkett. Lecky was a minor landlord, often an absentee living in London, with an aristocratic pride in his Irish heritage. As an undergraduate at Trinity College, he had developed an admiration for Grattan and the ideals of Young Ireland, seeking the maintenance of the ascendancy and the resurgence of an enlightened unionism; early in his career he had been an imperial home ruler as the following passage illustrates:

Ever since the dawn of public opinion, there has been a party which has maintained that the goal to which Irish patriots should tend, is the recognition of their country as a distinct and independent nationality, connected with England by the crown; that in such a condition alone it could retain a healthy political life, and could act in cordial co-operation with England; that every other system would be transient in its duration, and humiliating and disastrous while it lasted. To this party all the genius of Ireland has ever belonged ... Swift and

Molyneux originated the conception; Burke aided it when he ...
denounced the penal laws and the trade restrictions that shackled the
energies of Ireland; Sheridan, when he exerted all his eloquence to
oppose the union; Flood, when he formed the national party in
parliament; Grattan, when he led that party in its triumph and its fall. [39]

Lecky represented Dublin University at Westminster from
1895 to 1902,* his parliamentary career overlapping Plunkett's
by five years. His political development, however, was quite
different, for, with the rise of Parnell, he became an implacable
opponent of any form of separatism even arguing that Grattan's
parliament, which he admired, should not be taken as a
precedent for establishing a Parnellite parliament and executive
in Dublin. Apart from his vision of Irish history, Plunkett shared
Lecky's views on character formation, on the dangers of
excessive government intervention sapping the spirit of self-
reliance and, early in life, Lecky's belief that Ireland was not fit
for democratic government. Lecky was also mildly anti-clerical
and felt, like Plunkett, that catholicism lacked the industrial
virtues of protestantism. Emily Lawless the poet, daughter of
Lord Cloncurry and Plunkett's cousin, underlined the effect
which Lecky's writing had on his contemporaries when she
credited him with having broken down 'a barrier of prejudice so
solid and of such long standing that it seemed to be
invulnerable'. [40]

If Lecky's work influenced Plunkett's view of the past, George
Berkeley's *Querist*, published between 1735 and 1737 when the
great philosopher was bishop of Cloyne, proved a practical
stimulus to his planning for the future. After graduating from
Trinity College, Berkeley lived in London, Europe and America;
on his appointment to the see of Cloyne in 1734, appalled by the
poverty which surrounded him, he compiled an intensely
practical list of queries, a string of formally unrelated epigrams
bristling with home truths, directing attention to the need for
Irish currency reform and the development of Ireland's
commerce. He advocated the establishment of a national bank,
argued that the selfish aggrandisement of the ascendancy was
shortsighted, that the impoverishment of the masses
diminished the nation's wealth, undermining its credit, and
queried 'whether the way to make men industrious be not to let
them taste the fruits of their industry? And whether the
labouring ox should be muzzled?'

*Lecky died in 1903.

The bishop was both pastor and philosopher, a man of action as well as theoretician. In Cloyne where the *Querist*[41] was written, he moved from door to door among his people, experiencing their lot at first hand rather than from the vantage point of Dublin and the House of Lords. He could tell others to grow flax and hemp because he himself was growing them, employing more than one hundred in agriculture of one sort or another. This clothing of ideals with reality was to be Plunkett's forte. Inheriting Berkeley's zeal for social reform he made frequent use of his queries to stimulate thought which would lead to action. Among his favourites were:

Whether the divided force of men, acting singly, would not be a rope of sand?

Whose fault is it if poor Ireland still continues poor?

Whether it would not be more reasonable to mend our state than complain of it; and how far this may be in our power?

and, after his unhappy spell in the Westminster parliament,

Whether our parties are not a burlesque upon politics?

II

The Co-operative Movement and the IAOS

Robert Owen (1771–1858), the Welsh-born entrepreneur-philanthropist renowned for his New Lanark industrial community established around cotton mills on the banks of the Clyde, is widely regarded as the father of co-operation. However, the co-operative movement, as we know it, may be taken to date from 1844 when, on 21 December, 28 artisans (mainly unemployed weavers) came together to open a provision store in Toad Lane, Rochdale, thus writing themselves into the social history of England and of the world. The ideas which were incorporated in the rules of the Rochdale Equitable Pioneer Society form the core of co-operative thinking today:

1. democratic control;
2. open membership;
3. fixed or limited return on capital subscribed;
4. dividend on purchases;
5. trading strictly on a cash basis, no credit;
6. only pure and unadulterated goods for sale;
7. provision for the education of members;
8. political and religious neutrality.

Owen visited Ireland in 1823 and his ideas inspired a Clare landlord, Vandaleur, to set up a commune on his estate at Ralahine. Craig, a Lancashire co-operator came as manager making the Ralahine experiment into a great success. After two years however tragedy struck when Vandaleur fled precipitously having lost his estate on the gambling tables of Dublin.[1] Around the same time William Thompson one of the great co-operative thinkers proposed the formation of another commune on his own estate at Rosscarberry, Co. Cork but he died before the plan could be brought to fruition. There were other co-operative developments of a minor nature but the Irish co-operative movement may be said to have commenced in 1889, for that year witnessed both the opening of Plunkett's campaign as well as the foundation of the Belfast Co-Operative Society.

The associative power acquired by American farmers through the Grange (which reached its zenith when he was in Wyoming) must have impressed Plunkett for it was in the remote Mid-West that he dreamt of his campaign for co-operation.

For some years I led a rather lonely life thinking out the ways I would try to be useful in Ireland. A political career did not then commend itself to me ... a business life in America convinces a man that politics are by no means the most useful, or indeed the most edifying, of a nation's activities. And so my mind turned towards certain simple economic schemes ...[2]

The vigorous expansion of American agriculture made a stark contrast to stagnation at home. Irish farming was slowly overcoming the indelible marks of famine but emigration was high and morale low, while cheap, efficient transport and newly-invented processes of preservation had opened the British market to foreign competition. This led to a steady fall in agricultural prices between 1881 and 1887 reflected in the decline in the value of Irish agricultural produce from £72 million for the four years 1886-70 to £54 million for 1884-88.[3] The Irish tenant farmers had gained a considerable measure of security from a sequence of land acts (a process which would be completed by the Wyndham Act of 1903). The problem of land ownership was being settled but what about its use? The Land League, Plunkett observed, had given the people insight into the power of combination and had educated them in the conduct of meetings; but little progress could be made by the Irish farmer acting alone, harassed as he was, first by cheaper production from vast tracts of soil in the uttermost parts of the earth, and second by a nearer and keener competition from the better organised and educated producers on the Continent.

In 1885 he tried to organise Irish graziers to transform the shipping of cattle to England on the hoof into a dead-meat trade employing the newly invented process of refrigeration. The move was vigorously opposed by butchers and jobbers but failed principally on account of the lethargy shown by the cattlemen.[4] An early article, 'Co-operative Stores for Ireland',[5] written by Plunkett in 1888, shows the influence of the English movement which by then had 1,500 societies (most of which were consumer based), almost one million members and annual sales of around £37 million. But there was something more important than mere statistics:

Few have any conception how much the real movement, which has been defined as organised self-help, has done to raise the moral, social and material condition of the English working classes. [6]

An Irish exhibition held at Olympia (London) in the same year included a model dairy organised by Canon Richard Bagot, manufacturing butter and cheese by the most modern methods, while an audience of over three hundred listened to papers advocating the extension of co-operation to Ireland. The outcome was the formation of an Irish Co-operative Aid Association to promote co-operation in Ireland by means of propaganda and with loans of capital. The Association was soon dissolved when it was ascertained that the powerful Co-operative Union (representing the co-operative movement in the whole of Britain) would undertake this task. [7]

Plunkett was not directly involved in these proceedings, but publication of his article led to correspondence with J. C. Gray, secretary of the Co-operative Union, and to two visits to London to inspect the Whitechapel co-operative store. [8] In November Gray visited Ireland finding 13 co-operative stores in various states of existence including the one at Dunsany which, by then, had survived for 10 years. Significantly Gray's visit was the occasion of a spirited attack on co-operation in a Dublin newspaper by a body styled the Traders' Defence Association of Scotland. [9] A month later Plunkett returned the visit to the head-quarters of the Co-operative Union in Manchester, inspecting some of the local societies with Gray and discussing the extension of co-operative principles to Ireland at a quarterly meeting of the board. [10]

In June, 1889 he attended the annual Co-operative Congress at Ipswich.

I was greatly impressed with the tone of the arguments used by the representatives of the working men. Moderate, dignified speaking, always to the point. No one can realise what the working man has done for himself until ...[he is] heard speaking of ...[his] own aims and ambitions. [11]

Plunkett reported on conditions in Ireland; the Union undertook to promote co-operation there; he was made head of the Irish section of the Union of which R. A. Anderson later became secretary.

On 29 September, in Lord Monteagle's home, Mount
Trenchard, overlooking the estuary of the mighty river Shannon,
Plunkett opened his co-operative campaign. Their host, he
nostalgically recalled some forty years later, had

assembled a few of his neighbours, including the parish priest, to discuss
a scheme we had planned for re-organising Irish agriculture. In that little
gathering the agricultural co-operative movement in Ireland — some,
more bold, would say in the United Kingdom — was born. [12]

Progress would be slow, patience would be required for there
was no evading the obstacles which lay ahead.

The people are unbusiness-like, thriftless and improvident. They view
with suspicion any scheme which professes to be for their good. Their
sad history has taught them to trust no-one, not even themselves; and
while they have shown great power of combination for specific
purposes, their leaders have always had to rely upon some strong
political or religious incentive. When therefore we wish to organise a
combination which is wholly non-political and non-sectarian we start
under grave disadvantages. [13]

In fact the movement laboured under other prior
disadvantages for its leader was a protestant, a unionist and son
of one of the country's largest landowners, further, he was not an
orator, [14] in a land of great exponents of that art. Possessed of a
zeal untainted by fundamentalism, Plunkett's speeches were
constructive, logical and devoid of rhetoric — a difficulty with the
letter 'r' adding a quaint touch to his delivery. The parliamentarian, T. P. O'Connor thus described him addressing the Irish
Fellowship Club at Liverpool:

His speech had all his characteristic defects. He spoke slowly almost
stammeringly — he paused often to find the exact word, and there was
not a bit of colour, not a phrase of passion in the whole address. Yet the
fact remains that I have rarely heard an address which produced such a
profound effect. [15]

'He was', according to one admirer, 'the worst speaker one
could listen to and the most persuasive talker one could meet'. [16]
Plunkett's patent sincerity and obvious selflessness inspired a
total commitment to the emerging co-operative movement from
a remarkable group of men. First there was his old friend Lord
Monteagle from a family distinguished in imperial service, on
whose estate near Foynes, Co. Limerick considerable industrial

development had already taken place[17] and in whose house Plunkett launched his co-operative campaign.

Alexis Roche, now returned from Wyoming and settled in Co. Cork,* introduced him to R. A. Anderson who held a petty sessions clerkship at Doneraile and was sub-agent to Lord Castletown. 'P-P-Plunkett', Roche had warned Anderson (he had dreadful stutter), 'is the s-s-strangest being you ever met. In f-f-fact he is like nothing on earth'. This advance notice intrigued Anderson, who encountered a thin, spare man in his early thirties with a prominent nose, keen, kindly eyes and a limp handshake. Plunkett expounded his strange new doctrine of co-operation and though Anderson admitted at once that he grasped very little of what Plunkett was saying, the fascination continued to grow. 'Who is Mr. Plunkett anyway' he managed to whisper to Roche as he was leaving. 'Just another *** Honourable like myself', came the salty reply, 'but his father was Lord Dunsany, and so he c-c-couldn't help it'[18] Anderson was a blunt man, a dead shot and a competent horseman of a robust constitution. Undeterred by his failure to understand Plunkett's exposition of co-operative principles, he accepted the offer of a salary of £250 to turn co-operator.

A press report of a Plunkett speech in 1890 advocating co-operative dairying to the farmers of Munster led to fruitful contact with Father T. A. Finlay, a jesuit, recently returned from a study of rural economy in Germany. Finlay, whom Lecky described as perhaps the most universally respected man in Ireland, was professor of metaphysics at the Catholic University College; he had edited several important journals and was a fellow of the Royal University; later he became professor of political economy holding this post in University College, Dublin until 1930. Father Finlay's influence upon the co-operative movement, as well as on its founder, can hardly be under-estimated, 'he largely moulded my life's work' and was 'the kindest and most loyal friend I have ever had in a work which made my life worth living'.[19]

As the other co-operative leaders were mainly protestant, Finlay's presence helped to redress the religious balance in an essential way. From Co. Cavan, on the borders of Ulster, he numbered presbyterians among his ancestors and was as much at home among orangemen as with nationalists. Two stories told by Plunkett in tribute to Father Finlay pay eloquent testimony to his

*Roche had married Lucy Maude Goschen, daughter of a former chancellor of the exchequer.

resourcefulness in bridging the sectarian divide.

A last minute defection from a team of co-operators who were to address a meeting of Ulster farmers drawn from a predominantly unionist area led to Father Finlay joining the delegation.

He began by explaining the accident which accounted for his presence. He admitted its incongruity, but assured his audience that, so far as he was concerned, he saw no reason why either a jesuit or an orangeman should allow the events of two centuries ago to interfere with the practical affairs which they had come together to discuss. He understood that considerable feeling was occasionally aroused over a battle fought on a famous river not far to the south of where he stood. After all, he went on to remind them, the quarrel was not between Irishmen but between a Dutchman and a Scot. 'Surely,' he said, 'if these two worthies have not by now settled their little difference, we might leave it to them — that is, if too great a gulf does not divide them!' There followed a luminous and convincing case for the immediate establishment of a creamery. After he sat down, I was told by a friend who had met some of those present at the meeting a few days after it was held, an elderly, much-bewhiskered presbyterian rose and said, 'This mon has spoke raal worrds o' sense. Let's hae the cramery and ha' done wi' yon.' They had it, and it's a thing of joy to this day.

I remember attending a meeting in another part of the borderland where Father Finlay, who was among his own people, was to be the chief speaker. On this occasion the people of the district were about evenly divided, religiously and politically. I heard to my dismay that the orangemen and nationalists had both marched to the meeting with their flags and bands. I asked my friend if he did not scent trouble. 'Not at all,' he replied. 'I must just see the bandmasters.' By tactful diplomacy, the most provocative air on each side was deleted from the programme. It was not quite so easy to secure an agreement that they should play alternately and not together; but even this concession was arranged, and a pleasant and useful day was enjoyed by us both.[20]

The fourth of his main recruits came later. Plunkett wished to move the Irish from their obsession with politics; this was more a psychological problem than a practical one. He had learnt of Bishop Grundtvig's success in Denmark[21] and how a national feeling for the soil had been quickened by an interest in native literature and folklore. Might not the Gaelic revival and the Irish literary movement possess the inspiration to wean the Irish mind from political obsessions?

There is in the Irish mind today a yearning for a national life and dignity which the Irish believe existed long ago, and which they know has not existed, at any rate for centuries. It is remarkable that in all my work, having a purely agricultural aim, my friends and I succeeded by appealing to these old national instincts.[22]

Plunkett first met the poet Yeats but he was not the man; however, Yeats, in collusion with Lady Gregory, persuaded the northern poet, mystic, painter and philosopher George W. Russell (AE) to throw in his lot with the co-operators; until 1897 he had been a clerk in a large Dublin store. Plunkett recalled the Irish poet Goldsmith who sang of the 'Deserted Village' and 'had a clearer vision of the rural problem more than a century ago than any economist or statesman since'.[23] AE was an entrancing colleague but 'while he out dreams us all, none of us have as shrewd a business judgement or as nice a sense of humour'.[24] His compassionate nature plus an ability to reduce the complexities of co-operative organisation or the problems of rural credit to the simplest terms made a lasting impression upon the farmers among whom he worked chiefly in the poorer districts of the west of Ireland. In 1905 he took over as editor of the movement's weekly, the *Irish Homestead*, where, in Lady Gregory's picturesque phrase, he 'put his mystic light . . . into a turnip lantern, to the great advantage of the turnip, and it shines from there more clearly than ever before'.[25]

Plunkett was to be the intellectual force, Anderson the organising genius, Father Finlay the moral mentor and AE the imaginative inspiration of the Irish co-operative movement for its first forty years. As a shrewd observer wrote many years later, 'The friendship which bound together Sir Horace Plunkett, Father Finlay, R. A. Anderson and George Russell was touching to behold; seldom were four men of such diverse temperaments bound by so close a tie'.[26]

Strength through combination was to be the watchword of their movement (Ní neart go cur le chéile — no strength without combination — an old Gaelic proverb runs). Farmers must be urged to combine to buy their agricultural requirements at the cheapest rate and of the best quality; they must combine to avail themselves of improved appliances beyond the reach of the individual, whether it be in the erection of creameries or processing plants; they must combine to secure the use of the latest agricultural machinery and the most suitable pure bred stock; they must combine to buy their requirements and to market their produce thereby keeping the profit of the middleman within reasonable limits; they must combine to create, by mutual support, the capital for their industry:

In short, whenever and wherever the individuals in a farming community could be brought to see that they might advantageously
substitute associated for isolated production or distribution, they must
be taught to form themselves into associations* in order to reap the
anticipated advantages. [27]

They were to go into battle under the banner 'Better Farming,
Better Business, Better Living'. Agriculture was, henceforth, to
be regarded as an industry and as a business, as well as a way of
life. Into industry must be introduced the teachings of modern
science, into business the methods of combination to obtain
benefits of scale; and the life of the community must be made
more cheerful, more comfortable and more stimulating. The
emphasis was to be on self-help, but there was, when the
movement started, no effective agency for imparting the
technical knowledge essential to agricultural progress. This was
to be the government's prerogative.

* * *

The pioneers made a number of false starts before eventually
hitting on the key to co-operation in Ireland. A pamphlet of
Plunkett's, published by the Co-operative Union, explains his
initial idea which was, not surprisingly, based upon the English
model:

Whatever part co-operation may play hereafter in the encouragement of
Irish industries it is thought that for the present it is best to confine our
attention to the starting of co-operative stores with perhaps an early
development in the direction of finding the best markets for local
produce. [28]

This form of co-operation was being adopted, he explained,
because retailing was easier and less liable to disaster than any
form of productive enterprise, also the retail traders of rural
Ireland, by their inefficiency and slovenliness, instead of acting
as a beneficient influence, had lowered their standards to the
habits of the people. Country traders gave credit at exhorbitant
rates, their stores were usually untidy, their goods often

---

*Control of a co-operative society is vested democratically in the members; in a
joint-stock company it varies according to the size of the shareholding.

adulterated, most groceries in Ireland had bars attached and so 'the curse of drink is added to the curse of debt'. The wealthy and discriminating rarely patronised the country store but made their purchases in the bigger towns, or ordered direct from Dublin or abroad.

The Dunsany store had been set up to counteract these tendencies in the locality. After twelve years it had absorbed most of the trade of the surrounding district; there were then 189 shareholders, a capital of £340 and an annual turnover of £9,000[29]. In 1899 Plunkett established a co-operative store in Doneraile, Co. Cork with the help of Lord Castletown and Alexis Roche, two of the local gentry. Affiliated to the Co-operative Union and with an English manager, goods were purchased from the Co-operative Wholesale Society (CWS) in Manchester. The local bakers refused to supply bread so a bakery was added which failed as a result of the insobriety of the baker. The store stuttered on for a couple of years, ultimately becoming a proprietary concern but the experience had proved instructive; the English model of distributive co-operation was not the one to flourish in rural Ireland.

In the course of an address which he gave in 1890 to the annual congress of the Co-operative Union at Glasgow, Plunkett indicated the direction which his movement was going to take:

There happens to be in Ireland a most important productive industry, which lends itself in a very striking manner to co-operative organisation. I refer, I need hardly say, to the business of dairying, which, if I am not much mistaken, is destined to do more to illustrate the advantages of industrial association than any other form of productive industry.[30]

Ireland possessed remarkable natural advantages for, and a long tradition in, the production of butter, but, in terms of scientific innovation, education and business organisation, Irish farmers had fallen way behind their continental counterparts. The development by Laval in 1878 of the mechanical cream separator and steam-powered churn was revolutionising European dairying. Anderson, who visited Swedish creameries in 1890 found the farmers well educated, with a good business sense and most of them possessed a telephone! The output per cow was 33% higher than in Ireland and, in general, the land was not as good.[31] Denmark, where co-operative dairying had been in full swing since 1882, was providing particularly stiff competition for Irish farmers. In 1848, 379,000 packages of Irish butter had entered the port of London as against a total of 576,888 from overseas. By 1884 the number of Irish packages sold in London had been reduced to 5,618 compared to 1,703,772 from overseas. The average price, in that year, worked out at 6 pounds and 10 shillings per cwt., for Danish butter as against 4 pounds 19 shillings and 3 pence per cwt., for the Irish product. [32] It looked as if Ireland's English market would completely disappear while, even in Dublin, Danish butter had taken the lead.

The remedy was straightforward. Methods which had proved successful in Denmark must be applied to Ireland and, henceforth, European agricultural co-operatives rather than the urban British version were to be Ireland's model. Creamery plant was expensive so, in order to establish a creamery, farmers had to combine. The introduction of these ideas to Ireland was not only Plunkett's work. Possibly the first creamery (with separators) had been established in Midleton, Co. Cork in 1882 by Penrose Fitzgerald, Lord Midleton's agent, to serve his tenants. Canon Richard Bagot of Kildare, a pioneer of dairy reform, had set up joint-stock creameries at Hospital, Co. Limerick in 1884 and another at nearby Galbally soon after. [33] Plunkett saw that modernisation of the butter industry was inevitable but recognised the danger of the business falling into the grip of middlemen such as the unscrupulous butter merchants of pre-creamery days.

Together with R. A. Anderson, he set off to stump the country preaching the gospel of co-operation. They concentrated, initially, on the Golden Vale, the rich dairying area of the south and west but early results were discouraging. Farmers, in spite of Parnell's example, were suspicious of a movement spearheaded by a protestant landlord and, not unnaturally, it was regarded as a competing interest by traders and shopkeepers. The traders were often influential members of the Nationalist (or Parliamentary) Party, thus it was not surprising that there was opposition from that quarter from the outset. Meanwhile, in 1889, W. L. Stokes, the Co-operative Wholesale Society's representative in Limerick, in partnership with a far-sighted butter merchant — Robert Gibson, had, with the guidance of the Co-operative Union, succeeded in establishing Ireland's first co-operative creamery at Drumcollogher, Co. Limerick. [34] Over fifty meetings were addressed by Plunkett and Anderson before they recorded their first success. Anderson, whose life was threatened on at least one occasion (in Co. Clare) graphically described the difficulties which beset them:

It was hard and thankless work. There was the apathy of the people and the active opposition of the press and politicians. It would be hard to say now whether the abuse of the conservative *Cork Constitution* or that of the nationalist *Eagle* of Skibbereen, was the louder. We were 'killing the calves', we were 'forcing the young women to emigrate', we were 'destroying the industry'. Mr. Plunkett was described as a 'monster in human shape', and was abjured to 'cease his hellish work'. I was described as his 'Man Friday' and as 'Roughrider Anderson'. Once, when I thought I had planted a creamery within the precincts of the town of Rathkeale, my co-operative applecart was upset by the local solicitor, who, having elicited the fact that our movement recognised neither political nor religious differences — that the unionist-protestant cow was as dear to us as her nationalist-catholic sister — gravely informed me that our programme would not suit Rathkeale. 'Rathkeale' said he pompously, 'is a nationalist town — nationalist to the backbone — and every pound of butter made in this creamery must be made on nationalist principles, or it shan't be made at all'. This sentiment was applauded loudly and the proceedings terminated.[35]

1890 passed without a single co-operative creamery being added to the solitary total of Drumcollogher but Plunkett and company were not easily deterred and the tide turned when they established their first creamery society at Ballyhahill, near Monteagle's home in Co. Limerick. By the end of 1891, fifteen co-operative creameries had been founded and Plunkett had approached Arthur Balfour, the chief secretary for Ireland, seeking official support. Balfour was a member of the tory administration headed by his uncle, Lord Salisbury from 1886 to 1891. His rigorous application of coercive legislation (Edward Carson won his spurs as state prosecutor in this period) earned him the title 'Bloody Balfour', but he was also an enlightened administrator and, during his years in office, Ireland benefitted from a land purchase scheme, railway building and the Congested Districts Board. Plunkett admired Balfour.[36] 'In Ireland, a high courage, especially when it is combined with an understanding sympathy, always wins admiration and respect', he wrote in tribute.[37]

In 1891 Plunkett approached that august body, the Royal Dublin Society (RDS), to support his work. The Society is now best known for its annual shows, the Spring Show (of great importance to Irish agriculture) and the Horse Show held in August. Since its foundation in 1731 the RDS had taken a benevolent interest in raising standards in agriculture and industry. At the time of his approach, the Society had undertaken the first proper survey of Irish fishing grounds under the direction of an intrepid clergyman, W. S. Green*. Revolving in Plunkett's mind during his cowboy days had been the ideas of organising Irish farmers as a political force and of obtaining government support. Five thousand pounds, a large fraction of current state expenditure on agriculture, was channelled through the RDS and Plunkett hoped that a proportion could be diverted to his movement. In January he talked with Balfour and an RDS official, 'I wanted the government to get the Royal to apply part of the government funds for dairy purposes'.[38] The Society, however, rejected Plunkett's request on the grounds that it should not be seen to favour one form of trading over another and responded by setting up a working dairy at its next Spring Show; then making a grant of £50, not to Plunkett, but to the British Co-operative Union, for technical instruction in the Irish dairy industry.[39] This deliberate snub rankled with Plunkett; RDS backing would have been of the utmost value to his fledgling movement; a clash of personalities seems the most reasonable explanation. The RDS had many splendid achievements to its credit but it was very much a preserve of the ascendancy. (It was, according to one Dublin wit, 'only the Kildare Street Club daubed with cowdung!'). Land agitation in the nineteenth century had driven a great wedge between landlords and tenants and the benefits of the scientific work carried out by the Society were not filtering down to smaller farmers most urgently in need of them.[40] The RDS, as Plunkett saw it, must no longer be allowed to act as a buffer between farmers and the state. A sound system of agricultural administration had to be established!

As an added burden, relations between the Irish co-operators and their parent bodies the Co-operative Union and the Co-operative Wholesale Society were rapidly deteriorating. Initially there had been financial aid and assistance with propaganda from the Co-operative Union while purchases had been made from, and sales made to, the CWS. But the fundamental differences between producer and consumer-based co-operation were not easily reconciled; Plunkett somewhat grandly interpreting the domination of distributive over productive co-operation as the subordination of social to economic ideals, of things spiritual to things material.[41] 'I have often regretted', he wrote later, somewhat tongue in cheek, 'that the Rochdale pioneers continued to divide up a chest of tea instead of killing

*In 1882 he led the first successful assault on New Zealand's Mt. Cook and later became chief inspector in the fisheries branch of the DATI.

and curing a co-operative pig'.[42] In reality, conditions of urban Britain differed so markedly from those in rural Ireland that it was unlikely that, in the two countries, the same co-operative paths would be pursued.

In these circumstances friction was likely to arise. In 1893 the formation of the Irish Co-operative Agency Society, with a depot in Manchester to handle the sale of Irish creamery products, challenged the hegemony of the CWS. In the same year when a creamery at Castlemahon, Co. Tipperary collapsed, the CWS stepped in, bought the creamery and, as the farmers were unwilling to run it, the CWS took it on as a proprietary concern. Having taken this step the CWS announced its intention of setting up further proprietary creameries in other parts of Ireland. W. L. Stokes, the CWS agent, in a letter to the *Cork Herald*[43] argued that the CWS aim was to cater for their own members and obtain for them the best quality products, further

they wish it to be distinctly understood that they would prefer to see the farmers co-operating together and producing their own butter, it is only where this co-operation has failed, or where the farmers of certain districts have invited us to go amongst them, that we have decided on erecting creameries . . .

This led to protests by the Irish movement and to much inter-co-operative wrangling across the Irish Sea. The CWS creameries were afterwards transferred to Irish ownership but only after much bad feeling. An important consequence was the failure to establish real links between producer and consumer-based co-operatives, to the great detriment of the movement in both islands.

Arthur Balfour, at the end of his term as chief secretary, established the Congested Districts Board (CDB) inviting Plunkett to become a member. The Board was set up to deal with the appalling problems of deprivation in the over-populated and under-nourished west of Ireland. It purchased and amalgamated the smallest holdings, imported stock, built dwellings and established fisheries and home industries. By 1911 it had spent £10 million and bought two and a half million acres outright from the smallest tenants and sold them to more solvent neighbours. His travels, as a member of the Board, introduced Plunkett to a part of the country he had never seen but, while appreciating the Board's good work, he was never happy with its undisguised paternalism. He was, in fact, in favour of assisted emigration from congested districts (a policy which was fraught with political difficulty), making enquiries in that direction on a visit to the United States and Canada in the autumn of 1891.[44] The only real hope of success for the CDB lay, he believed, in the strict observance of the rule that a man should not, by state aid, be put in possession of a farm until it was ascertained that he was fit to run it. Typically he felt that 'permanent results can be produced only by working on character'.[45] Thus, although Plunkett was to remain a member of the Board until 1918, the underlying differences in philosophy meant that relationships between the Board and the co-operators were never entirely happy.

In July 1891 the *Freeman's Journal* reported an event 'of singular importance to the industrial history Ireland.'[46] It was the first conference of co-operative dairy societies, held at Newcastle West, Co. Limerick. 'Not a word except business', Plunkett enthusiastically recorded, 'the affair was unique in the industrial history of Ireland'.[47] Control of the processing and marketing of his goods would bring prosperity to the farmer; co-operators had no qualms at the thought that the inefficient middleman might be eliminated.

A measure of the energy and enthusiasm of the pioneers can be guaged from the fact that, during a twelve month period in 1892/3, Anderson addressed 440 meetings and over 10,000 copies of his pamphlet on co-operative creameries were distributed.[48] Some thirty co-operative creameries with a total turnover of £140,000 were in existence by 1893, and the need for a co-ordinating body was becoming increasingly clear.

There was a cry for advice on methods of organisation there was a demand for technical advice on creamery engineering, on the testing of milk for purity and butter-fat content, even on farm management, which it was beyond their scope to give. There was the problem of supplying fuel and salt and boxwood and the even greater problem of marketing co-operative creamery butter so that one creamery should not compete with another and none should be helpless in the hands of the wholesalers.[49]

The growing confidence of Irish farmers was emphasised at a meeting held in the Antient Concert Rooms,* Dublin on 18 April 1894 attended by some 250 people, representative of all sides of Irish life, at which the birth of the Irish Agricultural Organisation Society (IAOS) was announced. The Bishop of Raphoe, Dr. O'Donnell was there together with Lord Monteagle, Count

*Currently the Academy Theatre in Pearse Street.

Arthur Moore and Christopher Digges La Touche, managing director of the Guinness brewery. Messages of support were received from Edward Carson, Lord Iveagh, John Redmond and Sir Charles Gavan Duffy. Plunkett addressed the assembly for over an hour outlining the functions of the new organisation:

The keynote of our proposals is the proposition that the Irish farmers must work out their own salvation and further, that this can only be done by combination among themselves. [50]

The more business introduced into politics and the less politics in business, he advised, the better for both; emphasising the non-political and non-sectarian nature of the Society. Plunkett knew that farmers, through combination, had acquired political power elsewhere: the Syndicats Agricoles in France tackled the problems of land taxation, railway rates and customs duties as well as providing technical advice, setting up scientific experiments and acting as a trading agency for farmers. Speaking of proposals for the establishment of an Irish department of agriculture he stressed an essential ingredient of his co-operative philosophy:

An agriculture department is now a remedy, and so long as its functions are limited to what such departments have done successfully elsewhere it should certainly be created. But that any government assistance, whether legislative or administrative, can do one tithe of the good which can be done by organisation, is a popular fallacy. [51]

His speech was received with thunderous applause drowning the words of Lord Cloncurry who proposed the motion forming the IAOS. This was seconded by James Byrne, coroner, cattle-breeder and an influential nationalist from Co. Cork, and passed unanimously. Plunkett shrewdly terminated proceedings on this note of euphoria; further discussion would be anti-climactic, besides, the election of a properly balanced committee was a delicate matter. This having been duly done, at the next meeting Plunkett was elected president and Anderson secretary. The committee, judiciously chosen to span religious and political divides, contained the nationalist MP's John Redmond and Thomas Sexton (who though they never attended were of the first importance), Dr. O'Donnell, James Byrne, La Touche, Monteagle, Father Finlay and James Musgrave [52] (a prominent Belfast businessman).

Under the auspices of the IAOS the movement greatly

increased its scope. On account of opposition from the Nationalist Party, and to the great disappointment of 'whole hog' co-
operators such as Anderson, the establishment of consumer
societies (a co-operative store would have made a natural adjunct
to the village creamery) did not become official policy. However
agricultural societies for the purchase of high grade seeds,
manures and agricultural implements were a success as, initially,
were co-operative banks on the Raiffeisen[53] model introduced by
Father Finlay to provide credit particularly in the poorer areas.
Eggs and poultry, bee-keeping, home industries, horticulture,
flax and bacon curing (in Roscrea) were added to the objectives
for which societies were formed. In 1895 a weekly journal, the
Irish Homestead, appeared with Father Finlay as editor. AE filled
the editor's chair from 1905 and, under his guidance it achieved
an unrivalled reputation. Before the establishment of the
Department of Agriculture and Technical Instruction in 1900, the
IAOS maintained a staff of experts to encourage the formation of
co-operatives, and to give technical advice on cereal raising,
poultry breeding, fruit growing, the production and marketing of
honey, the packing, grading and marketing of eggs in addition to
servicing creameries.

The growth of the new movement may be traced from the fact
that, less than ten years later, over 800 co-operative societies had
been established; of these 360 were dairy and 140 agricultural
societies (for bulk purchasing and marketing), nearly 200
agricultural banks, 50 home industries societies, 40 poultry
societies and others with miscellaneous objects. The total
membership amounted to some 80,000 and the combined turnover to some £2 million.[54] A number of societies had started
village libraries and were helping in other ways to raise the
quality and to mitigate the hardship of rural life. Plunkett, in the
face of many obstacles, had succeeded in uniting protestant and
catholic, unionist and nationalist in a single movement with a
clearly defined goal. In the Ireland of 1894 this was a noteworthy
achievement.

III

Parliament and the Recess Committee

Plunkett's public work commenced just as Parnell's career was drawing to its tragic and dramatic close. As a landlord, Parnell had invested heavily in industrial development, mainly stone-quarrying and timber-milling, on his estate at Avondale in Co. Wicklow. Favouring a long term solution to the land problem by tenant purchase with government funding and without injury to the landlord, he held that compulsory powers should only be sought to deal with absentee landowners and the great London companies (with extensive domains in Ulster) but should not be used against resident landlords. Parnell believed, with Plunkett, that a role remained for the landlords to play in Ireland. Realising that the strength of the land movement stemmed from the tenants' desire to own the lands they worked, he emphatically opposed the formula of land nationalisation put forward by Michael Davitt. [1]

It was one of Parnell's most deeply held beliefs, that remedial legislation, rather than blunt the edge of the home rule demand, would sharpen it. In April 1891 he stressed this conviction in a speech at Irishtown:

I have always believed that by making the Irish tenant-farmer prosperous and independent of his landlord, by reducing his rents, by giving him and the labourers something to put in their bellies, we are not diminishing the forces of Irish nationality, but we are increasing them. [2]

To a companion on a railway journey in 1887, he proposed the establishment of a board of agriculture in Dublin with a staff of travelling lecturers, government subsidies for local agricultural societies and instruction for farmers in crop cultivation and dairying besides state aid for fisheries and forestry. [3] Parnell was never keen to spell out his economic theories in detail, nor in public, but these comments bear a striking resemblance to

36

Plunkett's thinking and were all, eventually, incorporated in his reforms.

At the outset of his career Plunkett had hoped to infect Parnell with some of his co-operative enthusiasm and, through the nationalist MP, T. P. Gill, as he recalled many years later, he arranged a meeting for June 1891 which never took place:

In the year 1889 I had a appointment with Mr. Parnell in the House of Commons, which he was unable to keep, and I never saw him. He wished me to explain to him the aims and objects of this movement, which a few of us were then starting. Who knows how different the situation we have to discuss today might have been had we met?[4]

Here Plunkett's memory was playing him false for the date on which he was due to meet Parnell in the House of Commons is shown quite clearly in his diary as 19 June 1891 (when he first met Gill) and there is no record in his diary of any proposed meeting in 1889. Having missed Parnell in the House of Commons he wrote to Gill on 20 June 1891, 'I hope to be fortunate enough to meet Mr. Parnell in Dublin on Monday';[5] again this meeting never materialised. One month later, after Parnell's failure in the Carlow by-election, Plunkett wrote again to Gill,

I am rather sorry Mr. Parnell did not take up co-operative dairying specifically at Carlow. It seems a pity to declare generally in favour of industrial reform and pass by what is practically the only industry in a large part of the country.[6]

By the summer of 1891 Parnell, who was fast going downhill politically and physically, and was, in any case, notoriously difficult to pin down on points of detail, had other things on his mind besides co-operative dairying (he died in October); but the importance of such a meeting to Plunkett was magnified in retrospect ('I happened to know that he had enlightened views on agricultural economics' Plunkett wrote in 1921),[7] for, had he received the Chief's imprimatur for his economic policy, it would have provided effective insulation against the subsequent attacks of Davitt, Dillon and the Parliamentary Party.

Plunkett, in 1892, was in sympathy a unionist, albeit a unionist whose views had been broadened on the plains of Wyoming, at the head of a co-operative movement the bulk of whose membership was nationalist. Unlike the majority of English politicians he had not been blinded by the dissention in Ireland which had followed the fall of Parnell, recording in June 1891, 'those who think the "national" spirit sick unto death are, I think, superficial observers'.[8] The co-operators formed a non-sectarian, non-political movement whose sucess depended upon 'a rigid abstention from party politics'. Had he concentrated his energies entirely upon social objectives, Plunkett would doubtless have encountered political opposition (as had Father Theobald Mathew in his temperance crusade of fifty years before).[9] Indeed the early 'commercial' outcry against co-operation by the Nationalist Party showed what a threat such a movement posed for the politicians; but the benefits which co-operation brought in its train plus the fact that many strong nationalists were keen co-operators had made the movement a difficult target. However Plunkett soon settled the politicians' problem by sportingly setting up as a target himself.

As the spearhead of co-operation he had become a public figure; inevitably his thoughts turned towards parliament. Polarisation of Irish politics ensured that non-party candidates stood little chance of success. To a member of the Dunsany family the securing of a unionist nomination was merely a formality. The temptation proved too much to resist; Plunkett gravely underestimating the effect which his decision would have upon co-operation. Arthur Balfour, whom he consulted, was mildly discouraging, indicating that he would not have nominated him to the CDB had he thought he would ultimately have become a parliamentary candidate,[10] but Plunkett pressed on. 'I adopted this course to strengthen my influence in Ireland and to facilitate my economic and industrial work!'[11]

Having accepted a unionist nomination, he could be sure of attacks from the nationalists and, during the election, he was accused, in parliament, of having used his position as a member of the CDB to political advantage. Balfour refuted the charge pointing out that South Dublin, the constituency which he had chosen, was not a congested district, adding that he had attempted to dissuade Plunkett from going forward.[12] Prior to 1892 the South Dublin seat had been held by the nationalists but his task had been made easier by the split over Parnell. Standing firm on the constitution but urging unionists to forget the past and to promote the industrial and material welfare of the country, Plunkett's vote of 4371 saw him comfortably home, ahead of French Mullen (2261), the Parnellite, and Grattan Esmonde (1452), the anti-Parnellite, and previous incumbent.

To the impatient, idealistic Plunkett his experience at Westminster came as a sad anti-climax. He spoke rarely but not well. Party manouvering and point-scoring he found boring and pointless. 'I had no idea the waste of time that was so cold-bloodedly indulged in. It really is outrageous. Our side is quite as bad as the worst section of the others'. [13] Worse still, having given himself as a hostage to nationalist fortune, his independent stance infuriated the unionists. However, his range of contacts in influential circles was greatly extended, his friendship with the Balfours prospered through frequent visits to their Surrey home at Fishers Hill, and to everyone he preached the co-operative gospel.

He had entered politics at an auspicious time. Gladstone was still prime minister but Parnell had fallen. The Nationalist Party was rent into two factions, the Parnellites led by John Redmond and the larger anti-Parnell group by John Dillon. This division was to prove of major importance to Plunkett.

Gladstone's second home rule bill came before the Commons in 1893. Plunkett referred to his family connection with Ireland extending back over centuries. In that time they had become more and more Irish while never failing to recognize the value of the English connection. It would be false to suppose that everyone opposed to home rule was out of sympathy with the Irish people but no solution to the problem of Ireland's development would be satisfactory if it failed to bridge the river separating north from south. If home rule were to be forced on Ulster, and he did not believe that this was possible, it would perpetuate and intensify a state of things, in which the Boyne would seem broader, deeper and stormier than the Irish sea; concluding, to his own party's satisfaction, that there was 'absolutely no nucleus to the home rule comet'. [14] The measure narrowly passed through the lower house only to founder on the rock of dominant toryism in the House of Lords. ('Thus perished all hope of a united, self-governing Ireland, loyal to the British crown', wrote Winston Churchill in retrospect). [15] The Grand Old Man of English politics retired and was succeeded by Lord Rosebery. Home rule was now in cold storage and was to remain so during the period of tory administration which was to follow.

Unthinking support for the Union formed the basis of the ascendancy's political faith, but Plunkett's education had been rounded off on the foothills of the Rockies. There he had learned to 'dilute his hereditary instincts with democratic ideals' and to 'forget and remember' enough of his country's history to choose a life of service. Considering himself a social reformer rather than a politician, he was, in his early phase, undoubtedly a unionist but one of that rare variety who,

> while recognizing the indisputable nationality of Ireland, has so little
> fear of its absorption or disappearance that the alleged material
> advantages of union with England appear more desirable than the
> chances of self-government. [16]

Having adhered closely to unionist orthodoxy in the home rule
debate of 1893, Plunkett committed his first breach of party
discipline when he voted against a conservative amendment to
exclude Irish representation from the Westminster parliament.
Carson threatened to denounce him in the Irish papers [17] but his
action failed to heighten his esteem among the anti-Parnellite
nationalists for he was the object of a series of attacks by Michael
Davitt on the grounds that his co-operative schemes were
distracting the Irish farmer from politics. [18]

Davitt, son of an evicted tenant from Co. Mayo, had spent his
formative years in Lancashire's cotton mills and was a socialist
whose economic theories were often at variance with Parnell's.
He wished to make ownership of the soil the basis of the fight for
self-government and was determined to abolish the landlords
root and branch. An admirer of John Stuart Mill's ideas for co-
operative re-organisation of industry, (Davitt quoted at length
from Mill's theory of co-operation in his *Leaves from a Prison
Diary*), [19] he failed to recognize that the form of co-operation
which Plunkett was advocating for Irish agriculture was, in
essence, that proposed for British industry by Mill.

Thus, at an early stage of his parliamentary career, Plunkett
had fallen foul of anti-Parnellite nationalism besides attempting
to widen the narrow context of unionist thinking. The sterile
slogans of 'law and order' and the 'status quo' must be
supplemented by a constructive social policy. Behind the scenes
he pressed his party colleagues to put forward economic rather
than constitutional opposition to home rule, believing that
commercial arguments emanating from Belfast were the most
serious which the nationalists had to counter. But his attempt to
alter unionist thinking was a failure; 'stupid, stupid unionists' he
wrote in his diary. [20] A compensation was the establishment of
good relations with the Parnellite nationalists in the lobby, and,
while disagreeing with their constitutional views, he showed an
enthusiastic anxiety to work with them for the common good.

A real tension was developing between his desire to serve his
country and his party loyalty. In May 1895 he wrote to Arthur
Balfour offering to resign his seat, [21] and to the South Dublin

unionists in the same vein.[22] But this time, with some apparent encouragement from Balfour, who remarked that little Irish legislation was contemplated in the next parliament (which Plunkett thought to be a mistake, missing 'the great — perhaps the last — opportunity they will have of making a unionist settlement of the Irish question')[23] he changed his mind and on 20 July was comfortably re-elected.

Rosebery's government was roundly defeated to be succeeded by the tories under Lord Salisbury. Gerald Balfour, the new chief secretary for Ireland and Plunkett's contempory at Eton (where they had been members of the same house) quickly set about continuing the constructive policies of his elder brother. Plunkett through his own efforts and his friendship with the Balfours was well placed to take advantage of 'Balfourian amelioration'. The split among the nationalists was, if anything, widened by Balfourian policy, for Dillon felt that each substantial reform granted by the government would make it more difficult to revive the national movement, while Redmond, following Parnell, held that the movement would only gather strength as the result of increased prosperity in Ireland. The Redmondites therefore, on the whole, co-operated in the new enterprises while Dillon denounced the government for dragging a red herring across the path of home rule. Dillon had an additional reason for disliking the co-operators for his family ran a large store in Ballagha-derreen, Co. Roscommon and country traders had always been the most vigorous opponents of the movement.

* * *

The state, in the latter half of the nineteenth century, was playing an increasing role in economic development overseas but English economic opinion, favouring a non-intervention policy dependent on private enterprise, dominated Irish practice. Foundation of the US Department of Agriculture in 1862 followed by the establishment of the land grant colleges marked the start of formal research work into agricultural problems. The Danish co-operative movement originated by the dairy farmers of western Jutland in 1881-82, swept across Denmark with government support, 'like a wave arising from the North Sea'. But apart from the land acts, generally extorted from the government by continued agrarian disturbance, there was a complete lack of government policy for, or intervention in, Irish economic development. Plunkett set out to remedy this defect in the agricultural sphere. He had crossed swords with the one body (the RDS) powerful enough to influence agricultural policy in Ireland, experience had revealed that parliamentary procedures were not for him, so now a bold initiative was required.

One evening in 1895 while I was coming to Dublin in a badly lit railway carriage, I wrote a letter inviting all interested in the material progress of Ireland, to a non-party conference for the purpose of formulating a demand for the kind of state assistance we needed both for agriculture and other industries. Next day I showed the letter to Father Finlay, who advised me to send it to the press. This I did, and the response, which astonished none more than myself, led to the formation of the Recess Committee.[24]

Splits in the ranks of unionism and nationalism cleared the way. T. P. Gill, a nationalist from Tipperary, was the key figure in enlisting Parnellite support. A graduate of Trinity College, Gill had practised as a journalist in Britain and America before becoming a Parnellite MP in 1885 and taking part in the 'Plan of Campaign'*. A skillful politician with a tendency to go the way the wind was blowing, his efforts to heal the split in his party after the O'Shea divorce case earned him the title of 'neutral Gill'. His nationalist contacts and administrative ability made him an essential ingredient to Plunkett's scheme but he was mistrusted by some of the co-operators including R. A. Anderson, and their suspicions were, ultimately, to be confirmed.

Ulster unionism, threatened by economic and class conflicts which ranged tenant farmers and dissenters against landlords and anglicans, always evinced a tendency to divide when not confronted by the bogey of home rule. The Ulster Liberal Unionist Association (ULUA), founded by the remnant of the Liberal Party in Ulster at the time of Gladstone's conversion to home rule and backed up by Joseph Chamberlain at Westminster, had at this time considerable influence. Comprised mainly of tenant farmers and businessmen of presbyterian and unitarian stock, its members, though resolute in their unionism, boasted of ancestors who had been United Irishmen or who had fought for American independence. The ULUA took the side of the tenants against the landlords and was a firm supporter of remedial legislation which favoured its agricultural and industrial interests; it sought an Irish department of agriculture with an Irish minister responsible for it, and its members formed

*A tenant campaign to withold rent from the landlords.

the backbone of Plunkett's northern support. Besides this, there was, in the linen firms and shipyards of Ulster, a demand matching that for a department of agriculture in the countryside. 'It is beyond all question that industrial instruction is the first and most pressing of all Irish requirements' argued the *Irish Textile Journal* of Belfast, [25] spearhead of the campaign for technical education since 1886.

Plunkett had put his finger on two glaring weaknesses in Irish administration under the Union. There was no single department to deal with the myriad problems of Irish agriculture (agricultural education being almost non-existent), neither was there any proper provision for technical or vocational education within the school system. The model farm at Glasnevin had been founded in 1838. But other attempts to establish model farms or agricultural training colleges, advocated by the Devon Commission of 1844, had come to nought in face of opposition from English free-traders with the ear of the government. Scientific education in Irish schools was in a similar plight; in 1901 only 6 secondary schools possessed laboratories (this had increased to 150 after two years of the Department's operation). [26] The drive for scientific and technical education came from Ulster and from the liberal unionists representing Belfast's mercantile class as well as the northern tenant farmers. In 1893, James Musgrave petitioned the Duke of Devonshire, on behalf of the liberal unionists, for 'the establishment of a state department for the promotion of the interests of agriculture in Ireland, with an Irish minister at its head', adding that this department should have an educative role vis-a-vis agriculture and other industries. [27] The Technical Education Act of 1890 enabling local authorities to raise a rate for the specific purpose of providing technical education had, by and large, been ignored in Ireland. (The Belfast Technical School, in 1893, was still a private institution, Musgrave was chairman of its council, receiving only a derisory grant from city funds). An Irish Technical Education Association was founded in the same year at a meeting held in the Antient Concert Rooms, Dublin to press for the provision of proper facilities throughout the country. The meeting was attended by Musgrave, the Church of Ireland archbishop of Dublin (a message of support arriving from Archbishop Walsh), Plunkett, Monteagle and George Francis Fitzgerald, professor of experimental philosophy in Trinity College. [28] In June Lord Salisbury, on a visit to Ulster, was petitioned by the Council of the Belfast Technical School that, 'the promotion of industrial and technical education, not only in connection with commerce and manufactures, but also in relation to agriculture, the principal occupation of the people, is urgently needed'.[29] Further impetus came from Prof. Fitzgerald*, famous for his work on relativity theory, in a lecture to the Irish Industrial League in 1896, demanding technical education in the schools and castigating his own university for its failure to promote the pure and applied sciences.[30]

By 1895, appeals from the Irish farming community, for the establishment of a department of agriculture were reaching a crescendo. The lack of technical education impinged most heavily upon the industrialists of Ulster. By addressing these two problems Plunkett had assured his campaign of support from protestants and catholics, from north and south, from unionists and nationalists. Thus when his letter, cunningly timed to appear in Horse Show week of 1895,[31] put forward a 'proposal affecting the general welfare of Ireland' the temperature had been tested and the ground assiduously prepared, for he was not the man to leave such matters to chance.

The possibility of obtaining home rule, during the life of the then government, was, he submitted, virtually nil, consequently all parties should unite to promote non-controversial measures for their country's good. He instanced two bills establishing Irish boards of agriculture and technical education which the government might be persuaded to support, and proposed that the leaders of the Irish parties should nominate members to form the nucleus of a committee with representatives of commercial, industrial and professional interests to be added to their number by the parliamentarians.

We unionists, without abating one jot of our unionism, and nationalists without abating one jot of their nationalism, can each show our faith in the cause for which we have fought so bitterly and for so long, by sinking our party differences for our country's good and leaving our respective policies for the justification of time.

He went on to give a remarkably honest appraisal of his own political position:

I am opposed to home rule, because I do not think it would be good for Ireland. Most of my colleagues are in favour of it because they think otherwise.

*Fitzgerald served on the Board of Technical Instruction until his untimely death in 1901.

I do not believe that home rule is dead, or that it ever will be while so many of my colleagues are sent to the imperial parliament pledged to vote for it. I go further to admit that if the average Irish elector, who is more intelligent than the average British elector, were also as prosperous, industrious, and as well educated, his continued demand in the proper constitutional way for home rule would very likely result in the experiment being one day tried. On the other hand, I believe that if the material condition of the great body of our countrymen were advanced, if they were encouraged in industrial enterprise, and were provided with practical education in proportion to their natural intelligence, they would see that a political development on lines similar to those adopted in England, was, considering the necessary relations between the two countries, best for Ireland, and then they would cease to desire home rule.

The letter met with immediate response, not all of which was favourable, but mostly so. Justin McCarthy replied on behalf of the anti-Parnellite nationalists to say that he could not participate in any organisation aimed at seeking a substitute for home rule. [32] Redmond however, after much pressure from Plunkett via Gill, consented to serve. Colonel Saunderson, the Irish unionist leader, vowed that he would not sit on any committee with John Redmond, in any case it appeared to him that the motivating idea smacked too much of independence. [33] The two principal organs of northern unionism were at first opposed to the idea (the *Irish Textile Journal* offering unqualified approval). [34] Plunkett headed for Belfast to see both editors and then in December mounted a major assault on the northern capital in the course of which he launched his co-operative campaign in Ulster as well as elaborating upon the proposals in his letter. The ULUA, which he addressed in the Ulster Reform Club, preferred its support with acclamation, and later that evening at a dinner given by Thomas Andrews, a liberal unionist stalwart with a large farm as well as a linen mill in Comber, unionists from both wings of the party gave him an enthusiastic reception. [35] The progressive section of Ulster unionism had been won over and the *Belfast Newsletter* and *Northern Whig* fell rapidly into line.

Against this background Plunkett showed real tactical appreciation in assembling a committee representing the widest group of interests. Lords Mayo and Monteagle (unionist peers), John Redmond and T. C. Harrington (nationalist MPs), Father Finlay, Sir John Arnott (representing southern commerce), Thomas Andrews and Thomas Sinclair (a Belfast provender merchant and the leading liberal unionist) served under

Plunkett's chairmanship. Gill, whom Plunkett praised as 'a practical Thomas Davis', provided a vital link with the nationalists and acted as secretary. An Ulster consultative committee chaired by James Musgrave and benefitting from the enthusiasm of Rev. R. R. Kane (a unionist and orangeman but also a member of the Gaelic League) met in Belfast. Sinclair, who missed the first meeting on 6 January 1896, in his letter of apology to Plunkett, showed the depth of favourable feeling in Ulster.

I am able to say that, as a result of your recent exposition in the north of the proposed work of the Recess Committee, considerable sympathy with its objects has been elicited, and a strong consultative committee, consisting of men of the highest standing in our civic and commercial life has been formed . . . [36]

Education, organisation and representation were to be guiding principles while the technical back-up so essential to such an undertaking was financed by Plunkett. Gill and Mulhall (a statistician) were appointed commissioners and sent to report on developments in nine European countries with instructions to differentiate between the parts played by state aid and by the efforts of the people themselves. The committee sat through the parliamentary recesses of 1895/6 and it was a tribute to the chairman's drive and to the secretary's draftsmanship that a unanimous report was presented to the lord lieutenant of Ireland on 1 August 1896, less than a year after Plunkett had floated the idea in the press. 'If', the committee explained, 'we should seem to claim exceptional treatment for Ireland in the course of this report, it is useful to remember that the state of things requiring to be remedied is largely the result of exceptional treatment of another kind which has already been applied'[37]

The report, which ran to 418 pages, analysed every aspect of the Irish economy and of the models which it might follow, from daffodil growing in Co. Cork to consideration of the 43 different categories of cottage industry in the province of Moscow. It described the existing economic position of Ireland and surveyed the unused or half-used potentialities. It reviewed the measures taken in Europe to promote agriculture and rural industries, fisheries and forestry, and offered a series of proposals for adapting these methods to Irish conditions. In agriculture there must be organisation of the people themselves, since no government could deal directly with the individual. There should be travelling instructors, model plots, experimental stations and laboratories. A consultative council of agriculture should be constituted, its members partly elected, partly appointed. Co-operative banking should be developed.

Technical education, which the Committee noted, was pursued more flexibly and more effectively on the Continent than in the United Kingdom should be strengthened to extend from primary school to university. The callings of commerce, industry and agriculture should be accorded professional status. Finally, there should be set up in Ireland a new department of agriculture and industries, absorbing such existing bodies as the Congested Districts Board, the Fisheries and Veterinary Departments and some sections of the Board of Education; in charge of a minister responsible to parliament, assisted by an appointed agricultural board and advised by the consultative council of agriculture. (In an appendix the French minister, Tisserand, outlined a possible structure for the administration of Irish agriculture). The Committee, it was stated in conclusion, placed their reliance on individual and combined effort rather than on state aid, and in asking for the latter insisted that it should be granted in such a manner as to evoke and supplement the former.

The report had a dramatic impact. Plunkett had effectively removed an important Irish issue from the Westminster arena and had united his fellow countrymen in a clear-cut demand for control of governmental administration of their major industry. Press comment on both sides of the Irish sea was mostly favourable (the *Belfast Newsletter* and *Northern Whig* being unanimous in their enthusiasm).[38] Standish O'Grady (whose translation of Gaelic sagas influenced Irish theatre and literature) described the Committee as 'a body of volunteers who, without authority or sanction from the higher powers, undertook to discharge the functions of a royal or parliamentary commission, and discharged them more brilliantly or effectively than has ever been done by any commission'.[39] The report's reception in government circles was somewhat cooler, which was hardly surprising in view of its hard hitting comments on past performance in which every attributed administrative shortcoming was verified by meticulous reference to impeccable sources — mostly English authors and official reports. Others took a dimmer view; the nationalist *Freeman's Journal* denounced the proposals as a 'burlesque substitute for home rule', arguing that their effect would be to arrange a 'large number of berths' for the 'disinterested guests at Mr. Plunkett's round table!'[40]

A major row, however, was stirred up by the report's disparaging comments upon the activities of the Royal Dublin

Society. Plunkett had his supporters in the Society for he headed the poll to its influential agricultural committee in 1895 as well as in 1896; but he must have still been smarting over the Society's rejection of his plea, in 1891, to divert a proportion of its government subvention to support co-operative dairying; for he seemed to go out of his way, on this occasion, to provoke the RDS. A pencil entry over Gill's signature in the margin of the (charred) minute book of the Recess Committee opposite the chairman's statement that he had prepared a draft report on the basis of the resolutions arrived at, contains the words:

It was I who prepared the draft report. I wrote every line of it save the passage — mostly references to the Royal Dublin Society. The passage about the RDS was written by the chairman in substitution for a different passage.[41]

The offending paragraph paid due tribute to the work of the RDS for Irish horse breeding and to the unrivalled success of its annual Horse Show but continued by quoting a criticism of the Society which had been published two years earlier by Plunkett:

With its great prestige, large membership, including most of the leaders of thought in Ireland, its efficient staff, ample funds, and a government subsidy, it is capable of performing well its chief function, namely, the advancement of agriculture, and yet its greatest admirers will not claim for it that it has succeeded in effecting any marked or permanent improvement in the methods of the Irish farmer.[42]

The Society was described as a quasi-academic body, unrepresentative of the majority of those engaged in agriculture, it was not elective (its members being admitted by ballot) and stood alone in Dublin without any system of branch societies throughout the country.

The RDS, not unnaturally, set to work and produced a pamphlet entitled 'Observations on the References in the Recess Committee's Report to the Royal Dublin Society, its Work and Position in Ireland'. Its efforts on live stock extended to other animals besides the horse and the annual Spring Show was evidence of this. The RDS, which had been in existence since 1731, was responsible for the foundation of the Royal Botanic Gardens; indeed there was also

Leinster House, the Society's historic home, which stands central in the midst of a group of flourishing institutions founded by the Society, namely: The Science and Art Museum including the Natural History Collections, the National Library, and the Metropolitan School of Art.[43]

The pamphlet contained counterproposals on agricultural administration and recommended, much to Plunkett's annoyance, that the Irish board of agriculture be simply a branch of the English board.

Quite undeterred by the acrimony, for which he was mainly responsible, Plunkett returned to the charge with an article in the *New Ireland Review*, 'The Apologia of the Royal Dublin Society'[44] besides an unsigned article in the *Irish Homestead*, 'The Royal Dublin Society and the Recess Committee'[45] written very much in the Plunkett style. A telling phrase gave the reason for failure of one of the Society's schemes: 'Its basis was aristocratic, and times have gone badly with the Irish aristocracy'. The tone of these articles was not an unfriendly one; as in the case of the CDB, Plunkett saw his struggle with the RDS as one of democracy versus paternalism. However he had managed to make some influential enemies, particularly Lord Ardilaun, president of the RDS from 1897 to 1913. Plunkett's failure to convince the Society of the efficacy of his schemes may have been inevitable but his series of attacks on that powerful body seem a serious error of judgement.

Publication of the Recess Committee's report brought him recognition in the form of a Irish privy councillorship but not immediate legislative results. In April 1897 Chief Secretary Gerald Balfour introduced the Agriculture and Industries (Ireland) Bill. It was deficient in two respects: the financial provision was inadequate and there was no reference to technical education. The bill was withdrawn pending the introduction, a month later, of the Irish Local Government Bill,[46] and Plunkett was given more time to perfect his scheme, enabling him to use the newly established county councils as the representative basis of his council of agriculture.

* * *

There had been general agreement among English statesmen since 1880 that reform was required in the government of Ireland but a wide divergence of opinion on the principles which should guide such reform. Gladstone had led the Liberal Party (not without some influential defections) to the conclusion that the Union was of itself, fundamentally unsound, so he, and his policies, were anathema to the Irish ascendancy. The tories, on the other hand supported the Union. But when the traditional defenders of property, law and order, in the Balfourian period, embarked on a policy designed to extend to the masses the benefits of union, Irish unionists, clinging desperately to their position of privilege, developed a persecution complex which ensured that no such policy would be treated on its merits.

In February 1896, the nationalists moved an amendment to the Address in favour of an amnesty for Irish political prisoners. Glasgow, Liverpool, Birmingham and London had suffered at the hands of Irish-American dynamiters, many of whom had been sentenced to life imprisonment some thirteen years before. Plunkett spoke in favour of the amendment (he abstained in the vote) stating that 'he should not join in such a movement as a politician; but he should simply join as an Irishman anxious for the peace and prosperity of his country.'[47] He was supported by Lecky representing Dublin University but his action brought a swift and unpleasant rejoinder from Saunderson on behalf of the Irish unionists (Lecky being excused on the grounds that it was his maiden speech).[48]

Plunkett and Saunderson soon again crossed swords, on this occasion in the letter columns of *The Times*; Saunderson, criticising a suggestion of Plunkett's that a national subscription be raised to alleviate the hardship suffered by tenants evicted during the Plan of Campaign, protested that a fund raised by nationalists would have been more appropriate. He failed to see why Irish loyalists and landlords should dip into their pockets to support those who were defying them and enjoined his readers to wait, as the tenants were gradually coming to terms with the landlords and their sufferings were a salutary lesson.[49] In a debate on an Irish evicted tenants bill in the previous month Plunkett had not spoken but had voted with the nationalists. The unionists were furious. Lord Ardilaun cancelled his subscription to the Dublin branch of the Unionist Registration Association on the grounds that the member for St. Stephen's Green (Kenny, a liberal unionist) and the member for South Dublin had voted for measures which were 'radical and communistic — both voted for a bill to rob the landlords, and one palliated crime to please the friends of criminals'.[50] Ardilaun was a formidable opponent. His statue in St. Stephen's Green, Dublin bears witness to his major benefaction, for he bought the city centre park from the house-holders, landscaped it and presented it to the nation. He was a wealthy member of the Guinness family and a champion of the rights of landlords. Plunkett's disparagement of the RDS must have irked him as the Society's then vice-president; his social theories would not have appealed to the conservative Ardilaun; while his dwindling attachment to the Church of Ireland marked him out even more as an object of suspicion.

Supporting Gerald Balfour's land bill of 1896 (bitterly opposed by unionists for introducing compulsory purchase of bankrupt estates) Plunkett said that it really looked as if older members of the House would see one Irish question settled by the imperial parliament in their lifetime, adding in tribute to his own class that 'it would be a very great calamity if the advantages of refinement, of education and grace of life and the traditions of an aristocracy were destroyed'.[51] He joined in the call for a catholic university for Ireland, as did Carson and Lecky, but the move was opposed by most other unionists and, when the first unsuccessful attempt was made in 1897 to set up an Irish department of agriculture, it was warmly supported by Carson. Carson and Plunkett for a while remained on friendly personal terms even though their political paths were rapidly diverging. Other unionists were not so friendly and, by 1896, his radical tendencies and his support for the policy of 'Balfourian amelioration' had aroused the strongest emotions among his unionist constituents. The campaign to unseat him, led by Lord Ardilaun and by Edward Dowden, professor of English in Trinity College, had already begun.

It was curious, and, according to John Dillon's biographer, 'slightly sinister from the nationalist point of view', that scarcely had the Recess Committee got underway, than another opportunity arose for inter-party co-operation on an Irish problem. In 1893, in response to persistent Irish complaints of over taxation, Gladstone had promised a royal commission on every aspect of Anglo-Irish financial relations. This was established under the chairmanship of Hugh Childers, a former chancellor of the exchequer, in 1894 and contained, in addition to various English financial experts, representatives of Irish unionism and of both wings of the nationalist party. In 1896 the commission reported and its findings, on the whole, justified the complaints. The principal argument was that while Ireland contributed roughly one-eleventh of the imperial revenue, her capacity for bearing taxation was estimated to be one-twentieth that of the whole UK, while the report was given a home rule flavour by the recommendation that, for purposes of taxation, Ireland should be treated as a separate entity.

The immediate outcome was that, during 1896, mass meetings were held in various parts of Ireland at which all classes and political persuasions united to protest their over-taxation. The situation was tailor-made for Plunkett and to the *Irish Times* he wrote, 'It is essential that a definite national claim shall be arrived at in support of which unionists and nationalists, north and south, can cordially unite.' He went on to suggest the formation of an ad hoc body (on the lines of the Recess Committee) comprising representatives of the Irish parliamentary parties and of the chambers of commerce in Belfast, Dublin and Cork which could enlarge its membership if required and should aim at presenting a unanimous report to parliament.[52]

By February 1897 this agitation had given birth to an all-Ireland committee, which, when the government showed signs of evading the issue, summoned a conference of Irish parliamentarians to discuss what immediate action could be taken. The circular calling the conference was signed by Saunderson, Plunkett, Redmond and Healy. (This time it was Dillon who demurred for tactical reasons). When the meeting took place, Saunderson, waiving the scruples which had prevented him from serving on the Recess Committee, was elected to the chair. He had become chairman by default, he explained:

If they had chosen a member of Mr. Healy's party none of the others would have been in the room . . . I walked into that committee room with my friend Mr. Lecky, with Mr. Carson, and Mr. Horace Plunkett, who were the only Irish unionist members who could harden their hearts to sit in such company . . . I will say this, that in no meeting was I ever treated with such respect or more willingly obeyed.[53]

A subcommittee consisting of Saunderson, Lecky, Healy and Clancy (nationalist) was given the task of finding a formula which would crystallise the issue and on 29 March a resolution was moved in parliament demanding remedial legislation. Plunkett vigorously supported the motion as did Saunderson who declared that he had been proud to preside over a united committee of Irishmen. There was not a constituency in Ireland, declared Saunderson, where their action was not warmly approved and he roundly repudiated the insinuation that the sacred principles of the Union had sufferred a moment's derogation.[54] Plunkett went into the lobby with the nationalists. Saunderson abstained, but most of the Irish unionists voted with the government which won the division by 317 votes to 157 and the problem of Anglo-Irish financial relations remained to plague future generations.

During the drafting of Gerald Balfour's ill-fated agriculture and industries bill of 1897, the *Irish Homestead* advocated that it should not create another Castle department, and to this end the new department should possess a minister responsible to parliament, a consulative council and freedom from treasury control.[55] When the bill was published, a critical memorandum from the Recess Committee pointed out that the financial arrangements were inadequate; that there was no mention of a vice-president (the chief secretary was to be responsible to parliament as in all other Irish legislation); and that the department and the board should be separate entities.[56]

Staunchly supported by the ULUA, Plunkett launched a campaign for the introduction of suitable legislation. The *Irish Textile Journal* protested that the dropping of the original bill (in spite of its imperfections) was 'as miserable an instance of the misgovernment of this country as all history could furnish',[57] while Sinclair (a mathematical graduate of Queen's College, Belfast) complained that 'every day lost means that the splendid equipments of our foreign rivals are increasing the balance against us at a rate that can only be measured by geometrical progression'.[58] In December 1897, as the *Homestead* enthusiastically recorded, a deputation from Belfast and Dublin arrived to press for the bill.

The largest deputation that ever came, as far as we know, to consult a member of the Irish government, was received in the Castle ... The deputation was composed of men of every political creed, of every religious sect, of all classes, practically of the community. They came to the Castle with one mind and of one accord in order to convey to the members of the Irish government their unanimous wish and their desire for the promotion of measures calculated to improve the material prosperity and welfare of their country.[59]

At Westminster two months later Plunkett expressed his frustration in forthright terms.

I am not myself a supporter of home rule, but until the unionist government has taken steps to deal with the economic condition of Ireland, I readily admit I cannot say they have done everything a home rule government would do.[60]

By this time not only was his brand of unionism becoming so unorthodox as to hardly deserve the party label but his espousal of nationalist causes seemed designed to arouse the ire of the unionist faithful. Besides this, there was a sneaking feeling that the establishment of a department of agriculture in Dublin would be the equivalent to home rule for Ireland's farmers (an early

IAOS pamphlet had been entitled *Home Rule in the Dairy*) so it was not surprising when adverse reaction from a section of his constituents reached unprecedented levels. On the credit side he felt that nationalist opinion had veered around to support the findings of the Recess Committee and the work of the IAOS, while at a meeting of Irish unionist MPs a strong resolution was passed in favour of the agriculture and industries bill.[61]

In the summer of 1899 Gerald Balfour introduced a new agriculture and industries bill for Ireland. Plunkett, on this occasion, had been closely consulted while the legislation was being drafted, but he was not to share in his one parliamentary triumph, for in March he had broken his thigh in a cycling accident in Kensington High Street, and on his return to the House in June, fell from his crutches re-breaking his thigh bone. Nationalist amendments moved by Dillon (including a proposal to prevent the Department from assisting the IAOS) were adeptly circumvented by the chief secretary and the bill passed through the Commons before the end of July. Lord Ashbourne guided it through the House of Lords and the Department of Agriculture and Technical Instruction (DATI) at last became a reality. Plunkett, who was shortly to be appointed vice-president, ('I begin to see that the Northern connection makes it almost inevitable that I must accept it if offered'),[62] had won a opportunity, denied to most men, of being entrusted to carry out a policy which he himself had conceived and had long and ardently advocated.

Resolutely determined to attract personnel of the highest calibre, he knew that, in view of the low level of scientific and agricultural education in Ireland, technical staff would have to be recruited from outside the country and the nationalists would be furious. The secretaryship had to go to an Irishman and the choice lay between T. P. Gill (catholic and nationalist) and R. A. Anderson (protestant and unionist). Gill had been an essential part of the apparatus of the Recess Committee, but Anderson, who had worked loyally for Plunkett since 1890 and was secretary of the IAOS, had a prior claim. Plunkett felt that the blunt and forthright Anderson would be unhappy with bureaucratic red-tape besides he was irreplaceable in the IAOS and, more important still, since he himself was vice-president, the delicate politico-religious balance would be preserved if Gill were appointed, so he was relieved when Anderson did not press his claim. Sinclair and Andrews supported the choice, Sinclair, writing to Gerald Balfour to stiffen his resolve not to give in to the old ascendancy party, pointed out that Gill was on the conservative side of nationalism, was largely unknown in Ulster and sought salvation in economic rather than political terms,[63] but other unionists were furious. Carson inspired an attack on Gill (made by Saunderson) for his part in the Plan of Campaign.[64] Plunkett, realizing the sectarian nature of the charge, was forced to defend him. In his diary he wrote 'the defence was weak. But the attack was contemptible'.[65] Less than a month later he learnt that the South Dublin unionists were seeking an alternative candidate and from that moment his parliamentary fate was sealed.

Military confrontation in the Boer War commenced, after considerable preliminary skirmishing, in October 1899. Opinion in Ireland was divided on the Boer question; unionists supported imperial intervention while nationalists took up the cause of the Boers. Five years earlier during a debate on Matabeleland he had recorded his view that the less interference there was from the imperial government in southern Africa the better,[66] but this was precisely the sort of issue to embarrass Plunkett who had just been appointed vice-president of the DATI and was desperately keen to maintain relations with both sides.

Having avoided making any public statement for as long as possible he was eventually cornered by his own constituents at a meeting of the Primrose League in Kingstown Town Hall. Scrupulously avoiding the jingoist rhetoric de rigeur on such occasions, Plunkett argued, perhaps against his personal inclination, that Boer treatment of the uitlanders had made British intervention inevitable. Suggesting that when the war was over, Boers should be treated with the generosity which their bravery deserved, he reserved most of his remarks for the Irish attitude towards the war. Nationalist rhetoric, including the suggestion that Irishmen in the imperial army should turn their guns on their own officers, was not taken seriously in Ireland. Moreover every Irishman was proud of the bravery of Irish troops. Unfortunately England took these sentiments to heart; they derived, he believed, from Irish feelings of hatred and revenge. However the nationalists, he observed to his audience's satisfaction, had been unable to devise a scheme of revenge against England which would not also have injurious consequences for their own country.[67]

Political pressure built up steadily during the summer of 1900; he was criticised by the landlords in the shape of the Irish Unionist Alliance,[68] savagely attacked by Professor Dowden at a constituency meeting,[69] letters appeared in the press concerning Gill's appointment and Ardilaun held a meeting of his opponents who called, unanimously, for his resignation.[70] But, fortified by Arthur Balfour's sentiment that 'Irish unionists were often trying enough but their opposition to the one Irishman of their party who had ever worked for Ireland without some selfish motive was beyond all bounds of political decency',[71] Plunkett met his constituency bosses and told them quietly but firmly that he was going to stand. The nationalists, detecting a split in unionist ranks, weighed in through Michael Davitt:

A vote for Mr. Plunkett would mean a vote for Mr. Chamberlain and Lord Salisbury, a vote for Dublin Castle, and a vote for Irish landlordism with all its bloody records in the process of the extermination of the Irish nation.[72]

Finally the Dublin branch of the Orange Order summoned a meeting in Rathmines Town Hall at which

the attitude of the Orange Institution in Dublin towards Mr. Horace Plunkett and his policy of Balfourian amelioration will be clearly defined beyond the possibility of doubt and misrepresentation.[73]

Plunkett agreed to attend the meeting if he were given an opportunity to defend himself in the presence of the press. But orange minds had been made up and the Order threw its weight behind his 'loyal' opponent, Ball*.

Orchestrated by Lord Ardilaun and Edward Dowden, and virulently pursued in the columns of the *Daily Express* (which was then under Ardilaun's control), the campaign was directed against Plunkett as the chief exponent of constructive unionism. Ardilaun was bitterly opposed to the land acts and the recent local government legislation. He had refused to meet Chief Secretary Gerald Balfour, referring to him as a 'common thief', and his efforts resulted in the loss of two southern unionist seats in St. Stephen's Green and South Dublin.

There were many messages of support for Plunkett. Lecky and Carson, both returned unopposed for Dublin University, deplored the split in Irish unionism,[74] Lecky, who referred to Plunkett as the 'only constructive statesman in Ireland', remarking on the 'folly or ingratitude of those unionists who are

---

*F. Elrington Ball (1863–1928) editor of Dean Swift's correspondence.

endeavouring to drive you out of the Irish representation'.[75] The *Northern Whig* derided Ardilaun as a 'porter peer' and a 'sour political fanatic',[76] while the ULUA pointed out, in an appeal to the South Dublin unionists, that the attack on Gerald Balfour and the government led by the 'extreme tory and landlord party' had been directed at Plunkett,

a man whose history and disinterested efforts during the last ten years for the betterment of Irish agriculture and industries in both north and south have placed him in the first rank of Irish patriots. Mr. Plunkett, whatever his errors of judgement may have been, is an enlightened exponent of that constructive and progressive unionism which seeks to grapple with and remedy the economic needs of Ireland and which aims to confer benefits upon all her people irrespective of class or creed.[77]

But all these were to no avail. Shortly before the nomination date Plunkett was presented with a memorandum signed by 750 of his unionist constituents demanding his withdrawal from the campaign. He was pressed on his appointment of Gill, his support for a catholic university, his attitude to the Boer war and, inevitably, to home rule. On the latter point he responded, 'I once said that if Ulster, by which I mean industrial Ulster — desired home rule — then I should be a home ruler', and stressed that 'a home rule Ireland without Ulster would be a political and economic absurdity'. Describing himself as a positive imperialist he argued that with proper development of her intellectual and material resources Ireland could play a governing and a civilising role in a world-wide empire.[78]

The returns on 10 October 1900 showed Mooney (nationalist) 3410; Plunkett 2909; Ball 1539. It was a humiliating blow, which he interpreted as a set-back to his policies, and broke down during the customary words of thanks to the returning officer.

Election	1892	1895	1900
Unionist	4371 (54%)	4901 (65%)	4448 $\begin{cases} 2909 \\ 1539 \end{cases}$ (57%)
Nationalist	3713 $\begin{cases} 2261 \\ 1452 \end{cases}$	2962	3410
TOTAL:	8084	7563	7858

The voting patterns of the three elections show that, apart from a slight rise in 1895, the percentage unionist vote remained constant; in 1892 the nationalists split and lost the seat, in 1900 it

was the unionists' turn, the nationalists having reunited under
John Redmond's leadership in the previous June. The figures
indicate that, in electoral terms, in spite of his policies, there was
no marked upsurge of nationalist support for Plunkett between
1892 and 1900. He had mistakenly believed that he would be
judged on his constructive policies by the electorate but this was
to underestimate the depth of ideological division in Ireland.

Plunkett was now in an extremely embarrassing position. The
vice-presidency of the DATI carried junior ministerial rank, and
while it was not mandatory on the vice-president to be an MP, it
would otherwise be impossible for him to deal with attacks on his
Department in parliament. He considered the possibility of
obtaining a seat in Belfast (too anti-catholic), [79] East Down [80] or
even Manchester. [81] The opportunity, when it came, was a by-
election in Galway City. The seat had formerly been held by a
unionist Morris, who had been created Lord Killanin. A
deputation of unionists and nationalists asked him to go forward
as an 'industrial candidate'. This appeal, combined with pressure
from the new chief secretary Wyndham, swayed him into
accepting the candidacy against the advice of his closest friends.
It was a disastrous decision. During his fortnight's campaign in
Galway he needed police protection, and the full panoply of
nationalist intimidation was unfurled against him. He was
'howled at by low fiends of women and children', 'to hell with
Plunkett' was yelled by 'hags and embryo hags' [82] and polling
day witnessed an easy victory for the nationalist candidate
Colonel Lynch [83] who polled 1247 votes against Plunkett's 472.

The whole affair has been graphically described in a letter,
written in 1938, by H.G. Smith, Plunkett's private secretary in
the DATI, to Lady Fingall:

What a time we all had trying to persuade Sir H. not to go . . . Nor shall
I forget my fortnight with him in Galway under police protection,
listening at night . . . [to] W. Redmond and others of the bevy of MP's
who came down to make certain that 'the man from Galway' would be
the Boer colonel and not Sir Horace . . .
I heard John Dillon denounce Sir Horace as a 'carpet-bagger', office
seeker, and similar epithets, and listened to the growls of those around
me, stirred up as we Irish are ever liable to be, by vitriolic speeches,
packed with the half-truths which are ever the worst of lies. [84]

Three years later Plunkett offered to stand as a unionist in
North Fermanagh but was turned down on account of his stand
for a catholic university. [85] One further attempt seems to have

been made to allow him to resume his parliamentary career. In a letter from Carson to the provost of Trinity College of June 1915, (a copy of which Carson sent to Plunkett) he refers to a movement to put Plunkett's name forward for a vacancy in the university constituency. The university members were regularly unionists and were often returned unopposed (Carson held one of the two Dublin University seats at the time). Carson pointed out to the provost that, if Plunkett stood, there would be a contest implying that an orthodox unionist would run against him. In a letter to the provost Plunkett replied carefully that, for the moment, he had no particular inclination to re-enter party politics. [86]

IV

Ireland in the New Century

The Act of 1899 establishing the new department envisaged, but did not require, that the vice-president be a member of parliament. Plunkett was thus legally entitled to continue in office but in a weakened position; however a unionist government under Arthur Balfour was returned to power in the 1900 election, so he was assured of official backing. The Council of Agriculture and the Boards of Agriculture and of Technical Instruction all urged him to remain as vice-president to supervise the growth of his fledgling department. At a banquet held in his honour in Dublin he was presented with a petition containing over 10,000 signatures (mainly nationalist) signifying support.[1] The new department was his own creation so he decided to stay.

The machinery of Irish government at the turn of the century was, in the words of the co-operative movement's historian, 'a bewildering hotch-potch of departments, boards and offices'. No single department was charged with overall authority for the development of agriculture or industry. Bits and pieces of administrative responsibility were assigned to different boards in a seemingly haphazard fashion. Some departments, for instance those dealing with finance and defence, were little more than branches of United Kingdom ministries. Several, including those in charge of law and order, came under the direct control of the executive (popularly known as Dublin Castle), while a few, such as the CDB, had varying degrees of autonomy subject to overall executive control in financial affairs.

This situation had been considered by the Recess Committee who pointed out that the administration of agriculture in Ireland was a perfect example of organised chaos. The Board of Works dealt with arterial drainage and land improvement, agricultural instruction was administered by the National Board of Education but technical instruction by the Science and Art Department in South Kensington, with its Irish branch in charge of the College of Science and the Botanic Gardens. Agricultural statistics were collected by the Land Commission, the Fisheries Board, the Registrar General and the Veterinary Department of the Privy Council. The Land Commission carried out agricultural experiments and helped the CDB with agricultural schemes. Fishery development might come under the Fisheries Board, the Board of Works or the CDB, thus the administrative cohesion vested in the DATI was, of itself, a considerable innovation.

The Boards of Agriculture and of Technical Instruction operated as if they were boards of company directors in charge of the two sections of the Department, formulating and overseeing the implementation of policy and controlling expenditure. An innovation was the Council of Agriculture which Plunkett called his Irish parliament; it was no accident that its membership of 104 was precisely the number of the Irish MP's at Westminster, for, as he wrote in answer to Dillon's continued sniping, 'The Recess Committee will be the natural transition from the present system to whatever substitute we may have for home rule'. [2] The Council was elected triennially and based upon the recently established local government, sixty-eight of its members were chosen by the county councils, thirty-four were nominated by the Department, and the president (the chief secretary) and the vice-president were ex-officio members.

The DATI's task, as Plunkett saw it, was to put the benefits of modern science at the disposal of the Irish farmer. Prior to 1900 some scientific work such as milk testing, animal and cereal breeding had been carried out in an ad hoc fashion by the IAOS or by the RDS. Now this work was to be done in style by the Department. The educational services provided by the DATI had a strong practical bias. Rather than set up a whole chain of agricultural colleges (as he was pressed to do) he sent out a team of instructors to meet the farmers in the field and concentrated on building up institutions (the Albert College at Glasnevin and the Munster Institute in Cork) already in existence. Parnell's estate of Avondale was purchased for the training of foresters as well as a vessel to survey Irish fishing grounds. Plunkett, at once, set up a statistics and information branch, and, for the first time, a complete picture began to emerge of the country's agricultural resources.

Efforts made by the DATI during Plunkett's term of office to improve the barley and the flax grown in Ireland provide a good illustration of his administrative philosophy working itself out in practice, for in both cases official backing was given to promising local initiatives. Barley is grown mainly in the southern and eastern regions of Ireland and a high quality is required to produce the malt which is a basic ingredient for brewing and distilling. But Irish barley was variable in its malting characteristics and, with the expansion of the brewing and distilling industries and, in particular, the growth of the Guinness Brewery in the nineteenth century, a great deal of barley had to be imported from eastern England or the continent. Prior to the establishment of the DATI some steps had been taken by the IAOS and by Guinness to rectify this situation. Experimental plots of old and new varieties of barley were grown in different parts of the country by maltsters under the supervision of an IAOS official, Sheringham from Norfolk. C.D. La Touche, one of the Guinness directors, a member of the IAOS committee and a friend of Plunkett's, was an enthusiastic supporter of the scheme. This initiative was greatly expanded once J. R. Campbell had been appointed to the senior scientific position in the DATI. Sheringham returned to East Anglia to be replaced by Hunter, a Yorkshireman appointed by the DATI, who won recognition as a leading agricultural botanist of his generation. The experiments proved successful in determining varieties of barley suited to Irish conditions and of a high malting quality; Irish growers were able to meet the full demands of the Irish brewers and distillers; and a cereal breeding and research station, jointly financed by Guinness and the Department, was established on the lands of one of the progressive maltsters, J. H. Bennett of Ballinacurra, Co. Cork, where it still continues its important work. [3]

The flax growers of Ulster had similarly taken the initiative by forming the Flax Supply Association in an endeavour to increase the quantity and quality of the flax grown in Ireland (much of the flax needed for Ulster's linen industry having to be imported from Holland and Belgium). A scheme was designed to supply three experts (two Dutch and one Belgian) to supervise the provision of high quality seed and the growing and treatment of Irish flax. This scheme, initiated by the Flax Supply Association and the progressive Barbour firm in Lisburn was then taken up by the Department to the benefit of the flax growers and linen industry of Ulster. [4]

Apart from agricultural education which fell naturally within its purview, the Department administered the grants for science and art which gave it control of several national institutions including the Museums, the Royal College of Science and the

Horace Curzon Plunkett, by Dermod O'Brien (ICOS).

Above: a modern view of Dunsany Castle. Courtesy the Irish Architectural Archive. Below: a ranch on EK Mountain, Johnson County, Wyoming in the 1880s. Photograph courtesy of Archives — American Heritage Center, University of Wyoming.

Above left: Lord Monteagle, by Dermod O'Brien (ICOS). Above right: R. A. Anderson, by Dermod O'Brien (ICOS). Below left: Fr. T. A. Finlay by Leo Whelan. Below right: George W. Russell (AE), a bronze by Jerome Connor, standing in Merrion Square, near Plunkett House.

Above left: a photograph of Sir James Musgrave (UM). Above right: a photograph of Thomas Andrews (UM). Below left: the Hon. Thomas Sinclair, by Frank McKelvey (UM). Below right: Harold Barbour, by Dermod O'Brien. Courtesy UAOS.

Metropolitan School of Art, all located in Dublin. On account of the primitive nature of Irish educational administration, Plunkett found himself in charge of scientific education everywhere but in the universities. It was not an opportunity he would have turned down, for scientific innovation and educational reform were two of his principal aims and, in his mind, they were inextricably linked:

Whenever I set out on a mental excursion into Irish political, sociological or economic questions, no matter where I start, I always come back to education as the condition precedent of all progress in Ireland.[5]

The lead given by the liberal unionists of Ulster was instrumental in ensuring that the new system of technical or vocational education should be non-denominational. During the preparation of the Recess Committee's report, the northern sub-committee put forward an amendment to the effect that the 'practical schools' should not be associated with denominational schools such as those run by either the Christian Brothers or the 'protestant committee',[6] while Sinclair urged Gill that the various denominations should not be mentioned in the educational paragraphs of the report.[7] Thus it was that the DATI administered technical branch of education was secular, unlike the primary and secondary branches which, to all extents and purposes, were denominationally controlled.

Plunkett kept in close touch with Sinclair and Andrews during the controversy over appointments to posts in his new Department. They backed him up in his determination to obtain expertise from outside Ireland, where that was necessary, and in his appointment of Gill as secretary; it was clear that if Plunkett was to be vice-president then the secretary must be a catholic. Significantly, however, Gill would not have been acceptable to Sinclair or Andrews in charge of technical education.[8] Dr. Walsh, the catholic archbishop of Dublin and an enthusiastic supporter of practical education, persuaded his hierarchy to accept this new scheme of a secular-controlled and rate-supported branch of education.[9] This made a striking contrast to the hierarchy's attitude to the 'godless' Queen's Colleges and its demand, which Plunkett supported, for a catholic university.

He had taken considerable pains to establish good relations with the catholic hierarchy, and had become particularly friendly with Bishops O'Donnell of Raphoe, Kelly of Ross and O'Dwyer of Limerick. Raphoe and Ross, running along the northwest and southwest coasts, were poor rural dioceses, the majority of whose parishes were congested districts whose bishops were keenly interested in the hope of improvement which the co-operative movement held out for their flocks. Dr O'Donnell was an IAOS committee member while Dr. Denis Kelly, an expert economist, sat on the Council of Agriculture; Bishop O'Dwyer of Limerick had other interests as his diocese incorporated some of the best farmland in the country, but the co-operative movement had originated there and Plunkett had been friendly with him since. The catholic hierarchy had welcomed the act establishing the DATI with a unanimous commendation while bishops Kelly and Clancy (Elphin) vindicated Plunkett's policy in making appointments to the DATI, often from outside Ireland, to a departmental committee of enquiry in 1907. [10] In November 1900, O'Dwyer wrote to Plunkett suggesting a confidential meeting with the bishops to discuss the university question. [11] Plunkett had to tread cautiously for, although he, personally, supported the establishment of a catholic university, his liberal unionist friends in Ulster directly opposed it. (At a party in Sinclair's house some weeks previously the university question had been taboo). [12] The result of these discussions was a suggestion of Plunkett's to the prime minister (Arthur Balfour) early in 1901 for the summoning of a royal commission to consider the problem. [13] The Commission on University Education was established later that year and Plunkett argued in favour of a complete system of Irish education open to all, thus eliminating what roman catholics regarded as 'the alternative between ignorance and Trinity'.

In his evidence to this commission he elaborated on his view of the vexed question of denominational control:

As far ahead as we need look, all attempts to divorce religion and education in Ireland, will be, as they have been in the past, mere paper restrictions, ineffectual because the Irish mind goes the other way; harmful because what cannot be done openly and directly will continue to be accomplished by sham and subterfuge. Besides, in my advocacy of the catholic claim I have learned that the real objection is, not to the element of religion in education, but to clerical control over secular education;

and then he added unexpectedly,

if an anti-clerical movement succeeded in Ireland, as it has done in some continental countries, in discrediting the priesthood, it would blight all hopes of a national regeneration. [14]

But while he did, at times, inadvertently offend catholic

susceptibilities, Plunkett never was anti-clerical. His efforts had been supported by the forward looking catholic clergy, particularly by those who had been able to surmount nationalist pressure:

I know, from my own experience, both in my work as an agricultural organiser and as a government official, that where you do get a priest who has been educated in economics his assistance is absolutely invaluable. [15]

The Church, he believed, had an obligation as well as the opportunity to foster both the material, and the spiritual welfare of its people. [16]

The magnificent new Municipal Technical College in Belfast, which opened in 1907, was one of a series of such institutions which sprang up around the country in the early years of the twentieth century. The vice-president's invitation to open the new Technical School and Workmens' Institute in Lurgan in 1901 disclosed that

The Town Council and Committee . . . are most anxious to associate the undertaking with the 'Pioneer' of the great social movement in Ireland, which must place our country in a position to cope with foreign enterprise and competition; [17]

while three years later at the opening of the Newtownards Technical School, Plunkett emphasised the benefits which would accrue to local employers, requesting them to 'assist its work, by criticism, by helpful suggestions, and by affording facilities within their power to the students [their employees] to attend classes' [18]

Other progress in scientific and agricultural education during Plunkett's vice-presidency of the DATI included a new programme in the primary schools to render the instruction more practical and to give it a more direct relation with the future occupations of the majority of the pupils; a much greater emphasis on science teaching in the secondary schools, and the establishment of a chair of agriculture in the Royal College of Science. In deciding to build up his two existing agricultural institutes in Dublin and Cork, the temptation to introduce with a few hold strokes some startling new developments with an embodiment in bricks and mortar, had given way to a wiser policy of treating education 'as an organic portion of the country's life, discharging its varied functions in a well considered relation with each other'. Insisting on the appointment of scientific officers of the highest calibre[19] (even if this meant, as it often did, recruiting from outside Ireland), Plunkett appointed J. R. Campbell, an able, fiery Scot to the principal position in agriculture. He was the tenth child of a small farmer from Shapinsay in the Orkney Islands who had been given 50 pounds on his eighteenth birthday and told to go and educate himself in Edinburgh — which he had done to such effect that he was professor of agriculture in Leeds University by the age of thirty five. A number of other posts were filled by applicants from outside the country leading to criticism from the nationalists but Plunkett was determined to get his new department off to a flying start by insisting on the highest standards. In 1905 he wrote to Hugh Law, a nationalist MP from Donegal and one of his staunch supporters:

It is typical of Irish life that we have in the Department conclusive evidence that our refusal to sanction the appointment of local persons where favours have to be dispensed ... is regarded by the county secretaries and their committees as one that relieves them of much embarrassment.[20]

A significant exception to this rule was made in the appointment to a chair of chemistry in the Royal College of Science. Douglas Hyde, founder of the Gaelic League, the spearhead of the Gaelic revival, wrote confidentially underlining the widely held fear 'so unhappily entertained' that 'no Irish catholic need apply'. That the applicant supported by Hyde, though highly competent, was appointed over opposition which appeared somewhat better qualified is an indication of the high regard which Plunkett held for the president of the Gaelic League.[21]

During his time as vice-president, Plunkett, who was always a mender of broken fences, managed to make it up with Ardilaun and to establish friendly relations between the RDS and the DATI. Although there was, naturally, some initial sparring between the two bodies, by 1904 the tone of correspondence between Plunkett and Ardilaun, in which the Department agreed to vacate its offices in Leinster House to make way for the Society,* was warm if somewhat formal. From Ardilaun's

*The RDS took over Leinster House (former Dublin residence of the Duke of Leinster) in 1815, but from 1877 the building had been shared with the government.

viewpoint Plunkett no longer posed any sort of political threat, while their organisations had every thing to gain by working together.[22]

Vice-presidential alertness to the importance of publicity led to Departmental participation in the Glasgow, Cork and St. Louis Exhibitions of 1901, 1902-3 and 1904, respectively. At Glasgow there was a small Irish pavilion involving only moderate expenditure; while the cost of constructing an Irish village at St. Louis was covered by an enthusiastic band of Irish Americans. The DATI involvement in the Cork Exhibition was of a different magnitude and aimed at interesting the Irish public and particularly the farmers in the whole range of departmental activities as well as in the country's potential for industrial and economic development. One exhibit which created extraordinary interest was a stuffed bullock on a pedestal and around him, in a glass case, all the articles of common use such as leather, glue, buttons, preserved meat, knifehandles, felt hats and artificial manures to be derived from the beast if it were slaughtered in Ireland. The emphasis, as always, was on the application of modern methods to Ireland's agriculture and ancillary industries and it was intended that, after ten years, another large scale exhibition should be mounted to illustrate progress along the lines indicated at Cork.

The continuing impact made by co-operation plus his success in marking out the guidelines and establishing the administrative machinery for the modernisation of Irish agriculture allied the forces of reaction to Plunkett's political opponents. His philosophy however, had a certain down to earth appeal so that he, and his movement, had to be attacked obliquely; he was soon to provide the opposition with an opportunity to attack head on.

Once the business of the DATI had settled into an established pattern Plunkett decided to give his philosophy a coherent form. His Wyoming experience had prompted him to reject paternalism. 'Alas I am old enough', he wrote shortly before his death, 'to remember those days when feudalism lingered everywhere in Ireland though the years as a ranchman in another, wilder, freer west has given me a different point of view.'[23] This led to the difficult admission (for a unionist) that Irish government should be with the consent of the governed. However, not just one system had to be rejected but two, for matching the Castle administration controlled by a protestant ascendancy, the nationalists had established a form of subservience via the Party and Westminster. Both blocked the way ahead; both had to go!

The depth of ideological division between the catholic-nationalist and unionist-protestant strands in Irish life often obscured the extent to which they shared objectives or stood upon common ground. Plunkett's work for co-operation and in the Recess Committee, by skilfully skirting constitutional issues, illustrated the advantages of a concerted approach to economic problems. Cultural links were simultaneously being forged between the two groups by the literary movement and by the Gaelic League. Convinced that what Irishmen held in common was of more significance than their many divisions, Plunkett looked for progress on a broader front. But, in order to prepare the ground, the focus of attention had to change. He needed to shift politics from the centre of the Irish stage or, it might less charitably be said, to change the question! Thus *Ireland in the New Century* represents a brave attempt to argue that the Irish problem was neither political, nor economic, nor religious but primarily a matter of character (the very problem which Plunkett felt himself best equipped to tackle). Once this diagnosis had been accepted and his remedy applied, the remaining difficulties would then appear in their true perspective and the Irish people would be in a position to resolve them for themselves.

He had always enjoyed hard challenging work and was happiest when tackling several full time jobs simultaneously, thus the book was written mainly between 5 a.m. (his customary rising time as he was a poor sleeper) and the start of his day at the Department. Published in 1904, it shows Plunkett in his true colours. He was both a visionary and a man of action, his interests were wide ranging and his energy boundless, but he was tactless and outspoken, he was not free from certain widely held Anglo-Irish prejudices, to a large section of his readers he appeared somewhat patronising, and, he was no politician. He had a tactical reason for rushing into print, for Gerald Balfour had left the chief secretaryship in 1900 to be replaced by the brilliant, but erratic, George Wyndham. ('Too optimistic for safety in Ireland' was Plunkett's comment when they met).[24] Wyndham took a grandiose view of the role of the state and was intent on a policy of centralisation. The two organisations of Irish government which had achieved most independence from Dublin Castle were the CDB and the DATI. Both now felt their autonomy to be threatened. Thus while Wyndham was preparing his land bill of 1903, Plunkett, suspecting a plot for 'castleising the Department', and worried lest his funds be impounded in the 'land bill juggle', wrote of his publication plans to Gill: 'It is a fight between two philosophies and we must win.' [25]

His book was prefaced with a characteristic optimism:

Those who have known Ireland for the last dozen years cannot have failed to notice the advent of a wholly new spirit, clearly based upon constructive thought, and expressing itself in a wide range of fresh practical activities. The movement for the organisation of agriculture and rural credit on co-operative lines, efforts of various kinds to revive old or initiate new industries, and, lastly, the creation of a department of government, to foster all that was healthy in the voluntary effort of the people to build up the economic side of their life, are each interesting in themselves. When taken together in conjunction with the literary and artistic movements, and viewed in their relation to history, politics, religion, education, and the other past and present influences operating upon the Irish mind and character, these movements appear to me to be worthy of the most thoughtful consideration by all who are responsible for, or desire the well being of, the Irish people. [26]

Ireland in the New Century is divided into two sections. The second contains a detailed description of the work, past, present and future, of the co-operative movement and the DATI; it is technical, factual and illuminated with wit and insight. The first part, in which he set down his views on Ireland and its institutions, on Anglo-Irish history and politics, on Irishmen and on the character of the nation, engulfed its author, as soon as it appeared, in a sea of controversy.

He started with an allusion to England's misgovernment of Ireland whose economic consequences she was at last beginning to acknowledge.

Although the nineteenth century, with all its marvellous contributions to human progress, left Ireland with her hopes unfulfilled; although its sun went down upon the British people with their greatest failure still staring them in the face, its last decade witnessed at first a change in the attitude of England towards Ireland and afterwards a profound revolution in the thoughts of Ireland about herself. [27]

'Whether it would not be more reasonable to mend our state than complain of it; and how far this maybe in our own power?' Berkeley's query of a previous century prompted him to suggest that

great as is the responsibility of England for the state of Ireland, still greater is the responsibility of Irishmen ... the most important part of the work of regenerating Ireland must necessarily be done by Irishmen in Ireland.[28]

'Whether our parties are not a burlesque upon politics?' asked another of Berkeley's queries. Irish unionists, he felt, had failed to supplement their unbending opposition to home rule with a progressive policy on other issues. The Unionist Party was supposed to unite all who, like himself, were opposed to the plunge into home rule but its propagandist activities were confined to preaching the status quo, and that only to the converted:

Now and again an individual tries to broaden the basis of Irish unionism and to bring himself into touch with the life of the people. But the nearer he gets to the people the farther he gets from the Irish unionist leaders. The lot of such an individual is not a happy one: he is regarded as a mere intruder who does not know the rules of the game, and he is treated by the leading players on both sides like a dog on a tennis court.[29]

When the home rule controversy was at its height, the chief strength of Irish opposition to Mr. Gladstone's policy, which weighed most with the British electorate, lay in the business objections of the industrial population of Ulster. The arguments then put forward remained unanswered by the nationalists:

'We have come', they said in effect, 'into Ireland and not the richest portion of the island, and have gradually built up an industry and commerce with which we are able to hold our own in competition with the most progressive nations in the world. Our success has been achieved under a system and a polity in which we believe. Its non-interference with the business of the people gave play to that self-reliance with which we strove to emulate the industrial qualities of Great Britain. It is now proposed to place the manufactures and commerce of the country at the mercy of a majority which will have no real concern in the interests vitally affected, and who have no knowledge of the science of government. The mere shadow of these changes has so depressed the stocks which represent the accumulations of our past enterprise and labour, that we are already poorer than we were'[30]

Two reasons were offered for the failure of Irish unionism. An over-rigid interpretation of Lord Salisbury's famous prescription 'twenty years of resolute government' had been made a sufficient justification for a negative and repressive policy, while the linking of the agrarian and political problems led to dominance by the landlords:

Had the industrial section made its voice heard in the councils of the Irish Unionist Party, the government which that party supports might have had less advice and assistance in the maintenance of law and order, but it would have had invaluable aid in its constructive policy. For the lack of the wise guidance which our captains of industry should have provided, Irish unionism has, by too close adherence to the traditions of the landlord section, been the creed of a social caste rather than a policy in Ireland. [31]

Plunkett had put his finger on the dichotomy at the heart of unionism, for British unionists were now aiming to make the Union work by shaping policies to benefit the majority of the Irish people; while Irish unionists (particularly the landlords) regarding themselves as a colonial autocracy, held that the primary thrust of government strategy should be to maintain them in power. On this issue he was perfectly clear. It was essential that the interests of a class should not be allowed to dominate the policy of the party. If there was to be a future for Irish unionism it must spring from a combination of the best thought of the county aristocracy and of the captains of industry.

Turning to the nationalists, he criticised the methods which had been employed to attain home rule as injurious to the development of a political and industrial character. They were justified, by nationalist leaders, on the grounds that the constitutional reforms which they advocated were a necessary precedent to industrial progress. The 'political backwardness' of the majority of the people stemmed from a lack of independent thought and self-reliance essential to a democracy which had never replaced the leader following habit. Parnell's rule he termed the one-man system; by abdicating responsibility to the Chief political development had been stultified.

The decade of dissention which followed the fall of Parnell will, perhaps, some day be recognized as the most fruitful epoch in modern Irish history. The reaction to the one-man system set in as soon as the one man had passed away. [32]

Nationalists were accused of moral timidity in contrast to their physical courage; the policy of giving trouble to the government was adjudged the one road to reform but, while he did not deny that past history lent credence to this view, there was now a new England to deal with. The Congested Districts Board had been established, local government had been set up in Ireland, the DATI was working effectively and the Dunraven Conference of the previous year had led to the concessions embodied in Wyndham's land act. None of this was a consequence of agitation:

Whatever may be said of what is called 'agitation' in Ireland as an engine for extorting legislation from the imperial parliament, it is unquestionably bad for the much greater end of building up Irish character and developing Irish industry and commerce. 'Agitation', as Thomas Davis said, 'is one means of redress, but it leads to much disorganisation, great unhappiness, wounds upon the soul of a country which sometimes are worse than the thinning of a people by war'.[33]

Of nationalist policy on Ulster he asked the question underlying the home rule debates of 1886 and 1893 — whether Ulster was to be persuaded or coerced to come under the new regime; and went on to warn that

those who know the temper and fighting qualities of the working-men opponents of home rule in the North are under no illusion as to the account they would give of themselves if called upon to defend the cause of protestantism, liberty, and imperial unity as they understand it.[34]

Besides the frequent references to defects in Irish character, it was his section upon religion and the churches which caused the most furore. This was included against the express advice of intimates such as Fr. Finlay and R.A. Anderson whom he had consulted. In the background were the bitterly anti-clerical writings of the catholic unionist M. J. F. McCarthy whose *Five Years in Ireland, 1895-1900*, published in 1901, followed by *Priests and People in Ireland*, in 1902, had helped to stir the sectarian pot. Plunkett was well aware of the danger for he wrote to Gill after the appearance of the first of them, 'The success of that ruffian McCarthy's book ought to give us a hint of what we have to meet'.[35] Unfortunately he failed to take the hint and his comments on catholicism (although in no sense comparable to McCarthy's) were to provide heaven-sent ammunition for his opponents.

His family had inherited a narrow evangelical anglicanism from their mother; Mary, his elder sister, has left a grim picture of a childhood devotion to a faith which was 'bigoted, intolerant and obstinately low church,' responding with a heavy irony to clerical railings against disestablishment, 'Oh Gladstone, Gladstone what thou doest, do quickly!'[36] Horace rejected this depressing dogma, giving throughout his later life the impression that he would have liked to believe but was too honest to set his scruples aside. 'I am sorely perplexed in my religious beliefs,' he wrote to the bishop of Winchester, 'my absorption in works, other people's mostly, leaves me little time to wrestle with the faiths which surround me'.[37] This passionless agnosticism lent a certain detachment to his comments but did nothing to deflect the wrath of his critics.

'While the protestants', he wrote, 'have given, and continue to give, a fine example of thrift and industry to the rest of the nation, the attitude of a section of them towards the majority of their fellow citizens has been a bigoted and unintelligent one. On the other hand I have learned from practical experience amongst the roman catholic people of Ireland that, while more free from bigotry, in the sense in which that word is usually applied, they are apathetic, thriftless, and almost non-industrial, and that they especially require the exercise of strengthening influences on their moral fibre.'[38]

The section on religion contained critical references to what he judged an excessive number of catholic churches and monastic institutions;[39] to the many celibate clergy and their influence upon the education and life of the people; and to the lack of industrial progress in other catholic countries. These remarks were not made in any bitter spirit, and each one was accompanied by an historical, or other, justification but they exposed some of the prejudices in Plunkett's way of thinking familiar among protestants at the time and had been included against the better judgement of his friends.

Indeed the number of Irish protestant clergy per thousand of their flock was, in Plunkett's day, double that for their catholic counterparts. The density of protestant churches, particularly in the south and west, was also considerably higher. Little potential investment capital had been diverted to church building and the apathetic and non-industrial character which he observed was more likely to derive from a lack of educational and commercial opportunity than from devotional practice.[40] On a global scale there was, then perhaps, a correlation between protestantism and capitalism, but now economic development is linked to national resources and patterns of world trade rather than to religious affiliation, while the commercial qualities of the Ulster protestant, which he noted with such approval, have not been sufficient to ward off serious economic decline.

The Irish educational system was criticised as being too academic and unrelated to practical affairs. Plunkett, who regarded the university as the foundation for the primary and secondary systems, found that Ireland's oldest university, the University of Dublin (Trinity College), had failed the test of actively influencing the majority of the people and of moulding their thought and directing their action towards the upbuilding of the nation's life.

I am bound to say, that Trinity College, so far as I have seen, has had but little influence upon the minds or the lives of the people. Nor can I find that at any period of the extraordinarily interesting economic and social revolution, which has been in progress in Ireland since the great catastrophe of the famine period, Dublin University has departed from its academic isolation and aloofness from the great national problems which were being worked out.[41]

The failure on the part of Trinity College strengthened the case for the establishment of a university acceptable to catholics which, he remarked, was 'not a concession of privilege, but of simple justice'.

The book concluded with sentiments in line with the emerging national spirit, shortly to crystallise in the foundation of Sinn Féin:

Ireland must be re-created from within. The main work must be done in Ireland, and the centre of interest must be Ireland. When Irishmen realise this truth, the splendid human power of their country, so much of which now runs idly or disastrously to waste, will be utilised; and we may then look with confidence for the foundation of a fabric of Irish prosperity, framed in constructive thought, and laid enduringly in human character.[42]

Initial reaction was favourable and the author was pleased and surprised with comments on his literary accomplishment. The *Northern Whig* observed that the author had demonstrated the existence of a higher plane 'on which we might all unite without sacrifice of convictions' while to Standish O'Grady (although he did not accept all of Plunkett's findings) the spirit of the book was 'fair, temperate, moderate, considerate and kind'.[43] The attack, when it came, was on religious grounds. The *Freeman's Journal* suggested that the author had demonstrated his unfitness for his position as his book was 'one prolonged libel on the Irish people'.[44] Provincial papers piled on more virulent con-demnation, his name was linked with that of M. J. F. McCarthy, and a succession of county councils and public bodies discussed resolutions calling for the banning of this filthy book. Cardinal

Logue issued a pastoral letter carrying a thinly veiled reference to enemies of the Church[45] and Monsignor O'Riordan, Rector of the Irish College in Rome, published a rebuttal running to twice the length of the original[46]; evoking a wry comment from the author that this amounted to a book about a chapter whereas a review was normally a chapter about a book!

If Plunkett's initial intention had been to seek publicity for his views, his wildest expectations must have been exceeded when, on 23 June, just five months after publication, *Ireland in the New Century* became the subject of a debate in the House of Commons.[47] Estimates for the DATI were under scrutiny as nationalist members (including T. W. Russell, the liberal unionist member for South Tyrone) waded into the vice-president on the religious issue. He was vigorously defended by Col. Saunderson who argued that he, personally, had never read a less one-sided work, but, to emphasise nationalist feeling, John Redmond resigned from the committee of the IAOS.

For a member of the ascendancy (however lukewarm his own religious affiliation) to cast aspersions on Irish catholicism was, at all times, a delicate task; for one in the exposed position of a minister without a seat in parliament it was an unforgiveable sin. Plunkett was misinterpreted, sometimes deliberately, generally with relish; many nationalists were turned against him who had never read the book; the co-operative movement was damaged by implication and his retention of public office made well-nigh impossible. The furious reaction to the contents of a few pages ensured that the author's incisive commentary on Irish affairs, his constructive arguments plus his blueprint for Ireland's future would be lost amidst the rantings of clerics and politicians.

Reactions, even catholic ones, from outside Ireland were predictably different. Alphonse Désjardins, the Canadian credit union pioneer, who ranks along with Plunkett in the co-operative firmament, fascinated by the parallel between the problems of Ireland and French Canada, confessed that he was inspired by the way in which Plunkett had overcome the most discouraging of obstacles,[48] while Dr. S. Welch, a prominent catholic priest and president of the Cape Town Irish Association, wrote of his delight at the prospect which the book opened up of uniting Irishmen for the welfare of Ireland.[49]

Plunkett added an epilogue to the 1905 edition in which he reprinted the text of a letter from John Redmond to Patrick Ford (editor of an influential American paper, the *Irish World*). The letter, written in New York and dated 4 October 1904 was widely circulated in Ireland and must have distressed both Plunkett and those who stood by him:

I am anxious before leaving for home, to say a word of warning with reference to an insidious attempt, which I find is being made in America by officials and agents of the British government, [50] to divert the minds of the friends of Ireland from the national movement, under the pretence of promoting an industrial revival in Ireland.

Promotion of Irish industries is so praiseworthy an object that I am not surprised that some of our people in America have been deceived in this matter. I myself, indeed, at one time, entertained some belief in the good intentions of Sir Horace Plunkett and his friends, but recent events have entirely undeceived me; and Sir Horace Plunkett's recent book, full as it is of undisguised contempt for the Irish race, makes it plain to me that the real object of the movement in question is to undermine the National Party and divert the minds of our people from home rule, which is the only thing which can ever lead to a real revival of Irish industry. [51]

The epilogue contained a spirited defence of Plunkett's motives. The object of publication, according to the author, was to combat the crisis brought about by emigration on the one hand and the social and economic revolution, consummated in the transfer of the land from owner to occupier, on the other. He reiterated his fundamental belief, that the Irish problem, was, above all else, a problem of character. As an illustration he recalled an anecdote of his ranching days. An Indian called at the ranch seeking work, carrying a reference from the agent of his reservation which ran 'Tinbelly is a worthless Indian. Anyone who gives him anything will be that much out!' Plunkett doubted whether an Irish testimonial would be expressed with such frankness. 'Does anyone know a country', he asked, where the testimonial would be phrased, 'Mr. P. J. Tinbelly is qualified to discharge, efficiently and faithfully any duties which may be entrusted to him?'

The epilogue was unlikely to make up any lost ground. Elizabeth, Countess of Fingall, recalled her daughter watching the author writing at the Fingall home. 'Uncle Horace', she asked, 'do you think that anyone will ever read that book?' 'Unfortunately', wrote Lady Fingall, 'they did, and it did him more harm than anything else could have done!' [52]

* * *

Prior to the establishment of the DATI, the IAOS, supposedly financed by affiliation fees of its member societies, depended, to a large extent, on private subscriptions from its most generous supporters. After 1900, Plunkett, with typical generosity, donated his official salary to the IAOS while the Department bore the cost of educational work carried out by the Society. Within a year it had taken over much of this work enabling the IAOS to concentrate its resources on co-operative organisation. The DATI gave further help in the form of low interest loans (eventually repaid in full) to the agricultural banks. But a drive to raise more funds for the IAOS through prompt collection of affiliation fees met with a poor response. Unfortunately, also, as soon as state funds were channelled into the IAOS, private donations tailed off proportionately.

Even with Plunkett as vice-president of the DATI relations with the IAOS were often strained. Anderson disliked Campbell and distrusted Gill, and Plunkett was cast in the role of peacemaker. He never lost his bulldog devotion to Plunkett but Anderson was for 'whole hog' co-operation which Plunkett opposed on the grounds that if the societies opened village stores it would lead to even fiercer conflict with the nationalists. In the Council of Agriculture there were signs of animosity between co-operators and non-co-operators (generally members of the Nationalist Party) which came to a head in May 1906 when a resolution to continue financial support to the IAOS was strongly contested but was carried. A scheme was then devised by which the Department would subsidise the general operation of the IAOS for the year ending February 1907 up to a maximum of £3,700; the IAOS having to find the balance necessary to carry out an agreed programme of work. Nonetheless, the Society's financial position continued to deteriorate; of a total income of £4,100 in 1906, only £425 came from affiliation fees.

Plunkett, with a ministerial post and without a seat in parliament, was in a delicate position. The ice became even thinner when, in January 1906, the liberals swept back into power with a huge majority. The nationalists, having regained their former political influence, determined to drive him from office. However, to his surprise and obvious delight, he learnt that the liberal government were not, at once, requesting resignation. The matter was raised in parliament in February when James Bryce, the new chief secretary for Ireland (who later became a close friend), and Campbell-Bannerman, the prime minister, replied that the government, as was its entitlement, intended to keep Plunkett in an office which they regarded as a non-party one. As a quid pro quo a committee of enquiry into the working of the Department was established, headed by Sir Kenelm Digby. The nationalists were unlikely to be mollified by such an announcement and on 3 April, Swift MacNeill asked the prime minister if he was aware that 'Sir Horace Plunkett's retention of his post for even an hour was distasteful to the people of Ireland?' Campbell-Bannerman replied that it would be inconvenient to make a new appointment pending the outcome of the enquiry.[53]

Anticipating criticism of DATI support for co-operative societies, the IAOS urged them to pass formal resolutions on the value of the Society's work and on the propriety of Departmental assistance. For once, the societies did not disappoint the parent organisation. Resolutions flooded in from all over the country worded in the most unambiguous terms. A moving tribute came from Townanilly Agricultural Bank, a tiny credit society in the Bluestack mountains of Co. Donegal:

When our little bank started a few years ago there were a number of us helplessly and hopelessly in the clutches of the gombeen man. Now he has not one of us, agus go raibh se go deo mar sin. Ta suimhneas, sean agus solas againn ó fuair muid amach as na crúba neamh-thrócaireacha [and it has been fine since then. We have peace and contentment since we escaped from his merciless clutches][54]

The nationalist campaign against co-operation, and nationalist jealousy of, and bitterness towards, Plunkett brought vigorous rejoinders from the *Homestead* edited since 1905 by AE. His barrage was concentrated upon Dillon and the *Freeman's Journal*; their opposition was ascribed to 'pure hatred of the founder of the movement' and the formation of a co-operative society in Ballaghaderreen*, Dillon's home town in Co. Roscommon, shortly after one of his most venomous attacks, was chalked up as a victory for the co-operators. Declamations against Plunkett by Dillon and his cohorts had the further effect of pushing nationalistically minded supporters of the IAOS away from parliamentarianism and into the ambit of the recently founded separatist movement, Sinn Féin.

In March 1907 the Department sent the IAOS details of a scheme to be jointly financed with conditions which were so restrictive that, in Anderson's opinion, the Department was gaining a complete stranglehold over the Society. Gill, who was trimming his sails to catch the nationalist breeze, was at the back

---

*Now the site of the giant Shannonside Milk Products Co-operative.

of it; however the Society had little option but to accept the conditions. Among other changes the IAOS was forced to sever its connection with the *Irish Homestead* in order to maintain the weekly's independence.

IAOS salaries were but a meagre fraction of those paid to DATI officials and after one unsavoury incident Anderson exploded with justifiable rage:

I found it hard to control the frayed tempers of my small staff. The monthly expenses diaries of the organisers, my own included, were subject to rigorous examination and criticism, so that much of our time was taken up by explanations as to why a telegram rather than a letter was sent, or why a organiser hired a car when there was a railway (but no suitable train!). The whole Irish Agricultural Organisation Society staff flared up when it was discovered that, an official at £1,000 a year salary, and first class expenses, had dogged the itinerary of one of our most trustworthy and zealous organisers, whose humble pay was £250, with third-class expenses, to verify his record of societies visited and inns slept in. Apart from the miserable meanness of this proceeding, the waste of public funds on such sleuth hunting was a scandal.[55]

Bryce, a liberal and home ruler of Ulster-Scottish stock and a keen Plunkett supporter, resigned the chief secretaryship under nationalist pressure in December 1906 to be succeeded by the pliant Augustine Birrell. At Westminister three months later Dillon pointed out that there had been no demand in Ireland for a committee of enquiry into the operation of the DATI and asked why the committee, which had concluded its evidence the previous July, had not yet reported, adding that the whole procedure was simply a device to keep Plunkett in office. Redmond underlined the further anomaly that, if Plunkett had continued to hold a seat in parliament, then, on the change of government, he would, automatically, have relinquished his post.[56] The nationalists, with the bit now firmly between their teeth, moved the following resolution:

That the position of vice-president of the Board of Agriculture was intended by parliament to be, and in fact is, a ministerial and parliamentary office, properly vacated upon a change of government, and that the retention of the office by an opponent of the government of the day is undesirable as a permanent arrangement.

To this motion an amendment was proposed that no change should be made in the vice-president's position until the committee of enquiry had reported. The thrust of the nationalist speeches was directed at the unconstitutionality of Plunkett's position. It was agreed by Arthur Balfour that the office was intended to be a parliamentary one but that, owing to the incumbent's exceptional qualifications, the previous government had decided to continue him in office, and, this he claimed, had been the right decision for Ireland. The nationalist MP who moved the motion observed that such diverse sources as the English press, the Belfast Chamber of Commerce, the Ulster Liberal Unionist Association and the sinn féin newspaper, the *United Irishman*, pleaded for his retention.[57] The *Homestead* linked Plunkett with Yeats and Hyde as Irishmen of ideas who had built up organisations to clothe these ideas with reality, noting the anomaly of Dillon flying to England to protect Ireland from itself, for:

the Department of Agriculture is unique in this, that it is controlled as to its expenditure by the representatives of the county councils in Ireland; and, in fact, that the Council of Agriculture is a miniature home rule parliament, and the Board of Agriculture a miniature home rule cabinet; and that Sir Horace Plunkett is the only Irishman who has succeeded in getting any form of home rule for Ireland.[58]

The *Irish Textile Journal*, reflecting liberal unionist opinion in Ulster, also leaped to his defence:

There would have been no Department of Agriculture but for the work of the Recess Committee in 1896, and there would have been no Recess Committee but for the work of Sir Horace Plunkett. From first to last Sir Horace Plunkett has been the mainspring of the Department, and whatever success it has achieved up to the present must be largely credited to him.[59]

The speeches in the Commons debate were, with one exception, moderate in tone, and the vice-president received a number of tributes from all sides, but Dillon, making no attempt to disguise his antipathy for Plunkett and all his works, launched a blistering attack.[60] He admitted that he had first met Plunkett on his return from America after his father's death. Plunkett, who, in 1891, was contemplating how state aid could best be channelled into Irish agricultural development, had called stating that he was free of political ties but loved Ireland and wished to devote his talents to its people. Dillon had replied that he could not expect to alleviate the condition of the people unless through politics and added, somewhat contradictorily, that if he could steer clear of any political involvement he would have his best wishes for his success. But Plunkett who had appeared momentarily to step outside the ranks of Irish unionism, then stepped back in again, and had become, in Dillon's view, a implacable enemy of the Parliamentary Party. He accused him of maintaining 'a band of agents paid by the taxpayer to blackguard and abuse' the nationalists, and of subsidising with public funds 'a scurrilous newspaper whose chief business was to sneer at home rule'. He had been ousted from parliament by the 'orange party' but they were foolish as Plunkett was in reality a most sinister unionist. The comparative failure of the DATI, as he saw it, was chiefly due to the personality of Plunkett as well as to the constitution which he had forced upon it. The amendment failed after a three hour debate by 247 votes to 108 and the motion was then carried without a division.

Although Dillon emerges with little credit from his confrontations with Plunkett, with the co-operators, and with the DATI while Plunkett was vice-president, some of the bitterness which he felt may stem from the fact that he seems to have been unintentionally misled concerning Plunkett's political leanings at their first meeting. Both men have left versions of this encounter, which agree apart from minor details, [61] and which took place on 18 August 1891 (and not in 1890 as Dillon suggested). Plunkett clearly indicated that he was more interested in social reform than in party politics and seems to have conveyed the impression to Dillon that he intended to remain politically independent. This, perhaps, reflected an aristocratic and somewhat condescending view of Irish politics that one might accept a unionist nomination while retaining one's independence, for, on the very day of his meeting with Dillon he records his consent to stand in the South Dublin election provided that Arthur Balfour approved of his decision. [62]

This misunderstanding goes some way to explain the abuse which Dillon constantly hurled at Plunkett, laced with the invective which members of his party generally reserved for their colleagues. But his enmity extended to the co-operative movement which he seemed to regard as an opposing political party. The Childers Committee on Financial Relations, the 1896 Land Act, the Local Government Act, the Recess Committee Report and the DATI all were objects of suspicion to Dillon. In the Land Conference of 1902/3 between representatives of landlords and tenants and the subsequent efforts of Dunraven and his colleagues to obtain a limited measure of devolution for Ireland, he detected the bogey of a centre party incorporating the moderates on both sides, and Dillon was as delighted as the Ulster unionists when the whole edifice collapsed in the crisis of 1904.

Events were to prove Dillon wrong and to vindicate Parnell's prognostication that remedial legislation would only strengthen the desire for home rule. Ironically for the Dillonites, when, in 1916, that desire did manifest itself, the parliamentarians, owing to their absorbtion with Westminster plus the emergence of Sinn Féin, were completely unable to exert control. The Nationalist Party never really recovered from the trauma of the fall of Parnell and the verdict must be that, from 1890 onwards, it was primarily a negative force.

Plunkett handed over office to the nationalist nominee, T. W. Russell, MP for East Tyrone, on 22 May. The final irony came a week later with the publication of the report of the Digby Committee which highly commended the vice-president and his staff on the execution of their departmental duty. Evidence presented by individuals and local bodies from all over the country indicated overwhelming support for Plunkett and for the modus operandi of the DATI. Marked tributes came from the north of Ireland as to the benefits which had been conferred upon the agriculture and industry of Ulster. Thomas Andrews pointed out that the Department's creation had been due to a understanding arrived at by the Recess Committee on behalf of the commercial north and the agricultural south.[63] Plunkett spoke of his initial insistence on the 'absolute necessity of freeing a Department, which was to introduce new principles into Irish administration, from the traditional influences of Irish government' for

there was a compact between the members of the Recess Committee who represented all parties that, as the expression was in those days, 'a new Castle Board should not be created', and it was held that a separate minister directly responsible to parliament was the main factor in keeping the Department free from Castle control.[64]

The committee, accepting the fact that the DATI's autonomy had now been established, recommended that the vice-president should neither be a member of parliament nor in the civil service, but should be someone of independent standing who would work closely with the president of the DATI — the chief secretary for Ireland — who would assume parliamentary responsibility. (Plunkett had turned down an offer by Wyndham to incorporate just such a change in the Land Act of 1903 preferring to adhere to the terms of the Recess Committee's report).[65] Needless to add, this recommendation, which supported Plunkett's position, was never acted upon.

Members of the Parliamentary Party at Westminster were pledged not to accept office, thus Plunkett's successor, T. W. Russell, was in fact an Ulster MP who had been a liberal, but opposed Gladstone over home rule and became for a time a member of the Ulster Liberal Unionist Association. Born at Cupar, Fife, the grandson of an evicted Scottish crofter, he had come to Ireland at the age of twenty to work in Donaghmore, Co. Tyrone and had risen to prominence in the temperance movement so beloved of the liberals in the nineteenth century. Russell was a exceptional orator who had taken up the cause of the Ulster tenant farmers, but his views on the constitutional issue were changing; by 1901 he believed that 'there was much to be said for the abstract principle of Irish self government'[66] and, by 1907, he was sufficiently close to the nationalists to be nominated in Plunkett's place.

He had been an MP since 1886 and had considerable administrative experience as parliamentary secretary of the Local Government Board from 1895 to 1900, but the stark contrast in official DATI correspondence between the periods 1899-1907 and 1907-1919 (when Russell retired owing to ill health to be succeeded by the unionist H. T. Barrie) exhibits the difference in style between the two vice-presidents. Plunkett's ideal of a self-help movement dovetailing in with a department of state was an experiment which attracted international attention, and his departmental correspondence was interspersed with a stream of enquiries from overseas; these tailed off sharply in 1907 and the only striking feature of the file covering Russell's incumbency is the frequency of requests for support from candidates for official position.

Russell, who by 1907 had distanced himself considerably from liberal unionism, took the official nationalist view of co-operation. In this he was supported by Gill, who, after the change over, felt no loyalty to the co-operators. In tune with nationalist feeling, Gill recommended tighter control over IAOS finances and that the DATI should take over the organisational functions carried out by Society. An unfortunate incident of late 1907 gave Russell just the excuse he had been seeking to cut off all financial support to the IAOS. Plunkett, at the meeting at which he resumed the presidency of the Society, had made a wide ranging, constructive speech redefining the IAOS's relationships to the farmer, to trading interests and to the DATI. The *Irish Times* carried his speech in full and Plunkett asked the writer, T. W. Rolleston, who had reported on technical education to the Recess Committee and had organized lectures for the DATI, to send copies of the report to some of his American friends from whom he hoped to solicit aid for the IAOS. Rolleston had little love for the nationalists describing them, somewhat unkindly on another occasion as, 'this damnable gang of swindlers and murderers';[67] his enthusiasm proved Plunkett's undoing, for he sent the paper accompanied by an injudicious covering letter to Edward Devoy of St. Louis, Missouri. The letter, which found its way to Redmond, was subsequently published in the *Freeman's Journal*.

Sir Horace Plunkett has asked me to send you a copy of the *Irish Times* containing a full report of his speech ... this speech is a very important event, and means an attempt to organise the Irish farmers to shake off the grip of the country publican and gombeen man, who has hitherto controlled the parliamentary representation of the country. No sort of attack upon home rule or upon home rulers as such is dreamt of. It is only insisted that Irish farmers will not use people who will use their power, as Dillon and the rest of the parliamentarians have been doing, to crush the farmer's movement for the better organisation of his business ...[68]

The nationalists claimed that the letter was the evidence they needed of a conspiracy against the Parliamentary Party. Even though Plunkett denied all knowledge of the letter and Rolleston admitted full responsibility, all hope of reconciliation between the Department and the co-operative movement vanished in a flood of vitriol. AE, in the columns of the *Irish Homestead*, chose attack as the best form of defence. Nailing down the facts he went on to deal with Dillon whom he described as the driving force and spinning tail of the torpedo of which Redmond was the 'rather blunt nose':

Mr. Rolleston began his now famous letter ... by saying Sir Horace asked him to forward a report of his speech. Then Mr. Rolleston made some comments of his own with which we personally agree but for which Mr. Rolleston, not the IAOS, not Sir Horace, is responsible ... Irish farmers are well aware that Mr. Dillon has been for many years the deadliest enemy to agricultural co-operation in Ireland ... He wants those he helps to be the enemies of his enemies, to espouse all his quarrels, to adopt all his narrow ideas and prejudices and to injure their own fortunes by refusing all benefits he is not the responsible agent for.[69]

The withdrawal of departmental aid[70] forced the IAOS back entirely on its own resources and Plunkett's appeal in May 1908 was reasonably successful. In 1909, when Lloyd George was introducing a development bill, Plunkett seized the opportunity to have a clause inserted (unsuccessfully opposed by Dillon) which would allow the teaching of agricultural co-operation to be designated a beneficiary of the fund which was being established. Agricultural organisation societies inspired by Plunkett's example, and modelled on the IAOS, had been founded in England and Scotland in 1900 and 1905, respectively. The three societies made independent applications for financial assistance to the Development Commission and without much delay grants of £3,000 and £1,000 were made to the English and Scottish societies. In accordance with procedure, all such applications required the approval of the relevant government department. The application of the IAOS was therefore referred to the DATI in January 1911. Ten months later Russell referred it to the Council of Agriculture and, under pressure from him, the Council endorsed his suggestion that the money should be granted to the Department which would supervise the co-operative schemes in question.

The *Northern Whig*, springing to the defence of the co-operators, underlined the anomaly that the IAOS should be attacked by a branch of the Irish government which, but for its labour, would never have been created,[71] while the journal *Sinn Féin* pounced on Russell's attempts to encroach on co-operative territory:

Mr. T. W. Russell, the tool of the political enemies of the IAOS, threatens to use public money to organise a counter co-operative movement which will in no way interfere with the butter rings or the gombeen men. If a hundred thousand organised farmers can't meet and beat such a move the co-operative movement has been in vain.[72]

More sensitive nationalists such as Hugh Law, Stephen Gwynn and T. M. Kettle,[73] realising that this sort of infighting could only act to the detriment of Irish progress, tried to make peace between the two bodies. (An obituary notice in the *Homestead* in 1916 revealed that Kettle had, with typical magnanimity, presented his collection of economic texts to the Co-operative Reference Library before departing to the trenches and his death).[74] Law pointed out, in a letter to the *Homestead*, how much harm and how little good was being done to the co-operative movement by debates in parliament and by the campaign of the tory press (which was using the IAOS as a stick to beat the nationalists) but though there were temporary cessations of hostilities the bitterness ran too deep and the dispute continued until everything was overshadowed by the outbreak of the war.

The Development Commissioners were, however, sufficiently independent not to be taken in by Russell's convoluted attempt to stifle co-operation with bureaucracy,[75] and the IAOS was, eventually, awarded a grant of £2,000 with an offer of a further £4,000 on a pound for pound basis. For a period during this debacle, the modest salaries of the IAOS officials had had to be withheld and were paid, only with the assistance of a subvention of £1,800 from Plunkett. Even more important was the endorsement given to the Society's work by the Commissioners, two of whom were co-opted onto the committee. With this support, both moral and financial, IAOS morale improved immeasurably and, in Anderson's words, 'a great peace seemed to fall upon us'.

V

Noblesse Oblige

Co-operation was by no means the only unifying theme in Ireland at the turn of the century. Dissention among politicians had led to disenchantment with politics. It seemed as if the fall of Parnell had released a force which formerly spent itself in political channels but which now sparked off a renaissance in Irish cultural life. The intensity of the literary revival, spearheaded by Yeats and Lady Gregory, focussed world attention on ancient Irish sagas and the modern Irish theatre. Inspired by Douglas Hyde, the Gaelic League's campaign to revive Irish language and traditions swept the country. The literary and linguistic movements cut across the divisions of creed, class or political affiliation (although the Gaelic League was ultimately to be politicised) and Plunkett, irresistibly drawn towards any movement for the regeneration of his people, was carried away with the idea of co-operation between 'the practical men and the dreamers of Ireland'.

This was the spring time for literary Dublin; some years later it was possible, in the full bloom of summer,

to spend a morning at St. Enda's School and discuss the ideals of Irish education with Pearse* and MacDonagh*, to catch a vivid minute with George Russell in Plunkett House, in the afternoon to see Yeats and Lady Gregory moving down the quays to rehearsal at the Abbey Theatre, and in the evening to hear a Synge play and pass a late hour with Kettle. An ambrosian night and day. [1]

Plunkett had his own contacts with the literary movement. Emily Lawless, the cousin who had influenced his view of Anglo-Irish history, was the author of a distinguished volume of hauntingly patriotic verse, [2] evoking the heartbreak of emigration and defeat for Irish soldiers on foreign fields after the collapse

*Teachers and writers who were to lead the Easter Rising in 1916.

of the Stuarts. The plays of his nephew Edward, later the eighteenth Baron Dunsany, achieved great popularity in America. His strange menacing fairytales predate Tolkien. Plunkett himself developed an attractive style. *Ireland in the New Century* is written in simple, flowing prose. He was not an orator but his speeches read well. Among his staff he was famous for last minute alterations to his script, he would, according to Alexis Roche, 'amend an order for a bag of coal!'

Having conspired successfully with Yeats and Lady Gregory to recruit AE, Plunkett and his movement soon became a focal point for Irish writers. Edward Martyn (another pioneer of the literary renaissance) and J.O. Hannay (the rector of Westport and novelist George Birmingham) along with Standish O'Grady and Douglas Hyde were keen supporters. T.W. Rolleston worked in various capacities for the DATI; Alfred Perceval Graves reported on agricultural and technical education to the Recess Committee; the Ulster novelist Shan Bullock served on the secretariat of the Irish Convention, while Plunkett counted Oliver St. John Gogarty (the Dublin doctor, writer and wit) and Bernard Shaw among his closest friends. The playwright Lennox Robinson worked under Plunkett (who was the organisation's Irish trustee) founding Carnegie libraries with such success that 'Mr Jack Yeats once made a picture of a village in the country, hiding itself in the shadow of a hill, in the hope that it might be overlooked by Mr Carnegie and so escape having a library thrust upon it.'[3]

In London for the parliamentary sittings of early 1897, Plunkett met the Irish literati with Lady Gregory who has left a fascinating account of the evening's conversation.

Dinner, Rt. Hon. Horace Plunkett, Mr. Barry O'Brien*, W. B. Yeats — some very interesting talk — Mr. O'Brien arrived first — and said that he would be glad to meet Mr. Plunkett — as all sections of nationalists have been agreeing of late that he is the only possible leader to unite all parties — Yeats, just back from Dublin corroborates this... Then Mr. Plunkett came and we went up to dinner — a little tentative conversation first — then Mr. Plunkett said his grudge against Parnellism is that Parnell so mastered and dominated his followers as to crush national life instead of developing it... Mr. O'B says it was necessary he should dominate for the campaign, and that he was a great general — I say we see Mr. P's contention is true by the helpless disorganisation parties have fallen into since his death and ask Mr. O'B what he would

*A nationalist MP and biographer of Parnell.

do at this moment in Ireland if he had power there — He says 'I would make Mr. Horace Plunkett our leader and follow him' — Yeats agrees enthusiastically and says 'we all want it' — Mr. Plunkett reddens and is evidently touched, tho' his quiet restrained manner is unchanged — Yeats asks him how far he would go — he says to a large measure of local government — but not separation — and not yet home rule, they are not yet ready for it.[4]

She followed this up with an invitation in the autumn to her home at Coole Park, Co. Galway. Again he met Yeats, 'the young poet — a rebel — a mystic and an ass but really a genius in a queer way' and Edward Martyn 'a clever writer of the more imaginative kind'. ('Galway', he wrote, 'has been a great surprise to me.')[5] Her farming neighbours were summoned to learn of co-operation:

We had asked the farmers to meet him, but it was a fine day after long rain and very few came, but he came and talked to them outside the hall door explaining the methods — with so much courtesy and earnestness that he won their hearts — his quiet manner with so much enthusiasm underneath, strike one very much.[6]

Lady Gregory and Yeats were instrumental in persuading AE to throw in his lot with the co-operators and he, she hoped, would inspire Plunkett with a 'spiritual nationality'. But the northern poet was given little opportunity to rest upon his literary laurels being promptly dispatched to the congested districts of the west of Ireland to organise Raiffeisen credit societies which Father Finlay had encountered in Germany. Overcoming his initial loneliness on discovering that, although a poet, he talked the farmers' language, as a co-operative organiser he became a great success. The *Irish Homestead* had started publication in 1895, in 1905 AE succeeded to the editor's chair. Under his inspired guidance the *Homestead* developed in a literary direction. While its main purpose was to provide news of the co-operative movement and of innovations in agriculture, also included were a series of poems in English and Irish (including a collection by An Craoibhinn Aoibhinn — Douglas Hyde), short stories (including three by Stephen Dedalus — James Joyce), and a special Christmas number which was purely literary and of considerable importance since it published the emerging young Irish writers, often for the first time. The first of these appeared just after AE had been recruited in December 1897, and contained contributions from Douglas Hyde, Emily Lawless, AE, W. B. Yeats, Standish O'Grady and George Sigerson. The Christmas number was illustrated by artists such as Sarah Purser, AE himself and Jack B. Yeats (whom the *Homestead* referred to as the artist of the co-operative movement although the title might, more correctly, have been conferred upon AE). It was hard grinding work, for with the help of his assistant Susan Mitchell — herself a writer of some talent — he often wrote the whole of the week's issue. Somehow he managed to maintain his output of poetry and painting. A seminal figure to his brother artists, AE was a decided nationalist whose simple charm broke down all barriers. Receiving his friends perched in his office on the top floor of the Plunkett House or at literary evenings at home, his encouragement of young talent, his remarkable breadth of interest and his flow of conversation made him, as he wished to be remembered, 'the friend of Irish poets — those who make the soul of the nation.'

Once the *Homestead* had been established as the journal of the co-operative movement. Plunkett, with his flair for propaganda, soon moved further, acquiring the Dublin *Daily Express* and its associate the *Evening Mail* plus a weekly, the *Warder*. The report of the Recess Committee was then in limbo; he was involved in urging the financial findings of the Childers Committee on a reluctant government, so a propaganda organ was needed which might sound a more political note. T. P. Gill, fresh from his triumph with the Recess Committee, was installed as editor. The *Express*, in tone conservative and unionist was to the right of Dublin's other unionist paper, the *Irish Times*, which explains Plunkett's writing to Gill on 19 May 1898: 'I shall be interested to see how you deal with poor old Gladstone's death in the *Express*. He was the man of the century but he disestablished most of your subscribers!'[7]

The new departure was signalled on 20 August. It would henceforth preach a gospel of reconciliation between unionist and nationalist, landlord and tenant; of reconstruction of financial relations between Ireland and Britain and of industry, agriculture and technical education along the lines of the Recess Committee's report. The annual meeting of the IAOS, a few days later, was reported in glowing terms:

Here, in actual operation, was the union' of classes and parties for common national interests which we have argued to be no longer an enthusiast's dream in Ireland but a matter of sober reality.[8]

The new management had pulled off a great scoop in the previous month by persuading the young Marconi to set up a transmitter on a steam yacht which followed the Kingstown Regatta to the Kish Lightship, and then publishing the first newspaper report to be transmitted by wireless.[9] More important was the literary bias given to the paper. Yeats, John Eglinton, Lady Gregory and AE became regular contributors while James Joyce was a reviewer.

Lady Gregory, a talented, ambitious member of the ascendancy, deeply committed to Irish regeneration and playing a dominant role in the development of Irish literature and theatre, was just the sort of person to appeal to Plunkett. She was, however, much more straightforward in her political views and acted, at this period, rather as a tutor (though he was to prove a somewhat recalcitrant pupil) as he took his first faltering steps towards nationalism. They dined again in February 1898:

Horace Plunkett and W. Yeats came and dined with me — the former anxious about the famine districts — says the distress tho' limited in area is very acute — he wants to get money just to keep the people from starving for the present, and he wants to make future famines impossible by teaching the people to help themselves — he is a good man, one feels the presence of goodness in the room.[10]

Yeats enlivened the evening with his feelings for Maud Gonne, and, when Plunkett suggested that Parnell was un-Irish, launched into a brilliant discourse arguing that the English were a masculine race with feminine ideals while the Irish were the reverse hence England never could accept a masculine ruler like Napoleon or Parnell, as Ireland would.

A year later at another dinner, Yeats read from Hyde's translations of his *Love Songs of Connacht* and she recorded; 'H. Plunkett quite for the language movement now'.[11] But, having taken one step forward, Plunkett, on becoming vice-president of the DATI in 1899, appeared to Lady Gregory to take two steps back.

Horace Plunkett in the afternoon, full of cares of his new board, and I think more unionist than before his illness — seems to think the grant for the board satisfies our financial claims and that we ought to be grateful. I say no, if we are owed the money let us have it, there is no question of gratitude, and we ought not to have to sit up and beg for it every time. He says he sympathises with the Boer farmers in the war — but if so, why did he go out of his way to make a speech in favour of it?[12]

Further differences arose over Yeats' letters of protest at Queen Victoria's visit to Ireland. Though a determined critic of the government of Ireland, Plunkett never lost his respect or affection for the monarchy. In May 1900 Lady Gregory talked to him again.

He lamented the Queen letters 'She was so nice and said the right things and it is so sad the "real and ideal" Ireland cannot work together.' Yeats had made such a beautiful speech that time they had a dinner[13] and he hoped we would work side by side — I defended Yeats and on his persisting I said that we could still all work together. 'You made a speech on the war that made angels weep, but we have not given up the effort to help you because of that' — He said his speech on the war had offended some of his S. Dublin people by not being strong enough — and then he vexed me by saying 'It is just as Balfour said in the H of Commons, the Irish wd be against England in any war'. It vexes me that he shd take his opinion of the opinion of Irish farmers from Balfour! However, we parted friends.[14]

In February 1899, Plunkett presided at a dinner for Yeats, George Moore, Edward Martyn, Lady Betty Balfour and Lady Gregory to strengthen the links between co-operators and the Irish writers.[15] This led to a celebrated Dublin banquet in the following May,[16] the editor of the *Daily Express* playing host to the members of the Irish Literary Theatre, currently performing Yeats' 'Countess Cathleen' and Edward Martyn's 'Heather Field'. Plunkett was absent, recovering in a London hospital from a fractured femur, the result of a cycling accident. The literary world was present in force with Yeats, Moore, Douglas Hyde, W. K. Magee (John Eglinton), Standish O'Grady, George Sigerson and T. W. Rolleston. Gill and R. A. Anderson represented the co-operators, (AE deciding, perhaps wisely, to stay away), Max Beerbohm came from the English theatre and Bernard and Tyrrell were present from Trinity College. The evening was memorable for a vigorous defence by Yeats of the 'Countess Cathleen' in the controversy which his play had aroused* and for the ominous pronouncement by an inebriated Standish O'Grady:

We now have a literary movement, it is not very important; it will be followed by a political movement, that will not be very important; then must come a military movement, that will be important indeed![17]

It was later immortalised by Moore in his extravagant satire on

*The Countess barters her soul for the safety of her people; although she is ultimately redeemed by the nobility of her intentions the play aroused the wrath of the catholic hierarchy.

Dublin life contained in his autobiographical novel, *Hail and Farewell*. Dublin's 'perfect acoustics' were not lost on a writer of Moore's talent and few of its characters escaped caricature (apart from AE and Father Finlay for whom he showed an almost reverential respect). Plunkett and Gill appear as Flaubert's clerks, Bouvard and Pecuchet, Edward Martyn, Moore's cousin, is mercilessly satirised as 'Dear Edward' but the balance is maintained as the author does not overlook his own foibles. The first volume contains a not unfavourable description of the co-operative movement including the perceptive comment that, at heart, it was 'a very simple idea, almost a platitude, but Plunkett had the courage of his platitudes'.[18]

Plunkett's star had risen during Arthur Balfour's chief secretaryship and, in his parliamentary days, he was a regular visitor to the Balfour's Surrey home, even persuading Arthur's sister Alice to present a cup for the most efficient co-operative society of the year.[19] Betty Balfour, Gerald's charming wife, inhabited the chief secretary's lodge in the Phoenix Park from 1895 to 1900. She became involved with literary Ireland staging Yeats' plays in her official residence, (the poet's republican scruples ensuring his non-attendance). Plunkett took the Balfours on a tour of the west of Ireland shortly after their arrival. Well aware of the value of influence in high places, he struck up a most useful friendship with Lady Betty, for she made an excellent channel of communication with the chief secretary. Their friendship, however, was more than one of convenience, its warmth preserved in the hundred letters which passed between them.[20] In February 1897 she contributed an article to the *Irish Homestead*, 'The Dalkey Co-operative Embroidery Society',[21] and Plunkett had won another important recruit for co-operation.

Yeats shared with Plunkett a belief that the explosion of pent-up energy released by the fall of Parnell heralded a regeneration in Irish cultural and economic life, but shared adversity was also a bond between them. The Parliamentary Party and the Trinity College establishment were among their common enemies and Yeats crossed swords with the two men who spearheaded the opposition to Plunkett in the South Dublin election of 1900. Edward Dowden, professor of English in Trinity College, was a scholar of international renown, yet he is best remembered for his controversy with Yeats over the definition and content of a national literature. Ardilaun appeared in the quarrel concerning the municipal gallery and the Lane bequest. Hugh Lane, a

nephew of Lady Gregory's, had amassed an important collection
of French impressionist paintings which he wished to bequeath
to Dublin if a suitable gallery were constructed. An imaginative
design incorporating a gallery on a bridge over the Liffey was
turned down on grounds of cost and Ardilaun's refusal to
support the project led to him being made the subject of Yeats'
poem 'To a Wealthy Man who Promised a Second Subscription to
the Dublin Municipal Gallery if it were Proved the People
Wanted Pictures'. In 1899, as a recognition of the bond between
them, Yeats paid Plunkett this remarkable (if over optimistic)
tribute:

The last few months have been of extreme importance to the Irish
intellectual movement, which began with the break up of the political
movement of Parnell, for they have done more than the preceding ten
years to interest the Irish leisured classes in Irish thought and literature.
Certain political impulses have helped; but the Irish *Daily Express*, a
paper whose policy is under the direction of Mr. Horace Plunkett has
been the chief mover in what had seemed an almost impossible
change. [22]

The bold experiment with the *Express* lasted a bare eighteen
months. The change in policy resulted in a decline in readership;
Plunkett's attempt to obtain a knighthood for the businessman
who had subscribed the initial capital was a failure; and Ardilaun,
already disenchanted with Plunkett's other activities, after discussions with Carson, bought up a majority shareholding
bringing this new departure in journalism to an abrupt halt. On
29 January 1900 it was announced in uncompromising terms that
the paper was changing hands:

It will cherish no dreams of a national millenium being convinced that
the interests of unionism and separatism, of property and communism,
are never reconcilable in the history of any country. It will offer a fearless
and energetic resistance to every fresh attempt of the government to
pander to treason by robbing loyalists. [23]

Gill moved smoothly from the editor's chair to the secretaryship
of the newly established DATI and the *Daily Express* became a
potent weapon in the hands of Plunkett's opponents which they
employed to unseat him.

Plunkett had been introduced to the work of the Gaelic League
and to the poetry of Douglas Hyde by Yeats and Lady Gregory.
A son of the rectory in Co. Roscommon, Hyde's ambition was to

make the language revival 'a neutral field upon which all Irishmen might meet', thus the Gaelic League (founded one year before the IAOS) of which he became president, was declared by its constitution to be non-political and non-sectarian. These characteristics, which were insisted on by Hyde, made it, as Plunkett observed, 'the object of much suspicion, because severance from politics in Ireland has always seemed to the politician the most active form of enmity'.[24]

There were other parallels, in Plunkett's mind, with his own movement. The declared objects of the League did not convey a true picture of its actual work in developing the intellectual, moral, and social life of the Irish people. Moreover, Ireland was perhaps, the only country in Europe where the national factor had been studiously eliminated from national education; where it was part of the settled policy of those who had the guidance of education to ignore the literature, history, arts, and traditions of the people. It was a fatal policy, he believed, for it tended to stamp their native country in the eyes of Irishmen with the badge of inferiority and to extinguish that sense of healthy self-respect which comes from the consciousness of high national ancestry and traditions. The Gaelic movement had brought to the surface a latent spiritual inheritance which had long lain undetected:

A passionate conviction is gaining ground that if Irish traditions, literature, language, art, music, and culture are allowed to disappear, it will mean the disappearance of the race; and that the education of the country must be nationalised if our social, intellectual, or even our moral position is to be permanently improved.[25]

These sentiments were given practical form, in 1901, by the establishment of a competition for co-operative societies (with prizes donated by Plunkett) whose objects were:

the revival of national sports and Gaelic pastimes;
the establishment of classes in Irish language, literature, poetry, and local antiquities;
the organisation of village libraries;
the revival of the ceilidh (Irish dancing);
the formation of choirs singing Irish music;
besides the beautification of rural villages and homes.[26]

On a visit to Dromore, Co. Down, where he addressed the local branch of the Gaelic League, Plunkett observed that, wherever the League thrived, there his own work was more appreciated.[27]

His commendation in *Ireland in the New Century* was backed up with a letter to Hyde enclosing a subscription of 10 pounds:

It has struck me that, as the sympathy I display towards the Gaelic League is rather from the business side of things, I ought to give my moral support something of a material character, especially now that my book has aroused such hostility that I may have done you more harm than good by my testimony to the practical value of your great movement. [28]

The friendship between the two men extended back to the beginning of the IAOS for an early leaflet entitled *Bancanna Tíre*[29] (Land Banks) was signed 'An Craoibhinn Aoibhinn' (the lovely little branch), Hyde's Gaelic pseudonym. (Land banks were credit societies based on the Raiffeisen model which flourished mainly in the western, gaelic speaking section of the country). During the fateful Dundalk convention of 1915 at which the Gaelic League abandoned its non-political stance forcing Hyde to resign, he emphasised the importance of Plunkett's support:

I had again and again said in public that the League was non-political and that I would never, while I was president, allow it to be made a political body. By speaking thus I had won a great deal of support in time past, Horace Plunkett and others ... By keeping the League strictly and sternly non-political we drew into it, or rather we earned the good will and kind words of such different people as Ford of the *Irish World*, Devoy of the *Gaelic American*, Cardinal Logue and Horace Plunkett. Horace Plunkett's kind words of appreciation were worth any money to the League ... [30]

Several of Plunkett's artistic friends, such as the nationalist historian Alice Stopford Green*, felt that, splendid as his economic movement was, it somehow lacked a spiritual side. 'Hitch your waggon to a star' advised Standish O'Grady in Emersonian terms. [31] But to which of the rising stars could Plunkett hitch his co-operative waggon without jeopardising its neutrality and alienating all its unionist supporters? Canon Hannay, writing in 1907, listed the movements inspiring regeneration:

The Gaelic League, in spite of the cowardice of its leaders, is one, the propaganda of the Sinn Féin Party is another. The literary, dramatic and artistic revival is a third, working indirectly but really. A fourth, perhaps

---

*Her brother, E. A. Stopford, a strong nationalist, was an enthusiastic member of the IAOS committee.

the greatest of all, is Horace Plunkett's work. In a few years I hope that our people will be sufficiently educated and awake to make a dissolution of the present union with England safe and highly advantageous to us. [32]

Co-operative ideals were synthesised with a concept of nationhood by AE. Irishmen should aspire to 'carve an Attica out of Ireland', to develop in rural Irish parishes an intensity of life such as had existed in the city states of ancient Greece or medieval Italy. The problem of creating an organic life in Ireland, a harmony of the people, a union of their efforts for the common good and for the manifestation of whatever beauty, majesty and spirituality lay in them must be resolved by Irishmen for themselves. [33]

*　*　*

On his father's death Plunkett's elder brother John had inherited the title. He was succeeded by his son Edward, the eighteenth baron. The Castle at Dunsany had been his home, but during his elder brother's last years, and with the marriage of his nephew, Horace had become a visitor there. There was a house at Mount Street in London and while in Dublin he inhabited the Kildare Street Club, but there was tension in the Club. Edward Martyn (who had to take an action to prevent himself being blackballed as a consequence of his connection with Sinn Féin) on being asked why he did not resign replied that he liked the food and that, anyway, he was not half as unpopular as Horace Plunkett!

In 1903 Plunkett took a house in Foxrock for the summer and repeated this in the following year. Foxrock was an attractive, undeveloped suburb south of Dublin between the mountains and the sea, with a railway station and within easy reach of the city by his newly acquired de Dion Bouton, one of the first automobiles in Ireland. The location appealed to Plunkett so he settled on it for his permanent home. Kilteragh, in Westminster Road, was completed in 1906. Lady Fingall arranged the furnishing, she often acted as hostess, and he indulged himself by laying out a miniature golf course around the house, so close that the balls often broke the window panes. Whirlwind golf, with Plunkett in full flight, was a compulsory relaxation. Bogey was 27 and the host held the record of 22 which was never equalled; except for diplomatic reasons he was rarely beaten. One guest has left this impression:

I have the happiest memories of playing 'golf' on his nine-hole course cunningly laid out in his garden. I do not think that the holes were more than 30-50 yards apart and we took only two clubs, a mashie and a putter, but some of them provided sporting tee shots aiming at blind holes. Negotiating rhododendron bushes and arbutus on the way while discussing the Irish question required the nerves of Hagen or Bobby Jones![34]

Immersed in the vice-presidency of the DATI, Plunkett left the design of Kilteragh to a Swedish architect and supervision to some of his friends. The house turned out to be rather ugly and bigger than originally intended, but AE added some magic touches (Kilteragh contained many of his finest murals) and with Plunkett's voracious appetite for friends who could be useful, it soon became one of the better known houses in the land. Lady Fingall has left this entrancing picture of the house, and of its owner, in her memoirs:

There was a stoep [verandah] facing south, built on the model of the one Horace had seen at Cecil Rhodes' house Groote Schuur. Horace had given up politics, having never been a politician, but he knew, too, that some form of government by Irishmen for Irishmen was inevitable, and his dream was that the new Irish constitution should be signed on that stoep. He built the house for his friends and for Ireland. For as long as it stood, it was to be at the service of both.

He had his own shelter on the roof, with a bed in it, where he slept, summer or winter, and which, by some mechanical device, he could turn ... towards the sun and against the wind ... From the roof Horace could see Dublin Bay with the mountains encircling it, the gleaming waters of the Irish Sea, across which so many of his guests came. Kilteragh was to be, as he had planned, a centre of Irish life. Every one interesting or interested, who visited Ireland, was entertained there ... Men and women of the most directly opposed views, who probably never foregathered elsewhere, talked to each other in those rooms.[35]

The Kilteragh guest book* is a remarkable record of famous Irishmen and women of the period: Collins, Griffith, Casement, Childers, Redmond, Dillon, Gogarty, Hyde, Yeats, AE, Bernard Shaw, George Moore, Edith Somerville and Violet Martin (Somerville and Ross), Lady Gregory and Constance Markievicz; and of distinguished English visitors anxious to share Plunkett's perspective of Ireland: Gerald Balfour, Alfred Lyttleton, Sidney Webb, Philip Kerr, John Buchan, G. K. Chesterton and H. G. Wells; Lords Londonderry, Midleton,

*Now in the Library of TCD.

Selborne, Milner and Grey; and Americans such as Gifford
Pinchot, the conservationist, Lawrence Lowell (president of
Harvard), Henry Wallace, of *Wallace's Farmer*, and Charles
McCarthy of Wisconsin.

Lady Fingall recalled her arrivals from England on the mail
boat:

There would be a lovely early morning drive across the country to the
foot of the Three Rock Mountain with my thoughts full of things to tell
Horace — the people I had met and what they had said. As the car turned
in at the gate, Horace would be on the steps. He was always up to meet
his guests with his delightful smile and handshake. Like George
Wyndham, he was such a good welcomer. After a hot bath you would go
down to the dining-room, where a beaming Curtin would have breakfast
ready, and Horace would start you and hear your news. Then — Ireland
claimed him again! You had thought only for a moment that he had
belonged to you; but Ireland was a formidable rival, and she won, as she
has always won. Horace was back at work. (He would have breakfasted
early, on tea made on milk, and toast which he always prepared for
himself. His own food was uncomfortable and strange — slops, fruits
and nuts, while he gave his guests the best of fare). And you were eating
your breakfast alone, under AE's pale magic shores and bluegreen seas
painted in a fresco on the wall. With only his dim sea fairies for
company![36]

When the opportunity arose Plunkett acquired some land
around Kilteragh which he used for practical agricultural
instruction. For years the problem of providing winter milk
(which depended on appropriate winter feeding) had bedevilled
the dairy industry. The problem was solved by the method of
continuous or 'catch crops', as they are sometimes called, which
require the sowing of rape, kale, turnips or mangolds in the
autumn, immediately following the harvest. The principal
exponent of catch cropping was Thomas Wibberley who started
as instructor with the Limerick and Kerry agricultural
committees.[37] His support for co-operative seed purchase in the
Russell era had proved uncongenial to the DATI so he left to join
the IAOS. Plunkett let Wibberly loose in Kilteragh with
remarkable results, as he reported to the annual meeting of the
Society in 1914:

I speak from experience in my capacity as milkman at Foxrock. I confess
I too had looked forward to a leisurely old age knee-deep in grass. Mr.
Wibberly organised me and now I walk erect waist deep in giant rape and
hardy greens.[38]

The Kilteragh experiment lasted until the outbreak of the war; Wibberly's methods (he also pioneered the making of silage) having an important influence on Irish agricultural practice. Edward MacLysaght, a Clare farmer and ardent nationalist, writing in 1916, thus described its impact:

During the three years the experiment lasted almost every Sunday the South-Eastern Railway discharged a cargo from one train after another at Foxrock Station, of farmers large and small, who had come from every county in the country to see for themselves the Kilteragh farm, and to hear Mr. Wibberley expounding his ideas on production of farm foods, with the actual practice of them at hand to illustrate his words. The fairy tales which Mr. Wibberly seems to tell in his writings on continuous cropping appear true when one visits Kilteragh. ... It is however a commentary on what the Department might have been, had Sir Horace Plunkett remained in office, to think of the numbers of farmers who have travelled from Clare and Kerry, from Wexford and Donegal, losing their time and paying their own expenses, to see a new idea put into practice.[39]

Plunkett's unorthodox sleeping arrangements were an indication of his chronic ill health. His early conflict with tuberculosis had left him with a slight stoop, a riding accident had forced him to give up hunting and recurring dysentery, which he had picked up on a visit to Egypt, affected his stomach. He suffered, also, from Meuniere's disease of the inner ear resulting in a continuous buzzing noise and dizzy spells. Not surprisingly, therefore, he was somewhat of a hypochondriac, he slept badly and was a vegetarian who shunned stimulants such as tea, coffee or alcohol. Compensating for this physical weakness was an extraordinary strength of spirit which gave him energy and a working capacity far above the norm. However the demands he made on his frail body frequently led to breakdowns and his annual visits to America always included a rest cure in Battle Creek Sanitarium, Michigan.[40] Plunkett had suffered at the hand of a God whose existence he doubted: 'God is there no future? Future is there no God?'[41] But he was to suffer more at the hands of men.

He was now an international figure and his work the subject of enquiries from across the globe. Formal recognition came with election to privy councillorship and fellowship of the Royal Society (1902); honorary degrees from Oxford (1906), and Dublin (1908). A knighthood was conferred on him by King Edward during his visit in 1903. Plunkett had enthusiastically arranged part of the king's itinerary in the west of Ireland and accompanied the tour hoping to indoctrinate the king with his ideas. But the obsequiousness of the courtiers overcame him; 'I think a week in royal atmosphere would make me a ramping socialist',[42] he wrote before escaping at Queenstown to catch the night mail to Dublin. His private secretary, H. G. Smith, wired the guard at Mallow and Plunkett was turned back to receive his knighthood. 'I rather think', wrote Smith later to Lady Fingall, 'that he was sorry that my wire caught him in time to stop his journey home'[43] H. F. Norman, an IAOS official, meeting Plunkett shortly afterwards, inadvertently called him Mr. and then hurriedly apologised for forgetting the honour. 'I wish you would forget it', the recipient replied with unexpected alacrity and reminisced of his cowboy days in America where 'life was not very safe and property was not safe at all, but there existed a real, if rough, fraternity unspoiled by the tomfoolery of corruption and politics'.[44]

Upon his enforced retirement from the DATI, Plunkett resumed the role of co-operative leader and president of the IAOS. Despite financial constraints it was a period of considerable progress. The co-operatives grew in number from 881 in 1908 to 985 by 1913 and the annual turnover in the same period from 2.2 to 3.3 million pounds. Symbolising the movement's new spirit of self-reliance, 84 Merrion Square, one of Dublin's finest Georgian houses, was presented to Plunkett as the headquarters of the IAOS.[45] Anderson organised the presentation unbeknown to Plunkett and when the recipient first became aware of the project he was anything but grateful, for, at a time when the Society's resources were so thinly stretched, he felt that the money raised could have been more usefully employed. Plunkett soon mellowed when he realised the value of such imposing headquarters to the co-operative movement. The presentation was made in November 1908, both Sinclair and Andrews from Belfast being prominent among the subscribers. The Plunkett House is still the headquarters of the IAOS (now re-styled the Irish Co-operative Organisation Society, ICOS). A brass plate in the entrance hall bears the inscription:

To Horace Plunkett this house was presented by his friends and fellow workers in recognition of his efforts for the well-being of his country, and as an aid to him in the further development of his work.

Portraits of Plunkett, Lord Monteagle and R.A. Anderson painted by Dermod O'Brien (nephew of Monteagle, president of

the Royal Hibernian Academy and a keen co-operator) adorned
the president's office. AE, as editor of the *Irish Homestead*, was
installed upstairs where 'the walls of his room cried out to be
decorated after his own peculiar fashion and every square foot
was embellished by his magic brush until it became a real
fairyland'.*

The intellectual arm of the co-operative movement was
strengthened by the establishment of a Co-operative Reference
Library in the Plunkett House. The idea behind this project
originated in the State of Wisconsin where Charles McCarthy,
son of an evicted tenant from the Cork-Kerry border and a close
friend and collaborator of Plunkett's, had established a
Legislative Reference Library to assist the state's legislators in
their labours. Plunkett's own collection formed the basis of the
library, the Carnegie Foundation provided financial support; and
the Plunkett House became a 'co-operative university' for
Ireland's farmers and for the rest of the world.

'Better Living' was the final component of his famous slogan
and, as time went on, Plunkett devoted more and more of his
attention to the regeneration of rural life. He had observed that
the great bulk of Irish emigrants with rural backgrounds settled in
American cities avoiding further contact with the countryside.
Thus it was not enough to make the farmer prosperous and
efficient; the amenities of the countryside must be improved to
staunch the drain of population towards the town.

Always sensitive to the feelings of the weaker sex (his first
political article had been entitled 'The Working of Woman
Suffrage in Wyoming[+]'),[46] Plunkett was only too well aware of
the unremitting drudgery and toil which were the lot of women
on the farm. In 1910, in conjunction with Daisy Fingall, Emily
Lawless and other prominent lady co-operators, he founded the
United Irishwomen, summarising their aims as:

firstly, to attend to women's business in the life of a community which
no man, least of all an old batchelor like myself, can understand;
secondly, to see that farmers attend better to the business of their
organisation and make them as helpful to women and the household as
they are to men on the farm; and thirdly, for Irish women to take up their
rightful part in the building up of a rural civilisation in Ireland.[47]

---

*Sections of wallpaper from AE's room in the Plunkett House are preserved in the
National Gallery.
+Woman suffrage was introduced in Wyoming Territory in 1869.

The United Irishwomen (since 1935 the Irish Countrywoman's Association) continues on its 'long and fruitful career of modest usefulness' to the present day. Plunkett had also been responsible for starting the Agricultural Organisation Society (AOS), as an English counterpart to the IAOS, and, in the period in which the AOS was active it was made the vehicle for the foundation of the Women's Institutes, following Canada's example, during the first world war. [48]

Having severed his connection with the DATI, Plunkett was entirely free, for the first time since 1892, of political constraints. He had remained a unionist under the Balfourian regime but had been sufficiently independent to cut loose from unionism when party policy regressed in 1905. Extension of the franchise plus the reform of land tenure and of local government had altered the balance of power without dampening the fires of Irish nationalism. Plunkett appreciated this fact (which had escaped most English politicians) recognising that neither membership of the Unionist Party nor of the Kildare Street Club would be sufficient to insulate the ascendancy from the upheavals which lay ahead.

Noblesse Oblige, a pamphlet written in 1908, was an appeal to those whom he termed the resident gentry. Gladstonian legislation had rendered it inevitable that the farmlands of the country would eventually be transferred from owner to occupier. The Dunraven Conference of 1902 between representatives of landlord and tenant had paved the way for the Wyndham Land Act of 1903. Together with the Local Government Act of 1898 this precipitated the final abolition of landlordlism and the grand jury system of local administration. 'The revolution', he wrote,' will soon be complete; and as it has been carried out on legal and constitutional lines, no reaction need be expected.' [49]

In a few years Ireland would truly become a country of small farmers; no other class would approach them in strength, in number, in political or economic importance. Whether they did, or did not, get home rule they would be masters of everything that mattered. Up to that time, although the land and national problems were essentially different, they were not susceptible to separate treatment since the leaders on the landlord side were practically all unionists and on the tenant side home rulers. Now that the land question was out of the way, the economic problem of agricultural development could be tackled without political or religious distraction. The gentry had seen their lands transferred and their privileges taken away; many of them were considering whether, or not, to throw in their lot with the country to which they belonged or with some other country where they saw a brighter future for themselves and their families.

'The abolition of landlordism', wrote Plunkett in typically optimistic fashion, 'so far from destroying the usefulness of the Irish gentry, really gives them the first opportunity, within the memory of living man to fulfil the true functions of an aristocracy.'[50] Pointing to Germany and France where, he claimed, the gentry had taken a prominent part in the movement for progress and co-operation in agriculture, he urged his fellow landlords to do likewise, 'In this choice the future of our class in Ireland is involved; on this choice will depend the world's judgement of our historic character and present worth'.[51]

But the story of the Anglo-Irish was to end in tragedy. After the sale of their birthright at the passing of the Act of Union, increased dependence in the following century on the British connection had prevented the development of a genuine national leadership which might, in the manner of the other colonies, have worked out a balanced harmonious relationship with the mother country. Acceptance of the status quo had increased their political impotence. They had remained unmoved by earlier and by sterner warnings.[53] It would require the trauma of the Easter Rising, followed by the failure of the Convention and the commencement of guerrilla warfare, to move a solid group — the followers of Lord Midleton who formed the Anti-Partition League — to adopt the stance so fervently advocated in *Noblesse Oblige*.

VI

Ulster and the Framework of Home Rule

The co-operative movement in the south of Ireland had become firmly established in the creamery districts of the Golden Vale before its tentacles eventually spread northward. There were sound commercial reasons for confining their efforts to areas with which the pioneers, Plunkett, Monteagle, Anderson and Father Finlay were familiar, and, in the early days, the founding fathers were practically run off their feet keeping things moving in the south and west. All this, however, did not go unnoticed in Ulster. The *Irish Textile Journal* of Belfast (which belied its title by taking a broad interest in the whole spectrum of industrial development) had, as early as 1891, become a keen supporter. Plunkett was described as 'the apostle of the good cause of co-operation',[1] the formation of each co-operative society as a 'capital object lesson in developed agriculture and associated enterprise';[2] while the IAOS appeared 'to afford every prospect of doing really good work towards advancing the prospects of Irish agriculturalists, and the prosperity of all interested in Irish land, whether as owners or tenants.'[3]

The resolution passed at the annual meeting of the IAOS in 1895 advocating the establishment of an Irish board of agriculture was welcomed by the *Belfast Newsletter*. 'The question is not, or ought not to be a party one', the editor noted with some satisfaction adding that representatives of all political opinions had come out in favour of the idea.[4] Later that year the *Tyrone Constitution* reported an initiative to found a creamery at Fintona and suggested that another was needed in Omagh 'and indeed in every district in Ireland'.[5] The Fintona creamery was the first to be established in the north, the second was in the Lagan area of East Donegal and when, at last, co-operation secured a foothold in the rich dairy districts of Ulster, the *Belfast Evening Telegraph* commented:

It is somewhat remarkable that it has been left to the south of Ireland to set an example to the generally more enterprising north in the way of co-operative farming. There now, however, appears to be an awakening. A few days ago the initiative was taken at Londonderry towards the formation of a branch; on Saturday last a meeting in favour of the movement was held at Newtownards, and Mr. Anderson, the secretary to the Irish Agricultural Organisation [Society] states that, during the last six weeks, he has had more applications for information than he could attend to.[6]

Once the movement was underway in Ulster it did not take long for the opponents of co-operation to raise their familiar cry. A letter from a firm of seed merchants to the *Coleraine Constitution* advised farmers of the district not to place themselves unreservedly 'in the hands of a few gentlemen assembled in an office in St. Stephen's Green, Dublin but to trust to the respectable merchants in Coleraine who had supplied them in the past', and, in a burst of local patriotism, maintained that 'the men who are engaged in this business in the town of Coleraine are much more competent to select seeds than such men as we notice on the committee of management in Dublin'.[7] This warning was obviously heeded for, a week later, an attempt to form a co-operative society in the town was postponed pending further information from Dublin.[8]

Plunkett's first co-operative foray into northern territory, organised by Thomas Andrews, took place in Comber, Co. Down in December 1895. Introducing Plunkett, Andrews made no bones about his own position, stating that

he had not the slightest doubt that before Mr. Plunkett left the room that night, he would tell them what was going forward in other parts of Ireland, and he would not be surprised if they all present — himself a farmer among the rest — felt ashamed that their countrymen in the south had taken the lead in regard to many matters in which they were vitally interested.

Plunkett, showing a shrewd appreciation of northern psychology, explained to the assembled farmers that

this was the first time he had ever pronounced upon this subject in the north of Ireland. He did not know how it was that they did not commence their movement in the north, where they should have been much more thoroughly and rapidly successful, but supposed that, being south of Ireland men themselves, they had a feeling that charity began at home. At any rate they knew this — that, whereas success in the north, would not necessarily be followed by success in the south, if they were successful in the south, they would have no difficulty in succeeding in the north. [9]

In the spring of 1891 Plunkett had met the Belfast co-operators, members of a 'small, struggling but very promising society which may be the seed of a great movement for the benefit of Ireland'. [10] On the same visit he established links with the liberal unionists of Ulster [11] joining in their campaign for technical education and industrial development; while at the start of his parliamentary career he had cultivated the editors of the Belfast papers. In 1895 the Recess Committee was established with its Ulster Consultative Committee and the support which he received from liberal unionists such as Musgrave, Sinclair and Andrews was essential to its legislative success. 'It is to their lasting honour', he wrote in 1910, 'that although their interests were commercial and industrial, these men of Ulster recognised the paramount importance of agriculture in the national life'. [12]

The first committee of the IAOS, elected in 1894, contained the names of Major John Alexander, later president of the Milford Creamery in Co. Carlow and of the Belfast industrialist James Musgrave. The Rev. E. F. Campbell, chairman of the Killyman Co-Operative Creamery in Moy, Co. Tyrone who was chaplain to the Orange Order formed a lasting friendship during his years on the IAOS committee with Father Finlay, while Dr. R. R. Kane, orange grand master and gaelic leaguer, had served on the northern branch of the Recess Committee. However the Ulsterman who constantly caught the eye was Harold Barbour, son of a famous firm of linen thread manufacturers near Lisburn.

A co-operative store based on the Scottish model had opened in Lisburn with the encouragement of the Barbours in 1882. [13] Other members of the family had been instrumental in the development of flax growing and scutching co-operatives and, when he graduated from Oxford, Harold, already infected with co-operative enthusiasm, devoted his services to the IAOS. He travelled the length and breadth of Ireland, often with R. A. Anderson, founding new, or encouraging existing societies. Plunkett regarded Barbour as his heir apparent. He was chairman of the IAWS (the Wholesale Society) for many years and became president of the Ulster Agricultural Organisation Society (UAOS) when political exigencies (and the receipt of government grants) made it necessary, in 1922, to form an autonomous body for Ulster. His death from pneumonia in 1938, while still in the prime of life, evoked a sense of loss among co-operators as intense as Plunkett's death in 1932 or the passing of co-operation's literary champion, AE, in exile in Bournemouth in 1935. A year earlier at the annual meeting of the UAOS attended by a strong southern deputation, Barbour had received a presentation from the Northern Ireland prime minister, Viscount Craigavon. Thanking the co-operators for their tribute, Barbour acknowledged the sources of his early inspiration:

I had the good fortune to have been taught and trained by Sir Horace Plunkett, Father Finlay and R.A. Anderson and the devoted band of workers whom they had attracted around them . . . In 1922, of necessity the Ulster Agricultural Organisation Society was formed . . . To the IAOS, our old parent body, I would say we have tried to keep the faith. [14]

The fact that the initiative in the north had been taken by the liberal unionists and that Plunkett was, in those years, a unionist MP meant that especial care was needed to encourage Ulster nationalists to believe that the co-operative movement had a role for them. The support of prominent northern nationalists was, therefore, of particular importance to the movement, a fact which Plunkett underlined by an entry in his diary for 1901 when, on a visit to the United States, he learnt of the death of the Newry solicitor, Michael J. Magee (under whose auspices a council had been formed in Newry rural district to co-ordinate the efforts of co-operative societies, stimulate home industries, and link voluntary with state-aided work).

He was an IAOS enthusiast and being roman catholic and nationalist his influence was invaluable. He managed to unite all classes and parties. His loss is irreparable. [15]

The co-operative movement in Ulster faced serious problems stemming from the political and religious divisions in the province. These were, on the whole, triumphantly overcome and, as the following extract from the *Irish Homestead* illustrates, it gave common cause to people from all quarters of a troubled community.

The new branch shop of the Enniskillen Co-operative Society at Ballinamallard was opened on Tuesday evening amid scenes of enthusiasm. There was a meeting in the Archdale Memorial Hall . . . There was likewise tea and the inevitable concert.
The hall is said to afford accommodation to 250, but it had nearly 500

people crowded within its walls. They were like sheep in a pen, with no opportunity of turning to the right or left. They hung over the gallery, they stared through the windows outside, they gathered in crowds upon the street. It was good of course to see the crowds and witness the enthusiasm but there was too much crowd ... The chairman traced the rapid growth of the society with a pride that was truly paternal. They had commenced with a capital of £300. Today they had nearly £3,000. Their trade had gone up to £300 a week, and they still looked for much larger things from Ballinamallard ...

The platform was so crowded that a lady who had been on the programme for a hornpipe heroically offered to dance upon the chairman's table, amid the deafening applause of the crowd. She mounted upon the table and awaited the music but the noise drowned the piano and she had perforce to descend leaving her dance undone. It was one of the evening's three disappointments ... [16]

The unifying power of co-operation is further illustrated in the following excerpt from the *Irish Homestead 's* report of the annual meeting of the Lowtherstown Agricultural Co-operative Society of Co. Fermanagh in the difficult year of 1922.

The meeting was followed by a concert and a dance and the event brought together almost all the elements of the community. There was the farmer, labourer and artisan, the banker and the humblest millworker, hibernian and orangeman, freemasons, sinn féiners (republicans and free staters) and unionists, together with representatives of the many modern forces for the protection or terrorising of the individual all vying with each other in the promotion of a happy and enjoyable evening. [17]

As its founder wrote in *Ireland in the New Century*, an object of his movement was to bring together, for business purposes, men who had previously no dealings with each other 'but who have now learned that the doctrine of self-help by mutual help involves no danger to faith and no sacrifice of hope, while it engenders a genuinely christian interpretation of charity!' [18] Co-operators, when they met and worked together, would begin to understand and respect opposing religious backgrounds and political views. The movement was to act as a bridge spanning the divisions in Irish society.

Upon no-one else was this effect more clearly marked than on Plunkett himself. His family possessed a national strain to which he was not totally immune, tracing a connection back to Hugh O'Neill, the sixteenth century Irish leader and Earl of Tyrone. New perspectives had been opened up by ten years experience of the American West, while intimate contact with Irish agricultural problems had underlined the paucity of the Castle administration. Contact with smaller farmers (mostly nationalist) had given him a sympathetic understanding of their political attitudes, while friendship with Yeats, Hyde and Lady Gregory had uncovered other facets of the new Ireland emerging after 1890. If these were grounds why Plunkett might be predisposed to re-examine his constitutional views, his gradual change of stance over the twenty years from 1888 occurred chiefly for pragmatic, unemotional reasons stemming from the lack of a proper system of Irish administration; from the need to develop an effective and accepted leadership; and from the realisation, as his own work progressed, that economic amelioration was not having the effect (predicted by English statesmen) of damping down the fires of Irish nationalism.

An Austrian visitor to Ireland, whom he had met in 1888, offered the opinion that home rule was Ireland's only chance. 'Even the present agitators would be sobered down and made conservative if given power'.[19] This foreign perspective set Plunkett thinking for he described himself afterwards as a 'pessimist about unionism. But I don't think home rule means such a collapse as some people think.'[20] Four years later he met Sir Charles Gavan Duffy, the former Young Irelander, a leader of the unsuccessful rebellion of 1848 who had emigrated to Australia, become prime minister of Victoria and had been rewarded with a knighthood. They discussed the home rule issue and Plunkett argued that

the capacity for self government has not yet been given to Irishmen. If only the right Irishmen were guaranteed for the first ten years of home rule they would make a record which would continue them in office. As it is, I think it better to try an improved partnership with an increasing control over local affairs. Perhaps my heresy comes from insupportable egotism. I feel I can do good under the present system and should be shelved under home rule.[21]

The meeting with Gavan Duffy came shortly before he entered parliament, and having become an active member of the Unionist Party, Plunkett took his stand on the Union whatever he felt on other questions.

Involvement in the campaign for technical education from 1893 had brought him in touch with the commercial life of Belfast. From his liberal unionist friends, the captains of northern industry, he learned of Ulster's economic objections to home

Portraits from *Vanity Fair*. Above: Arthur and Gerald Balfour. Below: George Wyndham and James Bryce.

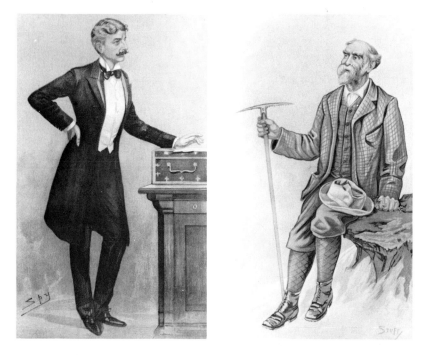

Portraits from *Vanity Fair*. Above: Edward Carson and John Redmond. Below: John Dillon and Charles Stewart Parnell.

Portraits from *Vanity Fair*. Above: President Theodore Roosevelt and H. H. Asquith, 1st Earl of Oxford and Asquith. Below: David Lloyd George and Augustine Birrell.

Portraits from *Vanity Fair*. Above: Col. Edward Saunderson and Arthur Edward Guinness, 1st Baron Ardilaun. Below: Windham Thomas Wyndham-Quin, 4th Earl Dunraven and T. W. Russell.

rule. These were the arguments, he afterwards maintained, which had to be met in detail by nationalist Ireland. During the home rule debate of 1893 there was a whiff of partition in the air and Plunkett had a significant interview with Lord Londonderry, the powerful Ulster unionist.

The object of my visit was to get Londonderry to pledge himself as an Ulster leader never, under any circumstances, would he consent to a settlement of the home rule question which separated Ulster from the rest of Ireland. He was very strong to stand and fall with the southern loyalists as well as the northern. [22]

Plunkett's views on some issues may have altered, as circumstances around him changed, but, until the break came, he was consistent in his opposition to partition; and, when he eventually became a home ruler, Irish and imperial unity remained his guiding principles.

During his time as vice-president of the DATI the outstanding problems of land tenure had been strikingly settled at a conference held over the Christmas period of 1902 between representatives of the landlords and tenants. The idea of such a conference had been floated in a letter to the press from John Shawe-Taylor, a nephew of Lady Gregory, then backed by Wyndham and afterwards taken up by representatives of the two interest groups. Lord Dunraven, who had led the landlord delegation, formed a working partnership with tenant representative William O'Brien, the independent nationalist MP with the slogan 'conference plus business'. Unwilling to dissipate the momentum which had been generated, Dunraven founded the Irish Reform Association which, in 1904, advocated a modest scheme of devolution for certain sectors of Irish government. The Irish unionists, increasingly uneasy as Wyndham pressed on relentlessly with Balfourian policy, rebelled when they discovered that MacDonnell, Wyndham's undersecretary, had been involved in drawing up the plan and the chief secretary was forced to resign. 'The Ulster bigots and a landlord clique . . . defeated us' recorded Plunkett[23] recognising the significance of this incident to 'fenian unionists' such as himself, working to find a modus vivendi between the opposing forces in Ireland. Dunraven's scheme, however, had not impressed him and he urged the prime minister, Arthur Balfour that his brother Gerald be re-appointed:

The talk about devolution has done much harm, which could be best counteracted by Gerald's resuming the administration of the Acts of 1898 and 1899* which gave more devolution and co-ordination to Irish government than any previous legislation, and perhaps quite as much as the Irish can assimilate for some time to come. [24]

But extreme unionists had the bit between their teeth and Walter Long was the safe appointee.

Dunraven, a reforming landlord and a moderate unionist, shared Plunkett's aims and background and the two men had everything to gain from collaboration, yet their relationship seems to have been deliberately cool. A careful examination of Plunkett's references to Dunraven shows that Plunkett had, in fact, an intense, apparently irrational, dislike of him; that he attempted to sidestep meetings proposed by Dunraven; and threw cold water on his most significant achievement, the land conference which paved the way for the Wyndham Act of 1903.

When recording his opinion of someone he had met for the first time it was Plunkett's practice to be somewhat caustic in his judgement ('tinged with Horacic acid' a contemporary put it). These judgements normally mellowed later. (Daisy Burke from Galway he referred to at their first meeting as 'not quite first rate but will become so, let's hope', [25] perhaps reflecting family opinion that Fingall was marrying below his station; shortly after, she became Lady Fingall and Plunkett fell in love with her!). His first recorded comment on Lord Dunraven on 20 October 1896 (they had certainly met before this) ran 'Intensely selfish and rather vain man. He will never have much influence', [26] and the comments in Dunraven's case became more biting as time went on.

He had been visiting the US during the land conference and took the precaution of issuing a press statement on his return to contradict aa assertion that he was entirely happy with the settlement, for he said, he had not yet had an opportunity of reading the report. [27] One month afterwards Plunkett, who was rarely averse to putting his views before the public, refused an invitation to comment on the report in the *New Liberal Review* describing it as 'a highly controversial subject which is about to engage the attention of parliament'. [28] In fact Plunkett had had prior warning of the whole affair, for he had written to Lady Gregory on 26 September:

Of course I am in favour of the — or rather a — conference. J.S.-T. [John

*The Local Government and DATI Acts.

Shawe-Taylor] came to me today with the draft of the letter the day before he published it. I gave him some advice involving 3 or 4 days delay which I thought would have insured the success of his conference but he was a bit feverish![29]

Later, when the situation in Ireland was reaching boiling point, he recorded a meeting with Dunraven at Adare, 'He wanted me to join him in working for a conference on the Irish question. I gave excuses',[30] while to Erskine Childers he wrote dismissively, 'Dunraven is pressing me to go down and see him at Adare, but I think it would be a mere waste of time'.[31]

Plunkett's other references to Dunraven in his diary are unusually bitter. In 1906 he wrote 'there is nothing in him but the political game';[32] in 1923, 'he really has been fond of Ireland all his life, though not as fond as he is of himself',[33] while Dunraven's 'amazing selfishness and extravagance' at the end of his life, Plunkett decried as 'robbing his heirs.'[34] The final thrust came in an obituary notice for Lord Monteagle, some years after Dunraven's death, in which he contrasted Monteagle's unassuming character with the 'notoriety of the late Lord Dunraven'.[35]

Such an irrational attitude demands an irrational explanation. It appears that Dunraven, who had been in the American midwest in the eighteen seventies, had been a backer of Frewen's ill-fated Powder River Cattle Company eventually liquidated by Plunkett,[36] although whether this led to such animosity is hard to tell. A more likely explanation for the intensity of Plunkett's feelings stemmed from Dunraven's friendship with Lady Fingall. Plunkett was in love with her but scrupulously respected the position of his cousin, the earl. Lady Fingall enjoyed the pleasures of society while her husband's interests were confined to the hunting fields of Meath. She regularly visited London for the season (rarely accompanied by Lord Fingall) and her memoirs give the impression of a number of liasons. One of these liasons may have been with Lord Dunraven. He had given her a pet name, 'the elusive lady', on her frequent visits to his home at Adare in Co. Limerick.[37]

* * *

On vacating the vice-presidency of the DATI in 1907, Plunkett found himself, for the first time since 1892, entirely free of political constraints, with an opportunity to reflect on his achievements and the philosophy which lay behind them. He and his colleagues had, with skill and perseverance, constructed a co-operative movement which spanned the political and religious divide. Plunkett and Anderson were unionists, AE and Father Finlay nationalists; this pattern was reflected throughout the organisation; the co-operative movement was the outstanding proof that Irishmen of different creeds or parties could work together. The movement had been established with initial help from the parent body in Britain; but it had soon become clear that, in order to develop, it had to strike out on its own. A similar idea underlay his work, via the Recess Committee, in the establishment of the DATI. Ireland's agricultural problems were so remote from Britain's and so poorly understood by the British administration, that autonomy was the only sensible remedy.

Obsessed with the need for his country's regeneration, Plunkett's judgement of political systems focussed chiefly on the question of how they would respond to his reforms. Thus under the Balfours he had remained unconcernedly unionist but Wyndham's fall in 1905 signalled the end of constructive unionism, its chief exponents in the ULUA losing their identity in a new coalition of Ulster unionists. Reversion to a policy of 'law and order' so beloved of his former colleagues held no appeal for Plunkett and having jettisoned his tenuous links with unionism he embarked upon an examination of alternative constitutional forms. Disagreeing fundamentally with the nationalist credo that constitutional change must precede social or economic progress, he stood at that point in the political spectrum where progressive unionism blended in with moderate nationalism; he was, as AE observed, 'the spirit of Sinn Féin, casting a rather misleading shadow before it as such politics as he possessed were vaguely unionist.'[38] But unionists had failed to seize their last great chance; the Nationalist Party had limited power but not full responsibility; the system must be changed. Plunkett and his compatriots had shown the way by which the gentry might put their talents at the service of the nation. Their example had gone unheeded and if leadership was not forthcoming from the aristocracy it must emerge from among the people. His aim had been to put into the hands of one section of the community the handling of its own affairs. Now this must be done on a wider scale, and if the problem was one of character, of strengthening the moral fibre of the nation, the remedy lay in giving to that nation the responsibility which nationhood alone could bring.

To Lawrence Lowell, the Harvard political scientist, he confessed that he had been unable to subscribe to home rule prior to the settlement of the land question, for he had never envisaged that problem being dealt with fairly by an Irish parliament.[39] Deeply conscious of Ireland's nationhood and guided by reason rather than the emotions, Plunkett developed no spiritual attachment to nationalism. He realised that, among the majority of his fellow countrymen, national feeling was by no means dead; and his twin successes in agricultural matters had shown that, in this sphere at any rate, Irishmen were proving capable of managing their own affairs. Might not the unionist argument that Ireland was unfit for self-government be dangerously tautological; for if Irishmen never got the opportunity, how could they develop the responsible attitude essential to the establishment of a sound administration?

Nationalist opposition to the Parliamentary Party had crystallised, in 1905, around the formation of Sinn Féin. The continuing barrage of criticism from the parliamentarians had the effect of driving many nationally minded co-operators to support this new body. In January 1908, AE brought Arthur Griffith to Kilteragh. The founder of Sinn Féin impressed his host as a 'remarkable young revolutionary',[40] but they appear not to have met again until after the Anglo-Irish Treaty of 1922. The interests of the two men, though parallel, ran along different lines; a spirit of self-reliance was basic to both their philosophies but Griffith confined himself to urban affairs, while Plunkett's concentration upon rural development had led him to overlook the slum conditions rife in Dublin. Besides this, there was a class barrier between them for Plunkett possessed a certain hauteur and at their next meeting in March 1922, his comment on Griffith ran 'narrow, bigoted against other classes, but also honest and fairly capable'.[41] There were no such barriers to AE's friendship so he and Griffith as literary champions of nationalism kept in regular contact and found much in common.

'Sinn Féin', Bernard Shaw explained to his English readers was simply the Gaelic for 'John Bull'. Implicit in the phrase is the concept of self-reliance (the literal translation being 'we ourselves'); it had originally been the motto of the Irish Industrial Exhibition of 1882. The movement aimed at self-reliance in industry, in agriculture and in politics and as the first part of this policy dovetailed neatly with Plunkett's philosophy, Sinn Féin supported the co-operators. Inspired by Deak's Hungarian policy of abstention from the Austrian parliament and of passive resistance in Austro-Hungarian affairs which he outlined in his 1904 pamphlet *The Resurrection of Hungary: a Parallel for Ireland,* [42] Griffith had worked out a programme based on abstention from, and non-recognition of, the Westminster parliament, the establishment of an Irish parliament based on the General Council of County Councils, self-reliance and trade protection, with a dual monarchy as the bridge between north and south. Although Plunkett would, at this time, have baulked at abstention from Westminster, his Council of Agriculture was, in Griffith's terms, a miniature Irish parliament while his own views were directly in line with the emphasis which Griffith placed on the regeneration of Ireland from within. Later, under Childers' influence, he came to accept an Irish parliament with fiscal autonomy, and while he was never sufficiently separatist to agree that the crown should be the only link between the two islands, Plunkett shared Griffith's marked aversion to violence.

Edward Martyn, first president of Sinn Féin, was a central figure in the literary movement, a friend of Plunkett's and a supporter of co-operation. *Leabhair na hEireann*, the Irish Year Book and Sinn Féin Directory, carried an article in every edition entitled 'The Irish Agricultural Organisation Society and the Co-operative Movement' written by H. F. Norman (assistant secretary of the IAOS). The first edition included an article on popular credit by AE and, in 1910, The Year Book reprinted Roosevelt's letter of tribute to Plunkett from the *Irish Homestead*. In 1909 Plunkett subscribed the handsome sum of £25 to the sinn féin newspaper[43] in which Griffith, from his editorial chair, directed a relentless stream of criticism at nationalist policy:

Shedding party prejudices for the moment, let any man look back over the history of Ireland and he will admit that our intolerance of one another has been the chief cause of the failure of all our movements.

One party gets strong — it uses its strength to force the weaker to join it or extinguish themselves. 'Be my brother or I will kill you'. Men with the ability and will to serve their country are forced out of public life . . .

Mr. William O'Brien is a man for whom, on half of his programme, we totally disagree. Sir Horace Plunkett is another man with whose programme we are largely in disagreement, and there are a dozen other such men with whom to an extent we are in disagreement — all of whom are either today in retirement or in semi-retirement from public life because the field is closed against them by party prejudice.

This is national folly. [44]

The constant stream of visitors to Kilteragh included many

other distinguished nationalists such as Albinia Brodrick, a sister of Lord Midleton, nursing in rural Ireland, the historian Alice Stopford Green (whom Plunkett introduced to the wealthy Irish-American Boss Croker seeking money for Patrick Pearse's school, St. Enda's)[45] and the tragic Roger Casement. All would have shared with their host a distaste for the methods of the Parliamentary Party plus an admiration for the idealism of Sinn Féin. In January 1908 he had been toasted by the Ulster Reform Club (home of the liberal unionists) as the 'greatest benefactor whom the Ireland of this generation has known'[46] but his northern friends looked askance at his flirtation with advanced nationalism. A letter from Sinclair retailed a rumour that he had become an imperial home ruler begging him to deny it. Plunkett replied cautiously that while he might some day take the plunge, Sinclair and Andrews would be the first to know of it.[47] As head of an avowedly non-political, non-sectarian movement, having severed his link with unionism, he was unwilling to make an opposite commitment. But, at the end of 1909 he recorded, 'I should not wonder if I have to become a home ruler before the year is out. I begin to think the time has come for it!'[48]

The general election of 1910 resulted in a liberal administration led by Asquith but dependent on the nationalists. A veto of the budget by conservative peers meant that a showdown between the houses of parliament had become inevitable. Plunkett, meeting Carson, argued that the Upper House should counter an attack upon its veto with a generous measure of democratic reform.[49] The struggle resulted in a liberal victory and the Parliament Act ensured that any measure passed in three consecutive sessions by the House of Commons would automatically become law. After the crucial vote he commended Monteagle, 'You were unquestionably right to vote with the government. The unionists who did so showed, in my judgement, the highest quality of courage'.[50] Another barrier to nationalist ambitions had been swept away; meanwhile Ulster planned resistance to the next instalment of home rule.

By August 1911, Plunkett was prepared to admit privately that he was, now, a home ruler.[51] To Sinclair and Andrews he denied Ulster the right to use force to oppose the imposition of home rule, but conceded the justice of forceful opposition to possible oppression by an Irish legislature.[52] Looking ahead at the end of the year he forecast social revolution and a European war. A letter, written around this time to Richmond Noble, an IAOS organiser working in Ulster, made his position clear.

I could not join either party as at present led. But, while the methods of both are bad, the main contention of the home rulers, is, I believe, true. I did not feel it right to admit this much until the unionists had an opportunity to frame and give effect to a real Irish policy under the Union. They failed to do this . . .

Progress was impossible in the current stalemate,

The best illustration of this is the proved ability of one or two political bosses to make the Irish Department of Agriculture refuse English money for our Irish Agricultural Organisation Society against, I am certain, the better judgement of every thinking nationalist in Ireland. This situation can, in my belief, be put an end to in one way only and that is by throwing on the people the responsibility of attending to these vitally important matters which they now have an excuse for leaving to the political boss or bosses. [53]

The unedifying dispute between T. W. Russell and the IAOS resulting in the removal of the government's subsidy to co-operation and the subsequent wrangle over the Development Commissioners' grant, besides driving a further wedge between co-operators and the Parliamentary Party had a disastrous effect on Plunkett's forward looking northern friends. 'I have reason to believe', he wrote in 1911, 'that unless T.W. is sternly rebuked and the matter put right quickly, many young Ulster politicians who were being mollified towards home rule will join Carson and his provisional government'. [54] While AE wrote of the same incident, 'Barbour, who is the . . . leader of the Ulstermen who will take the place of Sinclair and Andrews told me . . . 'I was hovering on the verge of becoming a home ruler. Now the thing stinks for me. I would not touch it for anything'. [55]

Three years previously Robert Barton, from a well known Wicklow family, just about to graduate from Oxford, had expressed an interest in working for the IAOS. Plunkett's response had been enthusiastic, prophesying of the future Treaty signatory, 'He looks strong and earnest and may prefer something more exciting and bigger politically and nationally for his wild oats period.' [56] In October Barton brought his cousin Erskine Childers to Kilteragh [57] and the two men followed this up with a co-operative tour of the west of Ireland. Childers had by then earned himself a considerable literary reputation. Thirteen years Plunkett's junior he had had a similar upbringing. Born in England he had moved to Co. Wicklow at thirteen, when his parents died, to be reared by his mother's family the Bartons of

Annamoe. Educated at Haileybury and Trinity College, Cambridge, he started his career in 1895 as a committee clerk in the House of Commons. Of indomitable courage, he joined up during the Boer campaign and won wide acclaim for his war diary published in 1901. If Plunkett's horsemanship had stood him in good stead in Wyoming, it was as a sailor that Childers excelled and his celebrated novel, *The Riddle of the Sands*, published in 1903, based on an intimate knowledge of the Baltic and the North Sea, served as a warning of possible German invasion from the Frisian Islands and influenced British naval strategy. Childers married Molly Osgood, a Bostonian of aristocratic lineage, in 1904. She had been crippled in a skating accident when she was three years old but overcame her lameness with great determination to become a competent sailor. The unbending republicanism of Childers' later years was to be inflamed by the impassioned Molly.

It is not clear when Childers began to develop a real interest in Irish political affairs. His 1908 visit to the west with Robert Barton was as much a holiday as an inspection of co-operatives, but Plunkett's movement did impress him and, having resigned his clerkship in the House of Commons to devote himself to his writing, they met again in March 1911, just as Childers started to work on the home rule theme. After this there were frequent contacts in Dublin and London. Childers read the syllabus of his book to Plunkett who responded by arranging for him to meet Sinclair and Andrews at Kilteragh to get the best Ulster view[58] and by the end of the year *The Framework of Home Rule* had been published. Another home rule bill was the price which the government had to pay for nationalist support and Childers' book was designed to concentrate thought and action on the forthcoming legislation.

Similar in background, with similar wiry physiques and with immense reserves of energy and determination it is not surprising that he and Plunkett soon became friends. Childers was deeply moved by Plunkett's work for Ireland, while Plunkett was certainly influenced by Childers' incisive political thought; as a convalescent in an English nursing home in August 1911, around the time of publication of the book, Plunkett informed a tory visitor that he was now a home ruler.[59] It was his first unequivocal statement to that effect although a month later he indicated his intention of maintaining a non-party stance.[60]

Childers wrote from a strictly imperial standpoint. He took, in turn, each of Britain's white colonies, America, Canada,

Australia-New Zealand and South Africa, outlining their struggles — partly violent and partly constitutional — to achieve legislative independence and to replace colonial by dominion status, or, in the case of the United States, by complete independence. The story of each of these emerging nations is then contrasted with that of Ireland and considerable weight is attached to Joseph Chamberlain's admission, made in opposition to the second Gladstone home rule bill of 1893, 'Does anybody doubt, that if Ireland were a thousand miles away from England she would not have been, long before this, a self-governing colony?'

The Act of Union between Great Britain and Ireland had been a failure because it had not been voluntary, neither had it preserved the freedom of the separate partners. 'It was', wrote Childers, 'accompanied by gross breach of faith, and it signified enslavement, not liberty'.[61] No white community of pride and spirit would willingly tolerate the grotesque form of crown colony administration, founded on force, and now tempered by a kind of paternal state socialism which Ireland then suffered; unionism was for Ireland in reality, anti-imperialist. The lesson of colonial history, which had yet to be applied to Ireland, was that government must be with the consent of the governed. Irish emigrants to the United States, he wrote, taking up a favourite theme of Plunkett's, had impregnated that nation with a hostility to Great Britain, which, though somewhat diminished in 1911, was still a grave international danger and an obstacle to the closer union of the English speaking races.

Childers shared Plunkett's view that character was the foundation upon which a nation should be built but went further in discerning the profound effect of political institutions upon human development:

Self-government in the community corresponds to free will in the individual. I am far from saying that self-government is everything. But I do say that it is the master key. It is fundamental. Give responsibility and you will create responsibility. Through political reponsibility only can a society brace itself to organised effort, find out its own opinions or its own needs, test its own capabilities and elicit the will, the brains, and the hands to solve its own problems.[62]

Moderate unionists, such as Plunkett, striving to unite Irishmen of all creeds to work for their economic and spiritual salvation, mistook cause for effect, failing to understand that their objects could never be fully realised without the satisfaction of the national aim. The success of the Recess Committee in establishing the DATI he interpreted as the granting of home rule in agricultural matters, and went on to praise the work of the co-operators in helping to build a new and vital rural civilisation. The Gaelic League was another important factor for good, but it was idle to suggest that these movements would not, particularly among the younger generation, strengthen the sentiment for home rule. Finally, describing Sinn Féin's proposal to abstain from Westminster as premature, he admitted that, although constitutional agitation had, so far, failed to produce home rule, the climate of British opinion had changed, while sinn féin policy would lead to total separation which, he felt, Ireland did not want. However, if the next home rule bill were to fail, Sinn Féin's stand would be justified and its strength redoubled.

In common with other writers from a nationalist standpoint, Childers made light of Ulster's objection to home rule which, he believed, would soon disappear under the new order, for Ulster's prosperity depended on her links with the rest of Ireland. Ulster unionists, he wrote, showing how little he appreciated their true position, would prefer real home rule to a half-measure, and in making that choice would show their virility and courage at its true worth. [63] This was the one area where the two men differed. Plunkett had arranged introductions for Childers to Sinclair, Andrews and their friends on his visits to Belfast and, before the final version of the book was ready, Plunkett wrote to the author suggesting a change in perspective by putting more emphasis on the reasons for his stance rather than on how it should be put into effect: 'I am thinking of the unionists who would not get over the first fence if you made it too much of an 'intrikkit lep' as we used to call the worst form of bank or ditch in my county'. [64] After publication he expressed the hope that the government would consult Childers about their bill. 'You must have shattered many of the bills they were considering' and worried that 'the old spirit may be stirred again by Generalissimo Carson, I am not sure that I did not feel that you a little underrated this feeling. Then, too, I should have liked you to have argued a little more with the business men of Belfast and their selfish business objection. For I am afraid Ulster is going to be more troublesome than is generally expected'. [65]

The scheme which Childers had proposed was dominion home rule, giving Ireland a bi-cameral parliament in full control of the police and judiciary with complete fiscal independence. Army and navy matters, the declaration of war and non-commercial foreign affairs were to be reserved for imperial authority. Although Plunkett's views were changing and, in private at any rate, by the end of 1911, he was prepared to call himself a home ruler he was not ready to declare for what were, for him, such radical proposals. A decade later when Childers was making his mark as a republican propagandist during the Anglo-Irish conflict, these ideas were adopted by Plunkett's Irish Dominion League, and in 1920 he described *The Framework of Home Rule* as the best piece of constructive work ever done on the Irish problem.[66] But Childers had moved farther and faster than his friend and, by then, deserved the nickname (coined for him by Anderson in the Plunkett House) of the 'Encyclopaedia anti-Britannica'.

If Childers' writings influenced Plunkett, they had a disturbing effect in other quarters. He had been a distinguished soldier, had affected British naval strategy with *The Riddle of the Sands* and his well reasoned case for home rule was bound to impact upon the political scene. The Unionist Party responded to the challenge by gathering the views of prominent unionist politicians in a series of essays under the title *Against Home Rule. The Case for the Union.*[67] The collection (which appeared in 1912) was intended, as is clear from the references to Childers, 'the ingenious apologist for home rule', as a counterblast to his book and was designed to put a constructive case for the maintenance of the Union; it was significant that one whole article (by Amery) was devoted to refuting 'the colonial analogy'. Essays by the Balfour brothers, Austen Chamberlain, George Wyndham, L. S. Amery, Walter Long, the Marquis of Londonderry, J. R. Fisher (editor of the *Northern Whig*) and Plunkett's Belfast friend, Thomas Sinclair were introduced by Carson with a preface by Bonar Law.

The main arguments put forward for the Union may be briefly summarised. Ireland had always been seen as a jumping-off point for England's enemies and control of the neighbouring island was still essential to defence of the kingdom. Moreover, England was now dependent on Ireland for a great proportion of its food supplies and military manpower both of which were vital in an emergency. Economic blunders under the Union, such as the laissez-faire policy of the famine period, were acknowledged but the marked increase in prosperity since 1880 was attributed to the link between Ireland and the mainland. Indeed Amery argued that the repression of Irish industry by the English parliament in the eighteenth century would have been impossible under the Union. This bore more heavily on the protestants of English and Scottish descent who consequently emigrated to America, where, by forming the backbone of the American revolution, they ensured that the same fate would not again befall them. The penal laws, he wrote, were in their turn a natural outcome of a political separation which made the security of protestantism in Ireland rest upon the domination of a narrow oligarchy in constant terror of being swamped. Under the Union they would never have been devised, or, certainly, could never have endured.

Plunkett's work in the co-operative movement and in the formation of the DATI received the warmest commendation particularly from Carson and from Gerald Balfour. Both men referred to the hostility which he faced from the main section of the Nationalist Party, and Carson pointed out that while Plunkett had been removed from the vice-presidency of the DATI on the pretext that it should be held by a member of parliament, T.W. Russell who had lost his seat in 1910, had been retained in office by nationalist intrigue.* The Marquis of Londonderry referred to the large body of Ulstermen who supported the co-operative movement in the belief that it was for the benefit of Irish agriculture and contrasted Ulster's welcome with nationalist hostility, while Gerald Balfour refuted Dillon's constant accusation that the IAOS was a propagandist body aiming, under the cloak of economic reform, at the covert spread of unionist opinion. He forecast that unionist policy would bring increased material prosperity and contentment which 'whatever their other effects may be, are not likely to strengthen the demand for constitutional changes.'

The inability of an Irish government, no longer linked to the imperial exchequer, to finance land purchase, industrial and agricultural development, social and educational reform was contrasted with the apparently endless bounty which would be extended to Ireland when the unionists were returned to power. But the strongest objection and, in the opinion of Bonar Law, the insurmountable obstacle to home rule, was the injustice of attempting to impose it upon an unwilling Ulster. Ireland contained not one nation but two, so utterly distinct in racial characteristics, practical ideals, religious sanctions and sense of civic and national responsibility that they could not live harmoniously together unless under the control of some impartial authority. This being the case, Sinclair argued, if

---

*Russell regained a parliamentary seat in 1911.

nationalist Ireland were to be granted its preference in relation to
the rest of Britain, the same choice must undoubtedly be offered
to Ulster; if this were not done, he warned, the alternative lay in
the establishment, upon the day on which a home rule bill
received royal assent, of a provisional government for Ulster.

In the United States early in 1912, by then under Childers'
influence, Plunkett found himself edging towards dominion
status, arguing for the retention of customs duties in Ireland
though he acknowledged that England was unlikely to allow her
manufactures to be taxed.[68] Developing this theme he wrote in
May, 'Thorough self-government, fiscal autonomy (as far as
possible) to teach Ireland to economise. Then, as free contracting
parties we may come into a fiscal union with England and
Scotland'.[69] A federal arrangement for the British Isles was being
floated by F. S. Oliver and taken up by politicians such as
Winston Churchill, Lloyd George and F. E. Smith. Plunkett was
not against the proposal in principle but felt that it was not
practical politics as it would take far too long to evolve; and he
ranked the various possibilities: first, dominion home rule;
second, the status quo; and third, a federal arrangement; in
descending order of preference.[70] When Asquith eventually
introduced his home rule bill in 1912, Plunkett felt it was an
improvement on the previous models but that it did not go far
enough. Ulster would fight, if coerced, but would yield, he
believed, to the dollar argument.[71] Reviewing the situation with
Milne Barbour (Harold's brother and president of the Belfast
Chamber of Commerce) he argued that home rule must come for
the reasons which he had already given and for the additional
cogent one, that Ireland would be unable to bear the cost of the
new legislation instituting old age pensions and social
insurance.[72] Then he talked to Arthur Balfour, now leader of the
opposition, who asked him why Ireland had not been able to
combine nationalism with unionism as in Scotland. Plunkett
gave three reasons: the position of the Catholic Church; Scottish
resources of iron and coal; and the fact that Scotland had
provided the Union with a king.[73] Sinclair wrote in September
imploring him not to go over to the nationalists. He replied
saying that he would not take any political pledge without letting
Sinclair know or consulting him, but he felt increasingly uneasy
at not having the courage of his convictions.[74] A month later it
was Plunkett and AE versus Sinclair and Andrews at Kilteragh;
'we did not of course shake their firm resolve but we drove them
from one fort — we simply pulverised the home rule means Rome

rule absurdity'.[75] While he had not officially declared himself, Plunkett had let his friends know that he was now a home ruler.

His political philosophy was working itself out between two rigid guidelines — the unity of Ireland and the unity of the empire. On a minor point he was equally certain; proportional representation was the voting system which should be incorporated into the forthcoming Irish legislation. He persuaded Bonar Law and Carson to treat as non-partisan the appropriate amendments which had been framed to the home rule bill and then led a deputation to the prime minister to press for their adoption.[76] These efforts were successful and the 1914 Act envisaged PR voting for both Irish houses of parliament.

Plunkett's contacts embraced the whole spectrum of Ulster opinion. The pressure caused by the onset of further home rule legislation had cemented over the crevices in Ulster unionism now dominated by Carson, so that, by 1912, the liberal unionists no longer existed as a separate political entity. Sinclair and Andrews had become two of Carson's trusted lieutenants and were counted among his most capable advisers. But not all northern protestants had fallen in behind Carson, and at a meeting of protestants against Carsonism held at Ballymoney, Co. Antrim in October 1913, Alec Wilson, a prominent Ulster radical, pointed out that Ireland then contained nearly 1,000 co-operative societies with a turnover of 3 million pounds. There were protestant and catholic members in nearly every one of these and no one ever heard of catholic members persecuting or injuring their protestant colleagues for the movement depended on the loyalty of protestant and catholic members to it and to each other.[77]

The home rule bill passed through the Commons in January 1913 but was rejected by the Lords. Asquith's parliament act had shackled the Upper House, and if passed in three successive sessions by the Commons, home rule would automatically become law. The Ulster Volunteer Force had been established with the support of tory extremists; Ulster was regarded by many of them as the weapon with which to defeat the liberals; Ireland had again become an English party political issue; whatever happened in the rest of the country, home rule would be bitterly resisted in Ulster. Not surprisingly, therefore, rumours abounded that Ulster was to be excluded from the home rule scheme. Plunkett, at the end of 1913, hit upon an ingenious way out of the crisis — the temporary inclusion of Ulster under a home rule parliament for a fixed period with the option of leaving at the end of that time.

Edward Carson, the Dublin bred lawyer-politician was just a month older than Plunkett and they had entered parliament together in 1892 (Carson making a special journey from his home in southern England to vote for Plunkett in the South Dublin constituency).[78] Both men had benefited from Arthur Balfour's patronage and, at the commencement of their political careers, would have been regarded as somewhat radical unionists. Carson, from Dublin's middle class, had been educated at Arlington School and Trinity College where he had followed a liberal line advocating women's rights, abolition of capital punishment and the disestablishment of the Church of Ireland, and, although at Westminster his tone had quickly changed, he and Plunkett had been at one in supporting the call for a catholic university.

They were formally friendly but the friendship did not run deep, early on Plunkett described him as a 'clever lawyer',[79] but 'not quite a first class man'.[80] Having made his name in Ireland as state prosecutor, Carson moved to London at Balfour's behest, to become one of the great advocates of his day, but a breach with the Balfours came over the Irish land bill of 1896 and it was Carson who overturned the nationalist jibe at Gerald Balfour, accusing him of 'killing Irish unionism with unkindness'. Carson and Ardilaun had struggled unsuccessfully to block Gill's appointment as secretary of the DATI but they did succeed in wresting control of the *Daily Express* from Plunkett on behalf of the supporters of true blue unionism; and though, on several subsequent occasions, Carson defended Plunkett from attacks in parliament, he was really using the IAOS as a stick to beat the nationalists. Plunkett's reforming unionism he regarded with suspicion but, since Plunkett had lost his seat and office, he was less of a political threat and the formalities were maintained.

The two men met in London in January 1914 and Plunkett emphasised Carson's responsibility should anti-catholic rioting break out in Ulster, for this would, inevitably, be followed by anti-protestant riots elsewhere. He argued the selfishness of the Ulster stand, which involved abandoning unionists in the rest of the island, and put forward his plan for temporary inclusion. Carson advised him to see Asquith but confessed his inability to control his own forces in a crisis situation.[81] The interview was followed up, two weeks later, with a letter in which Plunkett criticised Carson's scheme for the exclusion of Ulster (putting the onus on the south to coax them back in) on two grounds. Firstly,

Redmond and the nationalists could not possibly agree to it; further, the behaviour of the majority to the minority could not be fairly tested if the Ulster protestants remained out.[82]

Plunkett then put his scheme to Salisbury and Bonar Law. The former was prefectly frank, regarding Ulster as a weapon to use against the liberal government while Bonar Law was equally brusque in his rejection of the plan.[83] The prime minister indicated that he would accept the scheme if Ulster agreed to it, but he held out little hope of persuading the unionists to adopt the idea.[84] Then, in a typical burst of activity Plunkett met Gerald Balfour, Shaftesbury, Birrell (the Irish chief secretary), Simon and Austen Chamberlain. Carson remained friendly and was prepared to give him the names of, but not an introduction to, his chief lieutenants.[85] So on 6 February Plunkett met them on his own initiative in Belfast. The Ulster unionist delegation consisted of General Richardson (military adviser), Captain James Craig MP (second in command to Carson), Thomas Andrews, George Clark (of the shipbuilders Workman and Clark), Adam Duffin, Colonel Sharman-Crawford and a Belfast solicitor, McDowell. Their case rested on the following points:

that the Government was insincere and was simply paying off the nationalists for their 85 votes;
that Ulster had a right to be excluded if the majority so wished;
that the unionists were loyal, the nationalists disloyal;
that home rule meant Rome rule; and
that if his scheme were put into operation northern business would suffer and credit would be affected during the trial period.

He left the meeting depressed, but his diary entry was realistic:

I should have Ulsterism in an extreme form if I saw much of these people. Such intensity, narrowness of imagination, dour grim determination to fight for their own corner of this little island — God knows what will come of it all. I made no impression on anyone.[86]

He outlined the danger inherent in the Ulster situation to F. S. Oliver, exponent of federation of the British Isles, 'home rule all round', a few days later.

I had not realised how little control the leaders of the Carson army have over their rank and file. So long as the Tory Party think that home rule is their best card and stand by Ulster in their extremist attitude, neither my scheme, nor anybody else's except exclusion, will be listened to.[87]

In the same month the king's secretary let him know that the king, who was increasingly worried by the prospect of civil war in Ireland, favoured the exclusion of Ulster with the option of coming in later. [88] Redmond, whom he found to have no illusion as to the strength of Ulster's opposition, or the Ulstermens' determination to resist, was prepared to go to any lengths to meet their objections if only they would compromise. He agreed with Plunkett's ideas and was prepared to support them enthusiastically if only Ulster would. [89]

By this time the situation in Ireland had reached crisis point. The National Volunteers had been formed in the south to counter the Ulster Volunteers, while gun-running by the steamship *Clyde Valley* into Larne had been answered by the *Asgard's* celebrated voyage to Howth. The *Asgard*, skippered by Erskine Childers with his wife Molly and Mary Spring Rice, [90] daughter of Lord Monteagle, members of the crew, landed its cargo of arms for the National Volunteers on 26 July 1914. It was just two years since *The Framework of Home Rule* had been published whose reasoned constitutional arguments had so influenced Plunkett. But Carson and his followers had, since then, avowed their intention of taking the law into their own hands and Childers had followed suit. Plunkett remained unimpressed by his action, commenting that 'he is a rabid, radical home ruler and quite ignorant of the facts of Irish life which count most with me'. [91]

In February his proposals were expounded at some length in the columns of *The Times*. [92] Receipt of the king's opinion shortly after with the news that Asquith was proposing the exclusion of Ulster for six years, determined Plunkett to elaborate his scheme. A pamphlet entitled *A Better Way. An Appeal to Ulster not to Desert Ireland* appeared in June. Starting from the premise that the Union of the British Isles which had lasted for almost 120 years was coming to an end, he stood for a united Ireland as an integral part of a united empire. Explaining that leaders of professional and commercial life in Ireland normally avoided the bitterness and passions which political controversy aroused, he felt that the time had come

when our leading men of affairs and social workers must come to the aid of the politicians. Ireland sorely needs the council and advice of her best citizens, men who know their country, who see it clearly and see it whole, who possess the political imagination to grasp the British and imperial issues involved in the Irish controversy and who, above all, have a understanding sympathy with those of their fellow-countrymen whose honest opinions are in violent conflict with their own. [93]

The home rule bill had been amended to give each Ulster county the option (to be decided by majority vote) of excluding itself from the jurisdiction of an Irish parliament. Plunkett felt that this amendment, which had been designed to prevent a civil war, would probably provoke one. He pointed out that increasing prosperity and the settlement of the land question had not one whit diminished the desire for home rule in the south, and continued:

The evil of external government is seen at its worst where England, a rich country with eighty per cent of its population urban, industrial and commercial, makes laws for Ireland, a relatively poor country with over seventy per cent of its population rural and agricultural. [94]

This argument might also be used to exclude Ulster from an Irish parliament but the analogy was false for Ulster constituted a greater proportion of the wealth and political power of Ireland than the combined rural areas of Ireland, England, Scotland and Wales did of the UK. Further, in an Irish parliament the interests of Dublin and Belfast would be allied against those of the country districts; in any case it was hard to envisage the powerful, well organised, urban communities being disadvantaged politically by their rural brethren.

Carson and his followers, he knew, were not bluffing, and the military preparations in the north were being followed by others in the rest of the island. 'In the immediate future we shall have a quarter of a million drilled and armed men in the country whose preparations and organisation are for the sole purpose of extra-constitutional action'. [95] The government had failed to grasp the full implications of either the constitutional or the military situation, while the opposition was playing a purely destructive role. A major reconstruction of the bill was required though home rule was, by now, inevitable. Looking further afield, Europe was like an armed camp with Britain barely holding the ring. A war over Ulster could tip the scales precipitating 'that Armageddon which disturbs the dreams of this generation'. [96] Plunkett had just returned from the United States and it was his firmly held opinion (which he was to express again and again) that

the re-opening of Irish sores would seriously embarrass those who are engaged on either side in the friendly settlement of all open questions between the British empire and the western republic. [97]

The pamphlet's most striking paragraphs explained his

objections to partition:

The stream of life must come to the tree from the soil in which its root fibres are spread; it cannot draw the material of vital growth from a body to which it is artificially attached. Belfast, as an emporium of Irish trade, as a banking centre of Irish finance, has guarantees of permanent and ever-growing greatness which as an English or Scottish seaport town, it could not hope to possess. [98]

Further, partition would involve a betrayal of southern protestants:

These people are not consoled by being told that a protestant regime in Ulster is a guarantee of their fair treatment, on the assumption that the catholics in Belfast will be virtually hostages for themselves. [99]

Southern protestants did not fear religious persecution but they remembered how the Ulster unionists had championed the rights of the scattered minorities of their co-religionists in the south and west during the home rule controversies of 1886 and 1893. The Ulster Covenant*, in its opening sentence, declared that home rule would be disastrous to the material well-being of the whole of Ireland. Had Ulster now decided that, once its own interests had been looked after, the rest of the country could be left to fend for itself?

His proposal was three fold. Home rule should be applied to the whole country and Ulster would be allowed, after a stated period long enough to give the experiment a fair trial, to vote itself out should a majority so desire. An impartial tribunal would be established with powers to allow the option of exclusion to be exercised at any earlier time if it was proven, at the instance of the Ulster representatives in the Irish house of commons, that Ulster's interests were being affected in a material way. Secondly, the principle of temporary inclusion having been accepted, a conference of representative Irishmen, the constitution of which was to be agreed by Carson and Redmond, should be called to put forward amendments to the home rule bill. Thirdly, the two volunteer forces should be re-organised into an Irish territorial army.

The plan involved sacrifices from both sides:

The Irish minority are asked to risk some temporary inconvenience with

---

*A document signed by thousands of Ulster unionists in September, 1912 signifying their determination to resist the imposition of home rule.

ample provision against any serious permanent injury, and to stand by their co-religionists in the south and west in the starting of home rule. They are asked to give the majority an opportunity of showing that they have both the will and the capacity to establish, with the help of the Ulster leaders, a government fair alike to catholic and protestant, to the rural urban interests and to the Irish and Scot-Irish sentiment. The Irish majority are asked to recognize and guarantee the right of the whole province of Ulster to revert to its former constitutional position should it, after a fair trial, wish to do so. [100]

Plunkett judged the concession he asked of the majority far greater than that which the minority would have to make, but his appeal fell on the deaf ears of the covenanters some of whom had signed in their own blood. Then on 31 July, at midnight, Germany declared war on Russia. As the conflict spread the home rule bill was shelved for the duration of the war and his thoughts turned from Ireland to the Armageddon which he had predicted.

VII

America and the War

During his ranching period in Wyoming, Plunkett wintered in
Ireland and spent the rest of the year in the USA. From 1889
onwards, when his work for co-operation had begun, he
reversed the process, taking a Christmas break in America to
keep an eye on his business interests, normally penetrating as far
west as Cheyenne, although his visits were often too short for
more than a cursory inspection of his American affairs.

In 1895 he encountered Theodore Roosevelt* then engaged on
the daunting task of reforming the New York Police Department.[1] As a consequence of the assassination of President
McKinley, the next time they met, in 1901, was in the White
House.[2] The president was an easterner born and bred but he had
spent two years from 1884 ranching in North Dakota, and in that
period, had often visited Wyoming. Emphasising the need for
integrity in public life, he had brought the pioneering spirit and
the language of the West to Washington. To Plunkett he was 'the
strenuous advocate of the strenuous life'. It was not surprising
that the two men hit it off immediately.

Roosevelt's first term in office had not been marked by much
significant rural legislation. He had improved the postal service
and built good roads in the country but by 1905 he was set for
major innovation and conservation of natural resources was to be
his theme.

The early settlers to the great food producing tract of the Middle
West, Plunkett had observed in his Wyoming days, knowing that
the land must rapidly rise in value, invariably purchased much
larger farms than they could handle. They often sank their
available capital into the first payments for the land and went into
debt for the balance. The land was treated as a mine, or as a bank

---

*Robert Roosevelt, uncle of Theodore and a former US minister to the Nether-
lands, was married to a first cousin of T. P. Gill.

132

from which depositors were constantly withdrawing more than
they invested, in a system of farming unprecedented in its
wastefulness:

Land, labour, capital, and ability, I had been taught to regard as the
essentials of production, but here capital was reduced to the minimum,
and ability left to nature ... I remember writing home that I was in a
country where the rolling stone gathered most moss. [3]

Gifford Pinchot, [4] head of the US Bureau of Forestry and a
member of Roosevelt's 'tennis cabinet', was the apostle of
conservation. It was not to him simply a material problem, but a
moral issue. The American people would be judged, he insisted,
by the manner in which they applied their physical and mental
energies to the conservation of their country's natural resources.
Plunkett was infected by Pinchot's crusading zeal and, in return,
preached the necessity of improving the standard of life in the
countryside. The president was fascinated by the story of the co-
operative movement, the Recess Committee, and by the work of
the DATI. 'I wish you were an American and in the senate or my
cabinet', he wrote in 1906. [5] 'You take an interest in just the
problems which I regard as vital, and you approach them in what
seems to me to be the only sane and healthy way.' Plunkett
translated his Irish aim of self-help combined with judicious
government aid into an American context. His Irish slogan:
'Better Farming, Better Business, Better Living', became
Roosevelt's rural motto. 'By George! That's it!' said the
president. 'I'll megaphone it to the world!' [6]

Policy formation was entrusted to two commissions dealing
with conservation and country life. If Pinchot, after Roosevelt, is
regarded as the architect of the Conservation Commission, to
Plunkett belongs the credit for persuading the president to
appoint the Commission on Country Life. This commission,
composed of men such as Liberty Hyde Bailey, Dean of the New
York State College of Agriculture at Cornell University, 'Uncle
Henry' Wallace, American counterpart of AE and editor of
Wallace's Farmer and Pinchot himself held hearings in 30 different
locations and received 115,000 replies to a questionaire circulated
to half a million American farmers.

In his letter of February 1909 (drafted by Plunkett and Pinchot)
transmitting its report to Congress, the president stressed that
the object of the commission was

not to help the farmer raise better crops but to call his attention to the

opportunities for better business and better living on the farm. If country
life is to become . . . one of the most dignified, desirable and sought after
ways of earning a living — the farmer must take advantage, not only of
the agricultural knowledge which is at his disposal, but of the methods
which have raised . . . the standards of living . . . in other callings.[7]

Emphasising that it did not fall within the sphere of the state to re-
organise farmers' business or to reconstruct rural social life, the
commission's task was, he added, to highlight the problems of
the countryside and point out ways in which government policy
could help to improve the quality of country life.

The commissioners, arriving at many of the conclusions which
Plunkett had reached in Ireland, recommended a re-organisation
of rural schooling with its roots firmly based in the countryside,
and an improved system of communication incorporating better
roads and postal services, besides underlining the role played by
voluntary bodies in rural life. And although Roosevelt's
opponents, in subsequent administrations, did their utmost to
deride the work of the commission, many of its recommendations were ultimately given effect. Its report remains a charter
for US farm people — a major influence upon American rural
social philosophy.

Roosevelt decided, before he retired from office, to make a
formal acknowledgement of his debt to Plunkett in a letter to the
British ambassador Bryce (former chief secretary for Ireland).

You have, I know, followed with keen interest the work of the Country
Life Commission, which has pointed the way, as I think, to a better
handling of country problems and a more satisfying life on the farm. But
I do not know how far you are acquainted with the origin of the
movement in the United States. Of course, I have been interested for
many years in farm life, and especially in the tasks and troubles of the
women on the farm. But my interest did not reach the point of action
until I began to follow what was being accomplished through the
farmers' co-operative movement in Ireland. My old friend Horace
Plunkett, whom I saw on his periodical journeys to America, kept me
informed of the Irish agricultural situation and of the movement for
better living on the farms of Ireland. We Americans owe much to Ireland
and to Plunkett in the task we have been trying to do in the United
States, and before I leave the presidency I want to acknowledge our debt
and to send through you, my thanks for the help we have had, and not
only my thanks but the thanks of every man who knows what has been
done and sees the need and sure results of this great movement to help
the men and women who feed the nation and stand at the foundation of
its greatness and progress.[8]

The letter had a chequered history. The ambassador sent a copy to the foreign secretary, Edward Grey but Grey, after consulting Birrell who was in touch with Dillon, refused publication. It was just a year since the nationalists had forced him to retire from the DATI, and Plunkett was justifiably hurt by the Foreign Office's boorishness. In the meantime however, Pinchot, showing scant respect for UK officialdom, had sent a copy to the celebrated American agriculturist Henry Wallace who promptly published it in *Wallace's Farmer*. It was gleefully reprinted in the *Irish Homestead* and Plunkett was acclaimed and the Foreign Office derided. Dillon's last shot was to try to infer that Plunkett had himself published the letter in both America and Ireland. But few believed him and the letter received more publicity on account of its circuitous passage than it otherwise might have done.

Plunkett continued to influence agricultural policy during succeeding administrations. In 1910 he published his second book, *The Rural Life Problem of the United States*, in which he set the philosophy which he had been working out in Ireland into an American context. A Sociological Bureau was established in the Federal Department of Agriculture to carry out part of his plan and, in 1917, after trials and tribulations, the Carnegie Trust was persuaded to grant $20,000 towards the foundation of a National Agricultural Organisation Society which, however, collapsed when the funds were embezzled by one of the lieutenants Plunkett had trusted.[9]

His contribution had been to focus attention on the problems of rural life and economy in a country where words were quickly transformed into deeds and thoughts into actions. There was, throughout this period, a marked growth in co-operation among American farmers as well as between voluntary agencies and the state. In addition to the self-help side, a programme of government assistance had been established without a taint of paternalism. 'Some of these days', wrote Gifford Pinchot to Plunkett, 'it will be known that you are the man who stirred up the whole movement in America.'[10]

* * *

During his ranching days in the West, or, on his annual visits to the US thereafter, Plunkett had had ample experience of the tensions in the Anglo-American-Irish tripartite relationship. In 1898 he set forth his views on the Irish question in the *North American Review*. Written while still a unionist MP and 'an opponent of home rule in the accepted sense of the term', he thus described his own position, and that of his supporters:

Our chief offence is that we despise the so-called love for Ireland which is but a thinly disguised hatred for England. Our hopes for the regeneration of our country do not involve the destruction of an empire which Irishmen have taken a leading part in building up, and are today foremost in maintaining. [11]

'England does not owe us home rule', he wrote, 'and would give us, if only we would agree upon the need for it, remedial legislation of another kind'. Solve the economic problem, argued Plunkett, and then the Irish people would be in a position to solve the political problem for themselves.

Political opinion among Irish-Americans was as deeply divided as in Ireland; there were the constitutional Redmondites, the extreme Clan na Gael and a large non-partisan group 'liable to a supreme appeal . . . if the final fate of Ireland is at hand and can be affected from America'. [12] In times of crisis Irish influence in America was a force to be reckoned with, though, in the final analysis, Anglo-American interests usually prevailed. The Irish, Plunkett realised, had a peculiar attachment to their homeland:

They are not in the same position as the German or English immigrants who have no cause at home which they wish to forward. Every echo in the States of political or social disturbance in Ireland rouses the immigrant and he becomes an Irishman once more, and not a citizen of the country of his adoption. [13]

By the turn of the century his annual visits had become, as much as anything, propaganda tours on behalf of his work. There was opposition, as in Ireland, from the anti-Parnell wing of the Nationalist Party. Michael Davitt had been in the White House prior to Plunkett's visit in 1901. The president knew all about the Galway by-election, Plunkett informed Lady Betty:

He said to Davitt, he told me, 'Isn't Plunkett a good man?' Davitt replied, 'Certainly — that's what made it so important to defeat him', a delightfully Irish reason Roosevelt seemed to think. [14]

Three years later, with the publication of *Ireland in the New Century* and the ensuing letter from Redmond to the editor of the *Irish World*, Plunkett experienced outright hostility from a section of Irish-Americans. He promptly set about redressing the balance and felt that, although the Irish in the US were as determined as ever on home rule, they were moving away from the Parliamentary Party. Opposition from Redmond's followers had the effect of pushing Plunkett in the direction of more extreme opinion; and in America on Christmas Eve 1904, he used words which he might later have cause to regret:

Certainly one gets a far better love of Ireland from the non-parliamentary section. A good blow off now and again in the way of a rebellion is, I think, better than the eternal war of words. [15]

Theodore Roosevelt had followed the American presidential tradition of treating Anglo-Irish problems as an internal British matter, Plunkett confided to Betty Balfour in 1901:

I gathered one chief impression which was an immense relief to me. He is pro-English. His policy will be strict avoidance of foreign complications. There is not the slightest fear of any pro-Irish or pro-Boer indiscretions while he is at the White House. [16]

Though in 1911, now out of office, Roosevelt was able to write explicitly to T. P. Gill, 'I believe that the granting of home rule to Ireland would be of great importance in removing one source of friction between the United States and Great Britain'. [17]

Upon the outbreak of the war Plunkett diverted all his energies towards enlisting US assistance for the allied cause. He understood America better than most visitors; he had a real feeling for the Middle West, an area often overlooked at home; and was especially sensitive to the mutual misunderstandings which might arise between the US and the UK. Anglo-American wartime entente was not being helped by the personalities of the respective ambassadors. Sir Cecil Spring-Rice, the British ambassador in Washington and a cousin of Lord Monteagle, suffered from exopthalmic goitre making him hypersensitive leading to serious problems for President Wilson. Walter Page, on the other hand, American ambassador at the Court of St. James, was reputedly too anglophile and failed to make the American case, so there was desperate need for a suitable mediator.

Plunkett had contacts in the loftiest American circles; he had a long standing friendship with Arthur Balfour, who joined the war-time coalition cabinet as first lord of the admiralty in 1915, and who, unlike some of his colleagues, had a thorough understanding of attitudes in the US; but it was his friendship with Colonel Edward House which gave him a position of real influence in Anglo-American relations during the war. House was a Texan of independent means who had played a key role in Wilson's election to the White House. He had become the president's special adviser and, on his war-time visits to Europe, though consistently refusing public office, carried a letter giving him absolute authority as spokesman for the president.

The two men had met in London in 1913.[18] House regarded Plunkett as an eminent statesman and, knowing of his friendship with, and influence upon Roosevelt, intended to enlist his aid to forward Wilson's rural policy. A warm relationship developed at once and House accepted Plunkett's invitation to visit Ireland but later declined on account of his wife's ill health. Before the war House had been an advocate of a league of nations; after the outbreak his sympathies lay always with the Allies, and although this was also the case with Wilson, the president, guided by Washington's precept to steer clear of European entanglements, never allowed his personal feelings to override his political responsibilities.

Despite the presence of a vigorous and vocal German minority in the US, there was never any serious possibility of America entering the war on Germany's side. America, as a whole, was on the side of the Allies, but German propaganda in the US was well organised and there was always the danger, as far as Britain was concerned, that the Germans might make common cause with disaffected Irish-Americans — a possibility which Plunkett, through his Irish-American contacts, worked strenuously to counter.

He sailed for America in December 1914. Before setting off he had a meeting with Foreign Secretary Edward Grey to inform him of his wish to put the English case in the most effective way.[19] On arriving in New York the moderate Irish-American John Quinn informed him that anti-British influence among Irish-Americans was waning but the postponement of home rule and the inclusion, six months later, of two Irish unionists, Carson and J.H. Campbell, in the coalition government made this moderate position more difficult.[20] Earlier in 1914 Sir Cecil Spring-Rice, the British ambassador, had reported that

speaking generally an unfriendly feeling exists in this country against England . . . a great interest is excited by Irish affairs, and . . . American unfriendliness to England may and most probably will have serious results should affairs in Ireland become worse.[21]

Plunkett arrived to urge America to enter the war but found

Wilson determined on neutrality. The conflict, at that time, was not expected to last and Wilson, according to House, had peace proposals in mind, which Plunkett suspected were German inspired. A visit to the British Embassy, which was desperately short handed, convinced him that the UK government did not appreciate the importance of friendly relations with the USA; Germany, he felt, was making more headway in this direction. [22] He returned to London, after a final interview with House in February 1915, and reported at once to Grey on Wilson's proposed peace initiative. Grey replied with his hope that America would lead the neutral states into a league of peace, but to Plunkett this was not enough. Britain, he held, should take the initiative by herself proposing a generous peace and asking the neutral states, with America as their leader, to support her proposals. [23]

House arrived in London shortly after Plunkett who introduced him to Balfour, and, on his return from France and Germany, took him to see Lloyd George. House and Balfour struck up the rapport which Plunkett had expected, and on House's departure to America he and Plunkett agreed to keep in close touch. House had many correspondents and war-time confidants, but he put great store in his contact with Plunkett and through him with Balfour. The latter arranged for their letters to be transmitted in code and, in a letter to House of 8 June 1915, Plunkett felt it important to include a formal statement putting his position on record.

The friendship with President Wilson which led to Colonel House's unusual wartime role was briefly outlined:

As the war progressed and the relations of the United States to the belligerent powers became more and more complicated, the president required some agent who enjoyed his whole confidence to ascertain in the different countries all the facts which bore upon the right attitude of the United States towards the several powers. The obvious choice was Col. House. From the beginning of February to June 5, Col. House was engaged at this confidential mission. Having enjoyed his acquaintance in the United States and more especially having, in the months of December and January last, discussed with him in New York many aspects of the war which were of special interest to the United States, he invited me to keep in touch with him while he was in London, and this I did. When he left London, he wished to have someone with whom he could correspond on matters which were not ripe for official communication, but which had an important bearing on questions he would be discussing with the president ... I undertook to serve in this capacity and arrangements were made by a member of the British government to facilitate the correspondence by authorising the exclusive use of a secret code by Col. House and myself . . . I possess no authority whatsoever and my function will cease as soon as matters, in regard to which I may be of assistance to Col. House, come within the range of governmental action. [24]

Feeling the survival of western civilisation to be at stake, Plunkett believed that American involvement was crucial to an allied victory. Once the US had come in, its fleet could control the western hemisphere freeing the British navy for work elsewhere. Munitions and supplies would be available in large quantities to the Allies, and American troops would be directed to the front. But more important was the moral effect which America's entry would have upon the combatants.

American obsession with the restoration of international trade worried Plunkett, for when the time came to discuss terms, it might prevent the Allies from extracting concessions sufficient to secure world peace. House argued conversely that Germany must not be smashed in a way which would make European reconstruction impossible [25] and indicated that America would not support allied claims for territorial aggrandisement.

A key feature of British military strategy was the naval blockade which prevented munitions, war materials or foodstuffs from reaching Germany through its own or through neutral ports. The German response took the form of a submarine campaign. In February 1915 Germany declared the seas around the British Isles to be a war zone and warned neutral countries not to allow British ships to fly their flags. Both the blockade and the submarine war directly affected America; the former obstructing her trade with Europe; while the latter was likely to drag America into the war if American ships, or ships carrying American passengers, were sunk either deliberately or in error.

To counteract these dangers, Wilson, through House, put forward his concept of the 'freedom of the seas'. Contraband was to be confined entirely to implements of war. Trade was thus to proceed freely through neutral ports — belligerent ports could be blockaded — but foodstuffs etc., could get through by a circuitous route. The possible starvation of Germany would be avoided and in return submarine warfare on all except naval vessels should cease. House hoped that the freedom of the seas would be a forerunner of peace and that the concept would then be enshrined in international law by a league of nations. He believed that the restoration of imperial trade and the avoidance of submarine warfare would more than compensate Britain for her inability to starve Germany into submission. However German diplomacy, lacking much in subtlety, seized on the idea. The British response was an instant negative and the general misunderstanding which followed, served as an Anglo-American irritant for the remainder of the war.

By the winter of 1915 expectations of a short sharp war or of early US intervention had given way to pessimism. Plunkett remained convinced of Wilson's sympathy towards the Allies but, in spite of the sinking of the passenger vessels *Lusitania, Arabic* and *Ancona,* and the consequent loss of American lives, Wilson clung determinedly to neutrality.

Plunkett travelled to America in the winter of 1915 and found House (and Wilson) determined to see the Allies through, but unable to go further than American opinion would allow. English criticism of America's non-intervention was having an adverse effect and doubts were cast upon the efficacy of the UK ambassador Spring-Rice. Plunkett wrote that the president, Lansing (the secretary of state), and House wished that he be appointed in Spring-Rice's place, realising, at the same time, that this was beyond the bounds of possibility. [26]

Upon his return Plunkett consulted Balfour. They agreed that American intervention would be decisive, that the Pax Britannica could no longer be assured and that an alliance between the republic and the empire was essential to permanent peace. Although Balfour's immediate concerns were naval, he, too, was seeking a permanent basis for world peace and had prepared a memorandum for the cabinet incorporating this aim. [27] In this he reviewed various proposals — territorial changes in the interests of self determination, control of armaments and, finally, the creation of an 'anti-war federation' among nations sufficiently powerful, if they acted together, to prevent a repetition of such tragedies; expressing his view that the scheme was impracticable without American involvement.

'It is my own belief', argued Plunkett in an answering memorandum, [28] 'that if the United States were drawn into the war, peace would not only be immediately in sight, but the prospect of its enduring would be enormously improved'. It would facilitate the liberation of the democratic forces in Germany and the breakdown of the military bureaucracy in the only effective and permanent way — from within. Secondly, it would give the necessary sanction in the peace negotiations. When the war ended America truly would have become a world power; then Anglo-American entente would be necessary to sustain Britain's position as well as to ensure world peace.

In the spring of 1916, House paid another visit to Europe with a peace plan from the president which in essence meant the cession of Alsace-Lorraine to France, restoration of Belgium and Serbia, Constantinople for Russia and a league of nations. Germany, in the grip of the militarists, showed little interest in the plan. The Allies still wanted to smash Germany but House's aim was to end the war and he floated the idea that the president would demand a peace conference (its terms having prior approval from the Allies) and, if Germany refused, America would enter the war. On 24 March the *Sussex* (an unarmed passenger vessel, flying the French flag and carrying a number of Americans) was torpedoed in the English Channel and Wilson sent a peremptory note demanding instant cessation of the campaign against passenger and freight vessels which Germany grudgingly accepted.

In May the president announced the end of US isolationist policy and promised to play an active role in the world affairs of the future. He also put in a plea for the establishment of a league of nations. But to allied ears one unfortunate phrase robbed this important message of much of its influence. The offending words referred to the origins of the war: 'with its causes and objects we are not concerned'. The Allies felt that this struck at the basis of their struggle for democracy and the freedom of small nations and Plunkett cabled his concern at this transatlantic misunderstanding. [29]

Wilson fought the presidential election of 1916 on a peace ticket. His opponent Hughes had defeated the fervently pro-Ally Roosevelt for the republican nomination and Plunkett reported to House that, although there was a strong impression in London that Wilson would be defeated, he thought otherwise and emphasised the advantage to foreign policy of a second term for the president. [30] But Roosevelt 'who hates Wilson more than he does the Kaiser' was angry when he learnt that his friend and former collaborator was supporting Wilson. [31]

During the campaign in which he was faced with trouble in Mexico to add to the problems of Europe, Wilson challenged Hughes to state whether he would have intervened in Europe during August 1914, or May 1915, or would have engaged in a full scale war against Mexico. He was narrowly re-elected in the winter of 1916 and the prospect of American intervention appeared, if anything, to recede still further into the distance.

X-ray burns received at the hands of a Harley Street

dermatologist totally incapacitated Plunkett during the summer of 1916. Before the end of the year Asquith was succeeded by Lloyd George and Balfour replaced Grey as foreign secretary. Upon hearing this House wrote to Wilson:

If Grey had to leave the next best man in the kingdom for us is Balfour. This will give Sir Horace great influence upon American affairs, since Balfour and Plunkett are the closest friends and Balfour will look largely to him for guidance. This again is fortunate. [32]

In December, though his burn had not really healed, Plunkett decided to risk a visit to America. Wilson wished to propose a peace conference but House was urging him to wait for prior allied approval. On 12 December Germany published a note indicating her willingness to enter such a conference without spelling out terms. Wilson replied calling on the belligerents to tell neutral states their aims and on what terms they would accept peace. Again his message contained a phrase indicating that, in American eyes, all belligerents were equally guilty which was bound to offend the Allies, and on 22 December House wrote in his diary:

Sir Horace Plunkett was my first visitor this morning. He is terribly exercised over the president's note. He is sorry that he sent it and regrets the verbiage. He called attention to the fact that it contained the same old refrain. [33]

Plunkett, who was really too ill to intervene effectively, retired to the sanitarium in Battle Creek, Michigan, prior to facing major surgery in Chicago. With Plunkett out of action, House found a congenial contact, Wiseman, at the British Embassy. Events moved swiftly during the winter months. By February Germany had declared open submarine warfare causing Wilson to break off diplomatic relations, first with Germany, and then with Austria. The final blow came when German intrigue with Mexico was uncovered and the United States entered the war on 2 April 1917. Plunkett wrote in his diary the next day:

The president's speech to Congress last night leaves little to be desired. It justifies all I have said to our government about him. Roosevelt congratulated him on it and I congratulated Roosevelt on this fine example of patriotism. [34]

Plunkett arranged for an Irish-American delegation to meet Balfour who crossed the Atlantic in April to co-ordinate the war effort. The delegation was carefully chosen (with the assistance of Shane Leslie and John Quinn) and consisted of New York Supreme Court Judge Morgan J. O'Brien, John F. ('Honey-Fitz') Fitzgerald, Col. Robert Temple Emmet, and Lawrence Godkin (Emmet and Godkin were protestant Irish-Americans). The meeting which lasted for two hours took place on 4 May. The delegation asked for a generous settlement of the Irish question, pointing out how much of a irritant it had become in America, they ruled out partition as unacceptable in the US and Plunkett's proposals were argued with some force by Godkin. Balfour acknowledged the need for a resolution of the problem but underlined the difficulty of obtaining a settlement acceptable to north and south. Ulster's fears were understood in Britain; forcing them out of the United Kingdom would not be tolerated. He indicated that Lloyd George was involved in another round of negotiations with Irish leaders and promised to report faithfully on the views which the delegation had put before him.[35] The meeting was adjudged successful by both parties; it may have had no effect on British policy, but it helped, in the short run, to mollify Irish-American opinion.

Balfour's American visit was a tour-de-force and Plunkett's joy was unconfined:

I have always been a great believer in, and, indeed, a great lover of, Arthur Balfour, but he never used his personal charm to such advantage as in getting the Americans to understand the better side of the British people.[36]

He had written in his diary of his efforts in 1916, 'Undoubtedly the most useful work which I was able to do was in trying to get the British and United States goverments to understand each other'.[37] As he sailed for home the following May he received a telegram from House:

The president bids me send you greetings and wishes me to convey his deep appreciation of your unselfish efforts to promote good feeling on both sides of the Atlantic.[38]

VIII

1916

Mounting tension over the shocking conditions endured by the majority of Dublin's workforce with extortionately low wages and unspeakable living conditions had come to a head in 1913. Attempts had been made to unionise Irish labour spearheaded by Connolly and Larkin. A major strike in August led to a six-month lockout, to destitution for Dublin's workers and to AE's celebrated denunciation of the employers as 'blind Samsons pulling down the social order'.[1]

British trade unionists and co-operators rallied to the support of their suffering Irish colleagues. £70,000 was collected by unions and co-operative societies and fourteen shiploads of food were sent from CWS headquarters in Manchester to the starving Dublin families.[2] Plunkett, living in Foxrock and moving in exalted circles, was only vaguely aware of the problem. Lord Salisbury wrote in December wishing to subscribe to the distress fund without aiding the combatants, and Plunkett's reply was revealing:

The condition of the Dublin slums I always knew to be bad but had only realised one half the truth. The fact is, in common with the rest of my countrymen, I had been absorbed in the problems of our rural communities and had neglected all others. My feeling is that the poverty and destitution which has been revealed owing to Larkin's agitation, are so awful that temporary assistance, pending some radical scheme of permanent amelioration, can be provided without any appearance of taking sides in the Dublin labour dispute.[3]

In February the workers backed down, but not before they had formed the Irish Citizen Army. Everything was then over-shadowed by the outbreak of a European war. Plunkett handed the Plunkett House over to trustees and turned his whole attention to obtaining American support for the Allies and, ultimately, American intervention in the conflict.

145

Carson and Redmond needed to settle their differences if Ireland were to play her part, but Plunkett's last despairing appeal met with no response. Both men promised their forces to the allied cause, Carson doing so without difficulty but Redmond's House of Commons pledge of the Volunteers under his control to the defence of their homeland (releasing troops stationed there for service at the front) was ultimately, without the quid pro quo of home rule, to prove fatal. Plunkett, to whom Redmond's offer was 'one of the greatest political utterances of our time', [4] instantly recognised the danger for, on 9 August, he wrote to Redmond:

I would not 'hang up' the home rule bill indefinitely. I should like its passage postponed for a time, on one condition — namely that the unionists should agree to its passage the moment the present crisis, which makes the discussion of any amendment by consent impracticable, is over, or if the war goes on, or at some time to be agreed on in the near future. [5]

Staff in the Plunkett House, of unionist or nationalist sympathies, were fervently pro-Ally. Home rule was on the statute book, and though the enabling act was suspended for the duration of hostilities, Redmond's action in committing his National Volunteers to the allied cause had been applauded by the majority of nationalists. A small group remained sceptical; hard bitten nationalists disbelieved allied promises of freedom for small nations; Casement describing the suspended home rule bill as a 'promissory note payable after death'. 10% of the Volunteers opposed recruitment, breaking away from Redmond under the nominal leadership of Eoin MacNeill to form the Irish Volunteers, but in the early years of the war these remained a small disaffected minority and Irishmen generally supported the Allies. Tom Kettle, the nationalist MP, who was to die in the trenches, took an international view. Much as he loved Ireland he also appreciated Europe, and would not willingly allow western civilisation to be twisted from its hinges without some protest being made by Irishmen. Six years before the war he had laid down: 'My only programme for Ireland consists in equal parts of home rule and the ten commandments. My only counsel to Ireland is that to become deeply Irish she must become European'. [6]

The War Office, regrettably, showed a considerable bias in its treatment of the various Irish recruits. Carson's followers, organised into Ulster regiments, were allowed to wear distinctive insignia and to serve under the officers who had commanded the Ulster Volunteers; the National Volunteers who had supported Redmond, received no such recognition and were split up among English and Scottish regiments; it was notoriously difficult for an Irish catholic to obtain a commission; and the enthusiasm for service, whose mouthpiece was John Redmond, dwindled in the face of Kitchener's bureaucracy. [7]

A small group of dedicated fenians (having gained clandestine control of the Irish Volunteers through the oath-bound Irish Republican Brotherhood) led by men such as Tom Clarke and Patrick Pearse, decided to force the issue. Sensing that England's weakness was Ireland's opportunity, on Easter Monday 1916, in uneasy coalition with Connolly's Citizen Army, and to the amusement of their fellow Dubliners, they marched from Liberty Hall a few hundred yards through the city centre to the General Post Office and declared a republic.

The Pearse-Connolly coalition between republicans and socialists was unlikely to last, but it did indicate the directions from which an explosion was going to come. The fenian tradition of armed resistance to British rule had been kept alive by those such as Clarke, who had served fifteen years in jail for his activities as a dynamiter (for whose release Plunkett had appealed in the House of Commons debate of 1896). Fervent separatists, these men rejected the idea of Ireland's automatic involvement in a war which was none of her making, believing that they had been offered a heaven sent opportunity to reassert Ireland's independence, however futile the military exercise might be.

In March 1916, after a sojourn of some months in England where his attention had been completely absorbed by Anglo-American affairs, Plunkett returned to Dublin. On Easter Sunday 23 April, Mahaffy, provost of Trinity College, lunched at Kilteragh. [8] The events of the following week, as they impinged on Plunkett, are graphically recorded in his diary.

24 April. A black day — a dies irae. The policy of wait and see is a veritable sowing of the wind in Ireland. At 1 p.m. Daisy tried to get on the telephone* to the under-secretary's lodge. She was told from the Castle that a 'revolution had broken out' — that the police and sentries at the Castle had been fired at, that the gates had been closed and then the telephone stopped. In the afternoon I took Norman†, who knows

---

*It was a measure of the tactical inexperience of the insurgents that Dublin's main telephone exchange was never put out of action.
†Assistant secretary of the IAOS.

the mountain roads, to try and find Anderson, and his 'Methuseliers'*, who were picknicking in the mountains. I feared they would be ambushed and intended to get at them from the upper side and warn them. Near Sandyford we met some of them and heard they had marched to Dublin. We overtook them and found they had been commandeered. They were armed but had no ammunition, and four of them were shot dead, others being wounded. Then the force was taken into the Beggars Bush Barracks and furnished with ammunition. I came on to the Kildare Street Club and could find no one who knew anything. Spent an anxious night at Kilteragh.

25 April. Ambrose, caretaker at Plunkett House, got through to Kilteragh somehow, though the telephone was only available for military purposes, and told us that the milkman had told him that 'war was declared'. This turned out to be a proclamation declaring martial law. All day the city remained a strange mixture of peace and war. The inhabitants — men, women and children, ignored the official warning to remain indoors, though rifles were popping off occasionally, supplemented by machine-gun fire. The military occupied the Shelbourne Hotel, and thence sniped the rebels, who had dug themselves in in Stephen's Green. I went in and sent the staff of the Plunkett House home. Got the Fingall women folk ... to Kilteragh. There I worked the latter part of the day. I took letters to Kingstown but the mail service was suspended. Three barricades I had to climb to get to St. George's Yacht Club. Tom Ponsonby† came. He started Monday for the Cattle Show, but his train (which he was happily able to leave by motor) was held up 25 hours at Maryborough.

26 April. Still no news from the outside world. I went into Dublin with Tom Ponsonby and Bullard and to Nathan‡ at the Castle. There he was in the Master of the Horse's house, carrying on the government of Ireland. Birrell, of course, being in London where the papers (which have absolutely no news) say he 'made a statement in the House' yesterday! I drove my little motor to the Castle via Nassau and Dame Streets. Dame Street from South Gt. George's Street was deserted, the military at the Castle and in the City Hall, whence they have ejected the rebels, firing at the houses occupied by 'the enemy' on the other side. I went in to the Castle, which I had some difficulty in getting the guard to [let me] enter. I found Nathan surrounded by a queer lot of law officers, police and military. J. H. Campbell, now Attorney-General, was for 'thorough', and told me he was going to ask a lot of awkward questions about the management of the business of the authorities at the proper time. General Friend, GOC, was in England when the trouble began on Monday! One Kennard (an ass and a Christian Scientist) was his locum tenens.

I learned that there was no 'rising' elsewhere than in Dublin, that the

*Veteran Corps.
†Plunkett's nephew from Kilcooley, Co. Tipperary.
‡Birrell's undersecretary.

rebellion was organised and led by Sir Roger Casement, whom the government had captured. I had gone to the Castle to get a cypher telegram through to Arthur Balfour, telling him I thought it important to let the American people know of the German origin of the Irish trouble. I changed my cable to definite advice to give the capture of Casement as a piece of 'exclusive news' ...

Poor Anderson was shot*, but not I think seriously wounded in the afternoon.

27 April. To-day was to have begun with the meeting of the General Committee of the IAOS and to have been followed by a United Kingdom agricultural co-operative conference, for which I had elaborately prepared. Instead I had to visit Anderson in the Portobello Military Hospital where he was lying hit by three bullets — or buckshot, all wounds being slight. Went to the Castle, where I spent 5 or 6 hours at Nathan's office. He showed me the official file recording the landing of Sir Roger Casement from Germany on the Kerry coast, his capture and removal to the Tower where he confessed his identity, and deplored the way this poor dupe had been duped by the Germans.

All day the Irish Volunteers held their own, and demonstrated the enormous difficulty of dealing with an enemy in your own city. Troops were pouring in. There were some 700 or 800 raw boys, from the shires chiefly, in the Castle Yard, with artillery on its way. The GPO and Four Courts, the Royal College of Surgeons (which the Volunteers call their Military Hospital and call upon the authorities to respect under Geneva Convention!) and houses scattered over the city are held against the troops. Musketry pops away all day and from every quarter. Yet men, women and children still frequent the streets, unconcerned. Birrell has come over and is safely lodged at the vice regal. The provinces are reported quiet. But communications are badly interrupted. I got back about 7 to find Cruise O'Brien†... I had to tell him that his wife's brother-in-law Sheehy Skeffington† had been shot.

28 April ... A large military force has gradually been got together, and the city is gradually getting under control. There will be bad, very bad work, before the desperate men (those who will be shot or imprisoned for life) surrender — unconditionally, as they must. How much of Dublin may be destroyed Heaven knows ...

29 April. A dreadful day. The Food Committee‡ was to meet at 11 a.m. at the Castle. I took Lane in my little car and Tom Ponsonby took Needham. We went the way we were ordered. When we were coming along the west side of Merrion Square, the guard at the crossing of the tram at the NW corner opened fire on us. My car was in front, and at first

*Defending Beggars' Bush Barracks.
†Cruise O'Brien worked in the Co-operative Reference Library. Sheehy Skeffington was a pacifist; the officer who authorised his execution was tried and declared insane.
‡Commerical life in Dublin had ground to a halt.

a volley was discharged at it. The glass screen was shattered and Lane hit through the forearm. We held up our hands but they kept on firing for some time. Meanwhile Tom had got out of his car and lay down in the road. This was our undoing. The stupid young soldiers thought he was a rebel going to fire on them from behind the cars, and several of them fired at him while others kept up a fusillade on the front car. The poor fellow was hit three times, twice in the back near the spine if it was not actually hit. The spinal cord was not hit for there was no paralysis. Most fortunately we were opposite the houses of Dr Bewley, Sir Arthur Chance and Sir Andrew Horne, the first and last first rate physicians and the other a first rate surgeon. Bewley took in Tom and Horne, Lane . . . Needham and I did our best to get to the Castle, so as to have orders sent to the officers and NCOs not to extirpate friendly civilians. I asked Col. Kennard, second-in-command, to send a soldier to come with me. He sent a corporal and we sallied forth. When we got to Nassau Street the firing from the other side of the TCD grounds was so fierce that we had to turn back . . .

That evening R. A. Anderson telephoned with the news that the rebels had surrendered unconditionally.

30 April . . . I stayed at Kilteragh with the exception of a run down to Kingstown to inquire about the food distribution problem. Guns were booming from the Dublin side all day. It seems the Larkin (Labour-Socialist) element are desperate and have no idea of surrendering. I was glad to rest my nerves after yesterday.

1 May . . . Towards evening the sniping died down and the sheets filled. I took a look at the devastation in Sackville Street* and saw evidence that there must be in every modern city police preparedness for such attacks as this, e.g. a police hut at the NE and SW corners of Merrion Square would have prevented the snipers occupying its 4 sides.

2 May . . . Worked at getting the Volunteer Training Corps men to swear in as special constables to aid the DMP[†] . . . to search for arms and loot and generally restore order.

3 May . . . Only stray snipers in Dublin, and the Provinces, of which we have no news, are, at the Castle, reported quiet. Tom progressed well. Eddie[‡] I found in the King George Vth Hospital with a slight wound in the face. It seems that he was on leave at Dunsany when the rebellion broke out, came at once to Dublin and offered his services at HQ, was told to report to an officer at Amiens St. and while on the way there in his motor was shot, taken prisoner by the rebels and left (supposed to be dying which supposition he encouraged) at Jervis St. Hospital. He was treated very humanely.

---

*Now O'Connell Street.
[†]Dublin Metropolitan Police.
[‡]His nephew, Edward Dunsany.

4 *May* ... Birrell's resignation announced. He will have a great political funeral as he has done the bidding of the Irish MP's for 9 years. But more than any other living man he fomented this rebellion ... Wrote to Carson urging him to propose disarming the whole of Ireland.

5 *May* ... They are shooting the leaders of the rebellion, some 8 so far and Con Gore-Booth* of long ago — the Countess Markievics for some 18 years — has been condemned to death. She is deeply dyed in blood, but her motives were as noble as her methods were foul. I met Powerscourt, provost marshall, and he was, he told me, begging the authorities to shoot her. She is to have her sentence postponed till Sir John Maxwell returns. I shall urge her reprieve ...

7 *May*. A long talk with Sir John Maxwell, the commander of the force in Ireland, sent over to quell the rebellion, which he did effectively. My object in calling upon him was to get the necessary help in collecting all the available evidence of German initiative and direction of the insurrection. This would very likely smash the German-Irish alliance in America, as the Irish would be furious at having been duped into a mad revolt by promises of naval and military assistance. I have three other aims in wishing to make the latest Irish folly part of the big war. The reconciliation of the moderates and extremists in nationalist Ireland would be made much more hopeful, the destruction in Dublin and other costs of the rebellion would be pooled with the costs of the war and not fall upon Ireland, and the soldiers who had died or been wounded in this business would not go down to history as the victims of street riots. Maxwell agreed with all but the last point!

We then discussed disarming the people. I showed him my correspondence with Carson, in which I proposed that he should initiate disarmament with his volunteers, as everyone else would follow, and he replied that he could not as the women (especially) of Ulster wanted the arms kept while 50,000 of their men were fighting abroad, to defend themselves against enemies at home!

Maxwell sees that the labour section of the rebels — the Citizen Army whose desperation was the cause of the rebellion's outbreak against John McNeill's endeavours to stop it at the last moment — have a real grievance, and he proposes to embody in his recommendations an immediate inquiry into labour conditions in Dublin ...

Lastly, I urged clemency. If there have to be further military executions let them be restricted to cases where high treason was combined with murder ...

Maxwell is a good type of commonsense Englishman, with little imagination but with a sound judgement where the situation is fairly clear. He has done well so far. I hope he won't blunder when he has to deal with the aftermath of the crisis.

But the executions continued and Ireland looked on 'with

---

*A leading revolutionary from an Anglo-Irish Sligo family who were keen co-operators.

something of the feeling of helpless rage with which one would watch a stream of blood dripping from under a closed door'.

9 May. A very small meeting of the CDB over which I had to preside. Fr. O'Hara told me that the feeling in his parish had been strongly anti-Sinn Féin but a reaction was setting in with the executions. I saw Maxwell and General Friend today and told them the executions should now stop in the interests of the country.

Plunkett, realising better than most the effect which these events would have on opinion in the USA, wrote to the moderate Irish-American, James Byrne in the midst of the crisis:

The military executions will be a black chapter in Irish history. I do not think it was politically possible to avoid shooting a few of the ring-leaders who were not directly responsible for the killing of unarmed policemen, soldiers and civilians. Anyone who, in the midst of war, conspires with the enemy to overthrow the government of a country, stakes his life on the venture, and no government would be safe if the penalty were not paid. But three wrong things were done: too many were shot; the executions were too long delayed; and the disproportion between the punishment and the crime was given the worst possible appearance by minimising the gravity of the rebellion in order to save the faces of the civil government, who ought to have foreseen it, and to create the impression throughout the country that it had failed much more rapidly and completely than was the case, so as to dissuade others from joining in. I cannot really blame the military authorities when the whole matter was handed over to them, but it was criminal neglect of Asquith to allow them a free hand. [9]

The Rising itself had won neither Irish nor American approval but, as Plunkett predicted, the executions had a traumatic impact. Inevitable contrasts were made with the government's treatment of Carson, whose threats to resist home rule since 1912, had appeared treasonable. Charles McCarthy wrote to deplore the Rising but added that

There is great indignation all over America at the killing of so many of the men who are in the rebellion. America, in general, looks upon them as misguided men, and of course you know we have certain traditions here which come down from our own rebellion. [10]

President Lowell of Harvard described the Rising as a tragedy, but went on, 'To us here it seems that the executions of the Sinn Féiners after surrender was a great mistake', [11] while Theodore Roosevelt summed up American feelings in a letter written in July:

I regretted the executions of the Irish rebels because it seemed to me that the extreme leniency with which Carson and the Ulster unionists had been treated two years previously made it impossible to justify the extreme difference of treatment in the two cases by the far less dissimilarity of offence.[12]

Plunkett had been suspicious of German complicity in the Rising. 'I think the Germans undoubtedly did count on Ulster paralysing the British army, thereby misunderstanding the Covenanters as much as the English had in the opposite direction', he had written to Lowell in September 1914.[13] There were grounds for his suspicion. The guns for the two volunteer forces illegally landed at Larne and Howth had been of German origin, and now Casement's arrival on a Kerry beach from a German submarine, appeared to thicken the plot. But Casement had arrived to stop an uprising; his mission in Germany to recruit for the nationalist cause from among the Irish prisoners of war or to obtain substantial German support had proved an abject failure, while recent evidence indicates that messages requesting arms for the Rising passing from the German Embassy in Washington to Berlin had been deciphered by the Admiralty in London, but the intelligence staff under Admiral Sir Reginald Hall, in order to obscure their success in cracking the enemy code, never alerted Dublin Castle to the impending rising![14]

Plunkett crossed to London on 12 May to confirm his suspicions of German involvement, to seek clemency for the defeated and redress for the grievances of Dublin's working class, but made no progress on any front. He attended the opening day of Casement's trial believing him to be guilty of treason but undoubtedly insane,[15] having learnt from Basil Thompson, deputy commissioner of the Metropolitan Police, that 'Casement's diary which was captured showed that he was a vile creature living a double life — treason being his public, and unnatural vice his private taste'.[16] Casement's actions had certainly been treasonable; but Thomson and Hall[17] were now attempting to influence opinion against him by circulating copies of his diaries which purported to show him a homosexual. Thomson wrote to Plunkett early in June requesting information about Casement's movements in Ireland during 1913-14,[18] and Plunkett wisely referred him to the Royal Irish Constabulary saying that he had drawn a blank.[19]

Plunkett met Asquith during his visit to Dublin arguing that an Irish council of state representing north and south, consisting solely of Irishmen, should be instantly appointed and given executive powers for the duration of the war. The arrangement being temporary would have three advantages: the problem of partition would be left open; north and south would have an opportunity, without prejudice to work together; and when the war ended the home rulers would have a vacuum to fill instead of replacing an existing government. [20]

The English press had, quite erroneously, attributed the Rising to Sinn Féin, and Plunkett wrote to Asquith to underline the error:

Mr. Birrell told Lord Hardinge's Commission that what today is called sinn féinism is mainly composed of the old hatred and distrust of the British connection. In my judgement, it is at least equally composed of the old love of Ireland with a new desire and belief in the opportunity to serve her. It is a revolt quite as much against the handling of Ireland's affairs by her representatives in parliament as against British rule, which, during the last decade, has aroused no opposition if it has won little affection. [21]

He expanded on this theme in a letter to Charles McCarthy in May explaining that the nationalists, with all their power in Westminster, deserved a large share of the blame. They had proved incapable of drafting a decent home rule bill, 'had never done a hand's turn in reconciling the apparently, though not really, divergent interests of north and south', and had refused to allow any other movement to play a part in Irish public life. 'It was a revolt of those who wished to work in and for Ireland against the men who had transferred everything Irish to Westminster, and there made their country a pawn in the English party game'; [22] while a week later to House he explained that the sinn féin movement had 'an immense amount of justification on its side. I suppose my associates, in a sense all belong to it for most of them leave party politics alone and work for the material and social development of the country.' [23]

Asquith's response to the crisis was to hand the Irish problem over to Lloyd George (whom Plunkett never trusted) and when Lloyd George's solution was announced — involving partition with the immediate establishment of a 26 county parliament — Plunkett denounced it in forthright terms. The plan collapsed when it was opposed by the unionists (particularly by southern unionists) in the cabinet; and it emerged that Lloyd George, with the flexibility he was to show on other occasions, had given Carson and Redmond contrary impressions of Ulster's future.

In a postscript of the following year, Plunkett detected Connolly as the main influence behind the Rising. Recognising that he was an abler man than Larkin, he described him as

a unique combination of international socialist and Irish nationalist. He
carried with him the working classes of Dublin whose condition, ever
deplorable, had been aggravated by the war which brought them little of
the highly paid employment elsewhere available to compensate for the
enormously increased cost of living. A few old fenians — men of great
desperation — and a small group of dreamers, who displayed both
courage and humanity, were the backbone of the rebellion. [24]

Reared in the Edinburgh slums of Irish emigrant parents,
Connolly, a strange mixture of socialist and nationalist, was
courageous and talented. He and Plunkett never met, but he
admired Plunkett's work, shared his aim for the reconstruction of
Irish civilization (if perhaps along different lines) and, unlike
Griffith, had a detailed knowledge of the co-operative
movement. In his classic *Labour in Irish History*, first published in
1910, Connolly devoted considerable attention to the pioneering
efforts of Craig at Ralahine in 1831, while in *The Reconquest of
Ireland*, he pinned his faith in a co-operative commonwealth,
highlighted the role of the IAOS in Irish life, and heaped praise
upon the efforts of Plunkett, AE and Father Finlay. The main
political parties were singled out as their principal opponents: 'it
was early discovered that their attempts to regenerate Irish
agricultural life had no more bitter enemies than the political
representatives of the Irish people' [25]

The unionists, he wrote, foretelling the reaction of the northern
state after 1921, opposed the co-operative movement because it
brought protestant and catholic together on a fraternal basis, thus
undermining the bigotry and hatred upon which unionism
depended for its existence. The nationalists, on the other hand,
opposed the movement, because it would necessarily interfere
with profits of middlemen, dealers and gombeenmen who, in the
small country towns 'sucked the life blood of the agricultural
population around them'. Noting that distributive co-operation
had taken root in the north-eastern towns he stressed the benefits
of links with agricultural co-operatives and suggested that trade
union funds be put at the disposal of co-operative societies rather
than invested in the joint-stock banks. [26]

Plunkett and Connolly may not have met, but Connolly had
clearly been influenced by AE and, in *The Reconquest of Ireland*, he
reprinted the text of AE's attack on the employers of Dublin
during the lockout of 1913. Plunkett had, however, contact with
Connolly's widow and family after his execution for, together

with AE, he urged the authorities to grant them permission to move to America, where they eventually settled. Among Plunkett's surviving papers is a document written by Richard Tobin, the highly respected Dublin surgeon attending Connolly (whose leg had been shattered in the GPO) during his captivity. Plunkett used the document (a statement by Connolly to Tobin) to influence the authorities in his attempts to help the family emigrate to the USA.

Richard F. Tobin has attended James Connolly since he was wounded and, in presence of sentries, conversations took place in which the leader of the citizen army expressed his views with entire frankness.

Connolly believes that the Germans will win the war. When it was pointed out to him that, no matter how much the workers in whose condition he was chiefly interested had benefitted by the efficiency and paternal care of Prussian government, a military bureaucracy would be intolerable to the peoples of the allied countries, he replied that, if the war had been postponed for a few years, the labour element in Germany would have asserted itself and put an end to the Hohenzollerns. After the German victory he was confident that the combined forces of German, British and French socialism would wrest from the Hohenzollerns the power which had enabled them to initiate the war even though apparently their power might be increased by the victory they had won.

When it was pointed out that Ireland was geographically dependent upon England and that economically, as well as politically, an independent existence for the country was, for imperial reasons, impracticable. Connolly made it clear that he did not expect the British empire to survive the war.

In all their conversations Surgeon Tobin gained the impression that the prisoner is a man of high motives, of absolute sincerity and fixed opinions. He is widely read and his writings show advanced thought upon economic and social problems. He is an extreme socialist, with the exception that his writings show him to be very open-minded about the co-operative movement as a possible solution of labour troubles. When Surgeon Tobin said Good-bye to him last night, after the prisoner had been told that he was to be shot at 4 o'clock this morning, he said: 'Will you pray for me?', and Connolly replied that he would. 'And will you pray for the men who shoot you?' 'Yes', said Connolly, 'and for all other brave men who do their duty.'[27]

IX

The Convention

The news of Lloyd George's failure to settle the Irish question reached Plunkett in hospital. During the summer of 1916 he suffered from pruritis (itching) which, at that time, was often remedied by X-ray treatment. A Dublin radiologist treated him, then went on holiday; as the patient was not cured he consulted another Dublin radiologist, who wisely refused further treatment on the grounds that he was unaware of the strength of the dose already given. Soon afterwards, in London, Plunkett consulted a Harley Street dermatologist who brushed aside the idea that X-rays could do any harm and then gave him 'a powerful dose'. The result was a hideous X-ray burn with terrible pain which dogged him for the rest of his life. The internal injury required major surgery in Chicago a year later but, although the operation was a great success, it did not restore complete comfort. For the remainder of his life he had to take frequent doses of morphia to counteract the pain or to be able to sleep, for the burn had shattered his constitution and he was never able to do without the drug.[1] Plunkett consulted many doctors, few of whom he really trusted. A shining exception was T. G. Moorhead, professor of physic at TCD, who became his confidant and friend from 1912 onwards. Sadly Moorhead was in Egypt on war service at the time, for had he been on hand, since Plunkett generally listened to his advice, he would certainly have averted the disaster.

By December 1916 Asquith's indecisive wartime leadership was coming under increasing fire. A backbench revolt led by Carson and carried on by Bonar Law culminated in David Lloyd George becoming prime minister.

'How can I convey to the reader who does not know him', wrote J. M. Keynes,[2] 'any just impression of this extraordinary figure of our time, this syren, this goat-footed bard, this half human visitor to our age from the hag-ridden magic and enchanted woods of Celtic antiquity'.

As minister of munitions Lloyd George had made an outstanding contribution to wartime administration; he now turned his
attention to his fellow celts. Though a liberal he had never been
a crusader for home rule, his overriding aim was to win the war
and he was well aware of the barrier which Ireland posed to
American participation. To Carson he wrote dramatically:

In six months the war will be lost . . . The Irish American vote will go over
to the German side. They will break our blockade and force an
ignominious peace on us, unless something is done, even provisionally,
to satisfy America.[3]

Early in his premiership he showed an understandable
reluctance to re-open the Irish question but continued unrest, the
rise of Sinn Féin, pressure to extend conscription to Ireland and
America's entry to the war combined to influence him to try
again. By now he was aware, as Gladstone had been in 1885, that
the key to the problem on the British side was held by the tories.
On 10 May 1917 he wrote to the Irish party leaders with two
proposals: the first embodied home rule for the twenty-six
counties with a council of Ireland; and the second, as an after-
thought, contained the offer of a convention of Irishmen to
hammer out a solution. The constitution of the Union of South
Africa had been framed, a few years before, by a convention
representative of all interests and parties in that country, and
Curzon, in the House of Lords, indicated that the government
would give legislative effect to the convention's conclusions if
substantial agreement were reached on a form of Irish
government within the empire.

The convention idea had been around for some time. Plunkett
had written to Rolleston as early as May 1911 suggesting that
'something on Recess Committee lines ought to be done in this
constitutional crisis',[4] while to W. G. S. Adams, a week after the
publication of Lloyd George's letter, he expressed his unbounded optimism:

Things are moving rapidly in the Irish business and I have little doubt
that the convention alternative will be adopted and will succeed,
provided only they appoint a suitable chairman. I know from my Recess
Committee experience that anyone who really understands Ireland can
get the most antagonistic elements to combine once they consent to
meet.[5]

Adams, a recruit of Plunkett's as head of the statistics branch of
the DATI from 1905 to 1910, had become a fellow of Balliol

College, Oxford, and was now a member of Lloyd George's war-time cabinet secretariat. During his five years in Ireland he had come to admire Plunkett, to share his philosophy, and had forged close links with Irish politicians. He was now to be given special responsibility within the cabinet secretariat for the working of the convention; and became to a large extent responsible for deciding upon its format.

The nationalists rejected the first of Lloyd George's proposals out of hand, as Plunkett had reckoned, but Redmond, he thought, would accept the convention and, if there was sufficient representation from outside the ranks of the Redmondites, something might be achieved.

Plunkett at once perceived that the most difficult problem was to ensure sinn féin participation. The presence in English gaols of those arrested after the Rising was a barrier to any negotiation so he immediately petitioned Duke, the new chief secretary, for the release of the sinn féin leader, Eoin MacNeill. [6] With McNeill's brother James, a member of the Indian civil service, he agreed that a general amnesty granted at once was the only possible way forward; for, if Irishmen remained in gaol, a request for amnesty was bound to be made at the outset of the Convention; if it was deferred Sinn Féin would bolt, while if it was granted Ulster would withdraw. [7] Duke saw the force of this argument and on 15 June the prisoners were released.

Even though one obstacle had been removed, there remained another barrier to sinn féin involvement, for, along with the other political groups (nationalists, Ulster unionists, southern unionists) it was allocated five seats (there were seven representatives of labour). But the bulk of the membership was drawn from local authorities, and these, since the elections had taken place prior to the Rising, were dominated by the Parliamentary Party. Sinn Féin was sweeping the country with by-election successes in Roscommon, Longford, Clare and Kilkenny but its representation in the Convention would be in single figures while the nationalists would have nearer forty. This barrier proved insurmountable, however Edward MacLysaght and AE were nominated members who kept in touch with Sinn Féin. MacLysaght had regular contact with Eoin MacNeill, Bulmer Hobson and James Douglas but was disappointed and puzzled by de Valéra, [8] who regarded the proceedings as irrelevant (since the terms of reference precluded a republic) preferring to pin his faith in President Wilson's support for the rights of small nations. [9] Robert Barton, on the other hand, told

Erskine Childers, when he came to join the secretariat, that Sinn
Féin would accept an Irish parliament obtained by the
Convention and use it to achieve its aims, [10] while Tom Spring-
Rice (Monteagle's son) reported to Adams that moderate sinn
féiners would participate given amnesty for political prisoners
and a genuinely representative constitution. [11] Five places were
left open for Sinn Féin and, shortly after the Convention started
work in July, it was agreed that the problem could be overcome
by co-opting James Douglas, James MacNeill, Robert Barton and
Alice Stopford Green, but the co-option had to be unanimous
and Ulster turned it down.

AE explained to the Irish-American John Quinn that:

I accepted Lloyd George's nomination because I could not have it on my
conscience that I refused to help to bring about an Irish settlement if
there was a ghost of a chance. I think there is a ghost of a chance and I
will stick on it. [12]

Within the Convention he and MacLysaght sought full dominion
status, and AE warned the separatists in a series of *Irish Times*
articles in May that:

if they expect Ulster to throw its lot in with a self-governing Ireland they
must remain within the commonwealth of dominions which constitute
the empire, be prepared loyally, once Ireland has complete control over
its internal affairs, to accept the status of a dominion and the
responsibilities of that wider union. [13]

Drawing a parallel with the Boers in South Africa he argued that,
if Sinn Féin were not prepared to accept dominion status, the
alternative was the forceful coercion of Ulster 'and do they think
there is any possibility of that?'

Plunkett's ideas were set out in a speech which he made at
Dundalk in June, appearing later as a pamphlet entitled *A Defence
of the Convention*. The real stumbling blocks were Ulster and Sinn
Féin. Of the latter he wrote:

In some respects theirs is the most interesting political party in Irish
history. Most parties depend for their strength upon organisation, and
this is the weakness of Sinn Féin. Its strength is in its idealism, the central
idea being the concentration of all Irish thought and action upon
exclusively Irish service. That idea, in some of its implications, leads,
unhappily, to extreme courses, but none will question the nobility of an
aspiration for which many fine young Irishmen have laid down their
lives. [14]

Sinn Féin, more a movement than a political party, embraced a wide spectrum of opinion opposed to British rule. It must determine its role more precisely, felt Plunkett, and this could only be done in face to face encounter, under conditions favourable to frank discussion, with every section of the community to which, in common with the other groups, it wished to commend its policy. But Ulster unionists had their own version of sinn féin for they wished to be left to themselves alone; however they rightly claimed to their credit certain solid achievements, the result of certain sterling qualities:

There is not a thinking Irishman that admits the achievements and regards the qualities as absolutely indispensable to any prosperous and progressive Ireland in the future. But of all the misunderstandings which curse our unhappy country, the worst is the conviction among these Ulstermen that we of the south and west bear them no good will, and that we so little understand their industrial and commercial activities, that, even with the best intentions in the world, we should inevitably embark upon schemes of legislation and practise methods of administration fatal to their interests. Personally, I think we have neglected the duty of trying to allay — much we have done has tended to confirm these fears. [15]

He had put forward his plan for the temporary inclusion of Ulster when the crisis had been at its height. It was auspicious, Plunkett felt, that nationalist Ireland had appeared to accept this compromise, which led him to believe that the Ulster unionists would be astonished at their reception in the Convention:

There they will find an honest, unanimous desire not to coerce but to win them. All the alternative schemes for the future government of Ireland will be discussed in turn, and discussed in their severely practical, as well as their sentimental, aspects. Unless I am greatly mistaken, partition, in the last analysis, may prove to be administratively and financially disastrous to the north-east, as it is for other reasons to the rest of Ireland. [16]

This speech, delivered before Plunkett had been nominated to the Convention, betrayed an unfounded optimism — stemming from his experience of the Recess Committee — that co-operation on practical problems would, in the Convention, overcome the deepest ideological division. But this optimism had already been somewhat dampened by reaction in Ulster. Adam Duffin, the Belfast stockbroker who moved in inner unionist circles, wrote in June suggesting that 'Ulster will be driven back upon the unwelcome alternative of partition', 'our people's role will be to say nothing', their reaction would be negative, 'show us your programme and we shall proceed to demolish it'. He confirmed Plunkett's suspicion of his reputation in Belfast, 'You are, you know, looked upon as a very dangerous and insidious personality and anyone foregathering with you would be ''suspect'' '.[17] Plunkett then attempted to penetrate Carson's mind without success, but James Craig his right hand man, in a statesmanlike address to the orangemen on 12 July, indicated that Ulster would, without sacrifice of principle, assist the government in its search for a settlement by consent, adding that this would be a proper reward for the Ulster regiments on their return from the battlefront.[18]

The Parliamentary Party clutched at the straw of the Convention in a final desperate attempt to regain the prestige which it was rapidly losing to Sinn Féin. The 1914 home rule act (suspended though on the statute book) was unlikely to prove the final solution to the Irish problem. Southern unionists led by Lord Midleton had arrived at the conclusion that some form of home rule was by now inevitable. The Rising and its aftermath had exposed the ineptitude of the administration. If Ulster accepted partition effectively deserting them, could this government offer any worthwhile guarantees of security? Moreover Redmond's support for the Allies had touched a chord in every southern unionist heart and the bellicose nature of Sinn Féin had tended to push them closer to Redmond indicating that the time was ripe for a more positive attitude towards constitutional nationalism. Even so opinion was divided in their governing body, the Irish Unionist Alliance (IUA), as to the wisdom of participation, for that body's raison d'etre had been the maintenance of the Union. Once the decision had been taken, Midleton and his followers embarked on a course which was not approved of by the IUA, leading eventually to a split in the ranks of southern unionism.

The Ulster unionists took longer to make up their minds, many of their stalwarts taking the line that they should have nothing to do with the Convention. But Carson, under strong pressure from Lloyd George, argued that a home rule bill which included Ulster was on the statute book thus it was incumbent on the Ulstermen to obtain modifications, and to secure a position compatible with the principles for which they stood. The Ulster Unionist Council elected an advisory committee which contained J. M. Andrews (later prime minister of Northern Ireland and son of Thomas

Andrews), Sir James Stronge (orange grand master) and Hugh de F. Montgomery (a prominent northern member of the IAOS). The delegation was led by H. T. Barrie (an uncompromising Scot with a successful grain business in Co. Derry) and included Lord Londonderry and Pollock (later Northern Ireland's minister of finance). The Ulster delegates were not plenipotentiaries and every decision which they took had to be referred back to the advisory committee. Redmond had hoped that Lord Pirrie, the liberal and moderate home ruler responsible for building up the great Belfast shipyard of Harland and Wolff, would be among the nominees. But Lloyd George, probably unwilling to soften the uncompromising face of Ulster unionism, indicated that he could not be spared from his task of helping the government with the vital shipping problem. Of the 95 members who accepted the prime minister's invitation, there were 52 nationalists (including MacLysaght and AE), 24 Ulster unionists, 9 southern unionists, 6 labour, 2 liberals besides Plunkett and Mahaffy (provost of Trinity College where the Convention was held) who remained unattatched.

William O'Brien, the influential independent nationalist who had refused the prime minister's invitation, wrote to say that he would reconsider his abstention if a suggestion, which Plunkett had made in his Dundalk speech, that the decision of the Convention be tested in an Irish referendum, be made official. [19] The next day O'Brien's letter appeared in the press and Plunkett wrote to Adams to obtain cabinet approval. Lloyd George had promised government action on agreement by a 'substantial majority', the phrase was vague, Lloyd George was flexible and O'Brien was keen to pin him down. But the prime minister was too clever a politician to narrow his options, his main aim being to keep the Convention going and to persuade America that something was being done, and, on 3 July Adams reported from Downing Street that Ulster had turned the proposal down. [20]

Just as the Convention was about to commence its deliberations two events occurred which made the task of reaching agreement much more difficult. Carson (who like Dillon had decided not to participate) joined the war cabinet, and de Valéra was elected for the constituency of East Clare. Major Willie Redmond MP, the nationalist leader's brother, had died from wounds received in the attack on the Messines Ridge on 7 June. The resulting by-election resulted in a stunning victory for Sinn Féin; de Valéra 'the bravest and most determined of the rebels' polling two and a half times the nationalist vote. He had gone forward as an extreme republican advocating total separation. 'I wonder whether this will open the eyes of the English government ?' wrote Plunkett adding that the great majority of the clergy supported him in spite of an episcopal warning to leave politics alone.[21]

The first business on 25 July was the election of a chairman. The party leaders were ruled out as too obviously partisan and James Campbell, Irish attorney general, and Dunraven (both southern unionists) were among those under consideration, but the split between north and south was permeating the ranks of unionism and Ulster manoeuvred to ensure that Campbell's name would not go forward. In fact suspicions of southern intentions were such that it was unlikely that a southern unionist would be acceptable. Three months later things had reached such a pitch that Adam Duffin wrote of his southern colleagues to his wife:

They want to capitulate and make terms with the enemy lest a worse thing befall them. They are a cowardly crew and stupid to boot. We shall do all we can to stiffen them and help them in our ranks and they may be driven to reconsider their position.[22]

When the Convention sat for the first time in the Regent House of Trinity College, a committee of ten was appointed to select a chairman. Midleton proposed Hopwood* and got majority support for his proposal but AE argued vociferously for Plunkett indicating that if the committee decided otherwise he would re-open the debate in plenary session. Plunkett was not opposed by the Ulster unionists, his support for Redmond's war efforts had made up the differences between them, and Redmond, who initially had supported Hopwood, appealed to Midleton to withdraw his proposal. In the interests of peace he did so, although, as he wrote later, the Convention had occasion to rue his reversal.[23] On one point the Ulstermen were insistent, if T. P. Gill were appointed to the secretariat they would instantly withdraw.[24] Gill had already importuned Plunkett and Adams on the grounds that his work for the Recess Committee made him an essential ingredient to the Convention's success. After his gyrations at the DATI there was no likelihood that Plunkett would have accepted this suggestion, but there were times when his political skill might have benefitted the chairman. The Ulstermen did let one other Plunkett nominee slip thorugh the

---

*Sir Francis Hopwood (later Lord Southborough) who had helped to create the Union of South Africa and had been nominated to the Convention.

net, perhaps on account of his rank and distinguished service in the Royal Naval Auxiliary Service, for Erskine Childers, now a lieutenant commander and holder of the Distinguished Service Cross was granted leave from his duties to join the secretariat. It was common knowledge that Childers had run guns into Howth for the Volunteers three years previously and therefore somewhat surprising that he was not vetoed by the unionists. Even more surprising was the fact that another gun runner, Diarmuid Coffey,[25] held a minor position on the secretariat, however Coffey was soon eliminated by orange pressure for deliberately avoiding the loyal toast.[26]

Having unanimously agreed to the selection of Plunkett as chairman and Hopwood as secretary, the Convention promptly adjourned for two weeks. An ominous note, indicating the depth of southern feeling, was struck after the opening session. As John Redmond and Hopwood walked out of the front gate of Trinity College, two local nationalists standing between the lodge and the outer railings raised their hats, calling to the onlookers for cheers for the Irish leader. The crowd responded with boohs and groans, interspersed with cries of 'Sinn Féin', 'East Clare' and 'up de Valéra'.[27]

Plunkett had discussions with Lloyd George, the king and Carson during a visit to London before the main business began. On 15 August he had to approach Byrne, the under-secretary for Ireland, who, he was horrified to learn, was trying to arrest de Valéra.[28] If this happened there would be defections on the nationalist side and he was able to persuade the under-secretary not to molest de Valéra for the immediate future. A month later sinn féiner Thomas Ashe died after forcible feeding while on hunger strike in Mountjoy Prison. Plunkett intervened with Duke demanding immediate recognition of the incarcerated sinn féiners as political prisoners.[29]

The next question to be decided was that of procedure so that constitutional possibilities could be discussed without raising the spectre of partition. As Plunkett saw it, Ulster was the bogey to be overcome and a settlement was possible only if the Ulster case, as it was currently presented, was shown to rest upon a mistaken impression of how the northern province would be treated under home rule. But if Ulster remained unconvinced of the need to change its attitude, the remaining members of the Convention could be swung behind a report embodying the best features of home rule for the whole island within the empire:

I kept up my sleeve my trump card with the arrogant Ulstermen. At the proper time I may have to tell them that the Convention will report without asking their leave. They seem to assume that they alone count![30]

This final sentiment was based on pledges which Lloyd George gave to Carson which were known to Plunkett by early November, for he wrote to Lord Morley:

the whole difficulty is with the Ulstermen, to whom the coalition government in order to keep Carson and Bonar Law in good temper have given an absolute guarantee that, under no circumstances shall they be coerced.[31]

Just at that time, Ulster was enduring one of her periodic spells of unpopularity in Britain. The Tory Party had now nothing to gain from a non-possumus attitude which was interpreted as hampering the war effort in Ireland and America. The press, even the unionist press, was generally unsympathetic, emphasising the need to conciliate opinion in America and the dominions, while large sections of the media attacked the Ulster unionists' negative attitude as weakening the allied cause. The *Observer* wrote that 'the former unyielding exclusionist position of Ulster ... has become absolutely untenable', while the *Liverpool Courier*, hitherto a strong supporter of the orangemen, urged them to 'offer the government a basis for practical legislation ... in the noblest spirit of patriotism'.[32] In fact, as Ulster unionists noted with pained disgust, it was, by 1918, possible to depict Ulster as self-centred, not to say disloyal. As one of their number wrote:

'Noble-hearted Ulster' which was told only a couple of years ago that it held the key of the situation and was urged to resist to the last ditch, is then told by the same leaders that after all it takes but a narrow and selfish view of the question and instead of standing fast to save the empire, it must incontinently surrender to save the party. And the reason assigned in proof of the proposition that what was reasonable in 1916 is unreasonable in 1918 is even more quaint than the volte-face itself. It is that we are at a crisis in the war and that Ulster must now embrace home rule because the empire is in danger.[33]

His soundings indicated to Plunkett that if dominion home rule emerged as a solution, Sinn Féin would seize its chance to enter the political arena. The Convention did, in fact, succeed in narrowing Ulster's objections to home rule down to what he had always felt to be the essential economic one — that a home rule rule government in Dublin dominated by agricultural interests would be inimical to industrial and commercial Ulster. When the breakdown loomed over the question of fiscal autonomy or fiscal union, he believed that the onus lay on Ulster to prove the advantages of the latter for the whole of Ireland.

Even before he had been appointed chairman, Plunkett had sounded out Molly Childers[34] on Erskine's whereabouts so that he could be appointed to the secretariat which was to play a major role in his plan. Its main task was to supply constitutional and economic information for the draft schemes to be submitted to the Convention. Childers was joined by Diarmuid Coffey, Walter Callan, a lawyer, Cruise O'Brien (who had worked for Plunkett in various capacities) and Shan Bullock, the Ulster writer.

Finally, as if he had not already got enough on his plate, Plunkett decided to write a confidential report of the proceedings (which were held in camera) for the king. The report was compiled late at night or in the early morning, often after a tiring day at Convention business but shows little of the strain which its author must have been feeling. It is lively, candid and stylishly written and, in its comments on men and movements in Ireland, is pure Plunkett. No attempt was made to disguise the chairman's reaction to the obdurate Ulstermen or his efforts, first to bring them around, and then, when that failed, to isolate them. The document, which must have intrigued its readers, was secret only in name for he circulated copies to a select list including President Wilson, Lawrence Lowell, W. G. S. Adams, F. S. Oliver, John Dillon, Lennox Robinson and Bernard Shaw (who wrote in March 1918, 'The story becomes more thrilling as it draws to a end. I sometimes wonder if it will not be the only enduring achievement of the conference').[35] Too late he realised that Carson was likely to get his hands on a copy for, to Duke, he admitted his fears that Ulster would learn of his blow-by-blow account of proceedings with obvious consequences for the outcome.[36]

The presentation stage of the Convention consisted of wide ranging discussions on seven plans which had been submitted for the better government of Ireland. This lasted for two months and included sessions in Belfast and Cork. Redmond made a brilliant and conciliatory speech in Belfast, but in Cork he had to be spirited away from sinn féin demonstrators under a police escort. In Belfast, Sir William Whitla, a methodist, advocated inter-denominational education. Dr. Harty, the archbishop of Cashel, replied that the right to educate its own children was a fundamental principle of the Roman Catholic Church which it conceded to other denominations; and further consideration of this issue was avoided in the face of uncompromising clericalism.

The discussion had continued for two months (far too long in Midleton's opinion)[37] when a subcommittee of nine was set up to commence negotiation. Midleton and Barrie combined to ensure that Hopwood rather than Plunkett be made chairman. Considerable progress was made with major nationalist concessions on the composition of a bicameral parliament; not only were the unionists granted representation considerably larger than their numerical proportion, but Irish seats were retained at Westminster. The committee however reached deadlock on finance, the issue being, quite simply, fiscal union versus fiscal autonomy. The autonomists were led by Dr. Patrick O'Donnell, Bishop of Raphoe, supported by William Martin Murphy (influential owner of the *Irish Independent* who had led the Dublin employers in the lockout of 1913), AE, and Joe Devlin, the Belfast nationalist MP; the unionists on the committee argued the converse case, while Redmond was inclined to moderation. At this stage Plunkett intervened in an original but somewhat pedantic manner, by presenting the committee members with an examination paper designed to elucidate 'the precise cause of their inability to subordinate their differences of economic faith to the supreme need of their distracted country',[38] together with a covering letter which suggested that for the nationalists fiscal autonomy was too much a symbol of political autonomy while for the unionists fiscal union was too much a symbol of political union. The paper which consisted of ten questions, five to be answered by the nationalists and five by the unionists, had been prepared by A. C. Pigou, the Cambridge economist. The nationalist answer, that Irish development would be stultified if England controlled the purse strings was put so persuasively that Plunkett asked that it be transmitted direct to the unionists. Unfortunately, before doing so, a political postscript was added without the chairman's knowledge equating nationality to fiscal autonomy. This hardly helped matters and the Ulster unionist answer to the Plunkett-Pigou examination came in the form of a letter which stated bluntly that the problem was not one of detail but of principle, and a principle which they were unlikely to concede.

Up to this point the Ulster unionists had made no constructive suggestions whatever, remaining content to play their cards close to their chest and to criticise the proposals submitted by others. Londonderry made a brave attempt to break the deadlock by tabling a federal scheme, but the older Ulster heads got together and pressured him into withdrawal. Then Midleton intervened with compromise proposals that the Irish parliament should control taxation and excise duties, but that customs should be reserved for Westminster.

By Christmas it was clear to even the most optimistic of chairmen that a unanimous report was an unlikely outcome. Plunkett himself had been ill and had had to have his bladder cauterised three times in late December. Ulster was maintaining a solid front while pressure from Sinn Féin increased the likelihood of a split in nationalist ranks. Plunkett now aimed at agreement between the southern unionists and nationalists, if this could be achieved an entirely new situation would be brought about, for up to that time 3/4 of the people wanted self-government and 1/4 were for the Union, while this would mean 4/5 of the population in favour of home rule. The remaining 1/5 — the recalcitrant Ulstermen — would face increasing pressure at home and abroad until their position became untenable and they had to deal.

There remained in the minds of nationalists the idea of a pledge given by Lloyd George to Carson which ruled out the coercion of Ulster. On 7 March 1917 he had assured the House of Commons that no attempt would be made to force the population of north-eastern Ireland to live under a government with which it was not in sympathy.[39] But the idea persisted that in private he had been even more explicit, and on 11 January 1918 Duke admitted to Plunkett that 'things had happened which make it more difficult to put pressure on Ulster,'[40] which Plunkett interpreted to mean that Carson was supreme in the cabinet. But, depending on the circumstances, Lloyd George was able to handle Carson. He had removed him swiftly and efficiently from the admiralty when Carson had proved a failure as a wartime administrator, and later Carson resigned from the war cabinet.

Pressure on the Ulster unionists to compromise with their fellow Irishmen was steadily increasing. In January, Lloyd George wrote to Bonar Law, leader of the Tory Party in the House of Commons:

I take a very serious view of the Irish situation. If the southern unionists and nationalists agree, as they are likely to, the position of any government that refuses to carry out the compact will be an impossible one ... everyone in Great Britain and throughout the world — notably in America — would say that we were sacrificing the interests of the war to that of a small political section. In fact they would say we were doing it merely because Carson was in the government. The Irish in America would be more rampageous than ever and Wilson's position ... would

become untenable. The Irish are now paralysing the war activities of
America . . . This is the opportunity for Ulster to show that it places the
empire above everything, and if the little protestant communities of the
south, isolated in a turbulent sea of sinn féinism and popery, can trust
their lives and property to Midleton's scheme, surely the powerful
communities of the north might take that risk for the sake of the empire
in danger. If America goes wrong we are lost. I wish Ulster would realise
what that means. I am afraid they don't. Beg Barrie . . . to lift his province
to the high level of this opportunity.[41]

Indeed, in that very month, when accord, within the Convention, between the nationalist group and the southern unionists
appeared to be on the cards, the Ulster unionists, behind the
scenes, seem to have been considering some form of
compromise. The Allies, faced with a major German offensive on
the western front, needed the fullest backing from both Ireland
and the United States, and Ulster was perceived as an obstacle to
both. On 28 January Adams, the member of Lloyd George's
secretariat responsible for the Convention, saw their leader
Barrie who suggested the formation of an Ulster committee with
full powers of initiative in an Irish parliament plus the location of
some government departments in Belfast. He then put Barrie's
proposals to Carson who said he would try to deal with Ulster's
non possumus attitude, indicating that he had been considering
a bicameral Irish parliament with periodic joint sittings, but had
rejected the idea in favour of F. S. Oliver's federation of the
British Isles.[42] A speech of Carson's, made after proceedings
terminated, gives a good indication of the difficulties to be faced
by the Ulster delegation if agreement between nationalists and
southern unionists had materialised.

He might say that the Irish Convention gave him more trouble than anything with which he had to do in connection with the whole home rule
question, and it drove him out of the cabinet in the middle of the war.
Never was Ulster in a more dangerous position than when the Convention was drawing to a close, and for this reason: the southern unionists
lost their courage. They gave the case away, I do not believe that they
represented anybody but themselves. They said we were traitors,
whereas, as a matter of fact it was they, under the leadership of Lord
Midleton, who were prepared to say: 'If we go down, Ulster must come
down too'.[43]

The discussion of Midleton's compromise proposals took place
in early January. His scheme was opposed by the bishop of
Raphoe, W. M. Murphy, AE and MacLysaght but apart from

these delegates and the Ulster unionists it seemed to have achieved wide acceptance. Lord MacDonnell (formerly the undersecretary to George Wyndham) argued that he favoured fiscal autonomy but, appreciating that 'the southern unionists were for appeasement', said he was supporting Midleton.[44] Henry Whitely, representing the Belfast and District Trades Council, remarked that if Ulster working men could hear the debates in the Convention, they would see that the danger to their interests from an Irish parliament was wholly illusory.[45]

Barrie, for the Ulster unionists, replied that he had laid Midleton's scheme before his advisory committee and it had been rejected. The northern unionists had come to the Convention to find a compromise between the home rule act of 1914 and the partition proposals of 1916. There was no case on record, he said, in which customs and excise had been ceded to a local parliament. It would only prove a barrier to proper federalism. 'Once they were satisfied that it was wise and in the interests of the empire that further powers should be given to an Irish parliament, he believed that Ulstermen would be willing to join in securing a larger amount of elbow room for a parliament that had proved itself worthy of trust and confidence'.[46] Redmond, in his best vein, emphasized the sacrifices for the sake of agreement made by his own party, by the southern unionists and by labour. Then he attacked the Ulster delegates as pledge-bound to consult an outside body and for refusing 'to give an inch'. (Anderson, lord mayor of Londonderry, replied to this charge, pointing out that it was of little use moving without being sure of the position of one's supporters).[47] Surely this attitude, asked Redmond, which was so unworthy of Ulster did not represent its last word? For himself, his only remaining ambition, having brought the Convention to a successful conclusion, was to serve under the first unionist prime minister of Ireland. Then he tabled an amendment to Midleton's motion asking the Convention to agree to Midleton's proposals provided that they were adopted by the government as a settlement of the Irish question and legislative effect given to them forthwith. The amendment, drafted by a old parliamentary hand, was designed, to attract the hesitant nationalists by throwing responsibility for making a success of the Convention back on the government.[48]

The atmosphere had never been more cordial, a high water mark had been reached, it was essential to take it on the flood. But the chairman failed to realise his opportunity of obtaining maximum agreement along Midleton-Redmond lines, isolating the Ulster unionists and a few nationalist diehards (who would, in all probability, have come to heel before the decision point was reached). For ten days (much against Hopwood's better judgement according to Midleton),[49] the Convention dropped its discussion of constitutional issues and turned away to the problem of land purchase. By the time the constitutional question was reopened (though, in the meantime, an excellent system of land purchase had been agreed), the dissident (progressive) nationalists had regrouped, under Childers' influence, and Ulster's policy of sitting tight and saying nothing had been justified. Plunkett, who was always prepared to be hard on himself, was, perhaps, not hard enough on others. At that moment, on the constitutional issue, the Convention needed to be hard driven, instead it was allowed to wander down the pleasantly uncontentious by-ways of land purchase. Plunkett certainly misjudged Carson, who, he believed for some time after would be reasonable. Further, he was influenced by the proceedings of the Recess Committee which, however, had found a basis for agreement (on the need for a department of agriculture for Ireland) at its inception. Here, the opportunity for maximum agreement, if it ever came, was unlikely to occur again.

From that moment the fissiparous tendencies of Irish politics seemed to re-assert themselves and, although the chairman did not feel so at the time, the Convention went into a swift decline. Noble attempts to stem the rot were made by Plunkett himself, Midleton, Redmond, his successor as leader of the moderate nationalists Stephen Gwynn, and by Lloyd George himself. On 15 January Redmond, in failing health and out of touch, discovered, just as the Convention was about to go into session, that he had been deserted by a large group of nationalists, (including Devlin and three of the four catholic bishops), and refused to move his amendment. Tragically, too, the bishop of Ross, who was an economist and a keen supporter of the compromise, was too ill to attend the crucial session. Plunkett records that it was the worst shock of his political life. It was the signal that extremists had captured the nationalist delegation. All hope of isolating Ulster, and of utilising world opinion to bring about a settlement was gone.

By the beginning of February Carson had resigned from the war cabinet and MacLysaght and AE from the Convention. Carson was a great advocate and an outstanding defender of the status quo, but he was a failure as an administrator or as a constructive politician. Plunkett in a burst of incurable optimism (or it might more accurately be described as self-deception) wrote that his design was to leave himself unfettered in any action he might take on the forthcoming Irish legislation 'and many believed that he would use his powerful influence to bring about an Irish settlement'.[50] In fact Carson resigned because of disagreements with Lloyd George over the handling of the war and showed no interest in bringing matters to what Plunkett would have regarded as a satisfactory conclusion. MacLysaght and AE resigned both feeling that the Convention had lost touch with reality and that no formula which it might produce would now satisfy nationalist Ireland.

AE tendered his resignation on 1 February.[51] Plunkett, who was in London, replied asking him to postpone his decision[52] and, on 3 February, AE wrote confirming his intention to resign:

I have come to the conclusion that the Convention, constituted as it is, is simply a obstacle to an Irish settlement, and that the only thing to do is to let the new forces of nationalism manifest themselves in their full strength . . . The sinn féiners were right in their intuitions from the first. If I had followed my intuitions I would have remained away also. A man must either be a Irishman or an Englishman in this matter. I am Irish![53]

Plunkett saw Lloyd George and Bonar Law seeking pressure on Ulster to obtain agreement. He tried, also unsuccessfully, to get the southern unionists to change their line and to concede customs to the Irish parliament. Then he wrote to the prime minister suggesting that the government should settle for a report signed by three quarters of the members; what was needed, he said, was a declaration that the government would immediately set up an Irish parliament along the lines of the majority report. The customs problem could be postponed and eventually decided by a joint commission at the end of the war. A delegation of leaders of the various groups visited the prime minister all returning with different versions of what he was supposed to have said. On 25 February Lloyd George wrote to Plunkett and his letter was read to the Convention on the following day. He proposed the establishment of a single Irish legislature (leaving open the idea of a federation) with safeguards for Ulster and the southern unionists; foreign and military powers were to be reserved for Westminster as were customs and excise during the war and for two years after; the parliament was to contain an Ulster committee with power to deal with legislation affecting Ulster and to sit alternatively in Belfast and Dublin. Finally the department of trade was to be headquartered in Belfast and the report on land purchase would be given immediate legislative effect if the Convention were successful. Ulster was asked her attitude to these proposals and Barrie promptly replied that when the Convention had decided the fiscal issue the Ulster delegation might give its opinions. In Plunkett's view the letter represented 'the most generous concessions ever made by a British government to the wishes of the majority of the Irish people ... an Irish parliament is the obvious first essential of an Irish settlement, and should be taken upon any terms which do not mortgage the future'.[54]

On 6 March the ailing Redmond died and winding up of proceedings was postponed for a further week. Plunkett guessed that, even if he had lived, he would have been unable to unite the nationalists as he could not have convinced the progressives of the bona fides of the government. 'The Irish', he wrote, 'cannot be blamed for a deeply rooted conviction that pressure from Ireland is needed to supplement the efforts of her parliamentary representatives'.[55] That pressure was increasingly being exerted for, a few days before this, as he reported to the king, Sinn Féin had ordered a consignment of pigs for export to Britain to be turned back and slaughtered at the Dublin abattoir, the appropriate price having been paid to the vendor.[56]

Eventually Ulster showed its hand and presented a scheme for what might be termed partition and direct rule. It was a 'crude proposal', excluding the whole province of Ulster from the authority of the Irish parliament and placing it under a secretary of state, who was to administer it through such officers and departments as might be instituted by orders in council. Shortly afterwards, Dillon, who had suceeded Redmond as leader of the Nationalist Party, signalled a change in direction, following the progressive line in an attempt to regain the ground already lost to Sinn Féin.

A report along the lines of the prime minister's offer, somewhat reshaped in a series of proposals by Lord MacDonnell, was approved by 44 votes to 29. The majority consisted of the southern unionists and the moderate nationalists led by Gwynn, the minority consisting in the unlikely combination of northern unionists and extreme (or progressive) nationalists led by Devlin and O'Donnell. The latter group submitted a minority report 'of great ability and moderation' drafted by Childers, based on ideas which he had developed (with Plunkett's help) in *The Framework of Home Rule*. The chairman, who by now was utterly exhausted and on the verge of collapse, bore no rancour towards the

Above left: Lady Fingall, an undated photograph published in her autobiography *Seventy Years Young* (1937). Above right: Colonel E. M. House in C. C. Seymour (ed.) *The Intimate Papers of Colonel House* (1926). Below left: Lennox Robinson, 1918, by Dermod O'Brien (UM). Below right: H. F. (Gerald) Heard, Laguna Beach, 1952. Courtesy the photographer, Jay Michael Barrie, and The Vanguard Press, Inc.

Above left: Michael Davitt, by Sir William Orpen (HLMG). Above right: T. P. Gill, 1898, by Sarah Purser (NGI). Below left: Robert Barton, a portrait by Sir John Lavery (HLMG). Below right: a photograph of Erskine Childers, c. 1920. Collection: Colin Smythe.

Above left: Bishop Berkeley, by James Latham. Courtesy Trinity College, Dublin. Above right: W. E. H. Lecky, 1878, by G. F. Watts, courtesy the National Portrait Gallery. Below left: Edward Dowden, by John B. Yeats (HLMG). Below right: Douglas Hyde, 1906, by John B. Yeats (NGI).

Above left: W. B. Yeats, 1898; above right: Standish O'Grady, 1904; below left: George Moore, 1905; below right: Lady Gregory, 1903. Four portraits by John Butler Yeats (NGI).

progressives who had effectively torpedoed his Convention plan:

I know business men who recognise the essential importance to Ireland of the closest trade relations with Britain, and yet feel that this end will be best attained by giving Ireland, in the first instance, a free hand in negotiating these relations. I confess I have a great deal of sympathy with the main lines of the progressive policy ... To my mind the end which the Convention should have set before it, to which all other ends should have been subsidiary, was an united Ireland.[57]

At lunchtime on Monday 8 April the Convention wound up and the chairman, who (with the secretariat) had spent the whole of the weekend finalising the report, crossed to London by night mail with the precious document. Redmond's defection had been one great shock, the next day Plunkett received another. Having spent the morning with Adams at 10 Downing Street handing over his report, he spent the afternoon at the House of Commons listening to Lloyd George introduce a military service bill which extended conscription to Ireland. 'I was witness', he wrote, 'of one of those perverse misunderstandings which ever darken the pages of Anglo-Irish history'.[58] The prime minister promised in the course of his speech, to introduce legislation based on the report but this was clearly a political feint. The main impetus to the rise of Sinn Féin had been the threat of conscription and the sinn féin taunt which brooded darkly over the whole Convention — that it was merely another British ruse to keep Ireland (and America) quiet — now seemed justified. Plunkett wrote a memo to Lloyd George asking him to appeal to Ireland to provide her quota of men for the final crisis of the war on a voluntary basis. The Parliamentary Party withdrew sadly from Westminster to join Sinn Féin in the struggle against conscription. Plunkett, throwing caution to the winds, wrote a strong letter to the press denouncing government policy[59] and, having done so, he collapsed with bronchial-pneumonia.

In his confidential report for the king, which was completed sometime later, he fired a parting shot at

the most mischievous formula of Anglo-Irish politics: 'Ulster must not be coerced'. The amazing thing about this is that it is absolutely without foundation in fact; it is a figment of the Ulster conscience. The people of Ireland outside the north-east corner, loathe coercion and have no wish to have it applied — still less to apply it — to the one community in Ireland which, for generations, has not suffered coercion. But we are told that all this is beside the point — that as Ulster will not come into a all-

Ireland settlement voluntarily and must not be coerced, there can be no settlement. The answer is simple. Ulster cannot and ought not to be coerced physically; moral coercion can and ought to be applied. All the free peoples of the world are today demanding the universal application of the principle of self-determination. How long can the British government, with its clear mandate to ensure the satisfaction of that demand throughout the civilised world, refrain from impressing upon north-east Ulster the moral obligation to accept it?[60]

X

Dominion Status

The Convention's deliberations, under Plunkett's idiosyncratic direction, stretched from July 1917 to April 1918, ensuring that, for a critical nine months of the war, the Irish question remained off the centre of the stage. Lloyd George's decision to impose conscription on Ireland, which, to Plunkett, was 'as devoid of military advantage as it was fraught with political disaster',[1] exposed the prime minister's real intentions. The Convention, as far as he was concerned, had proved a useful delaying tactic and, having made up his mind on partition, he simply disregarded the constructive side of its report.

For the first time since the death of Parnell the whole of nationalist Ireland had found a rallying point. The parliamentarians returned ruefully to Ireland to join with Sinn Féin in the campaign against conscription; from that moment their fate was sealed and the party's extinction in the forthcoming election became inevitable. Total nationalist opposition to conscription marked the real rejection of British administration in Ireland and the de facto ending of the Union between the two countries. Extremism was set to take over, the day of the moderates was past, for the next four years they were to exert little influence upon Irish affairs.

Lord Midleton's valiant effort to reach a compromise in the Convention had led to a split in southern unionism. The diehards, in March, issued a 'call to unionists',[2] supported by Carson, urging a return to a rigid line on the Union, which, they felt, had been abandoned by the Midletonites. This spurred Plunkett into print, denouncing the government's policy of conscription now, with the promise of home rule later; calling on them to implement the majority report. He expanded on this theme in three articles which were published in the press in July and later as a pamphlet entitled *Home Rule and Conscription*. The government had offered four reasons for postponing home rule:

177

a newly discovered German plot; a bitter hatred of England expressing itself in disloyalty and treason; the hostility of the Catholic Church, its hierarchy sanctioning and approving resistance to the law of the land; and the failure of the Convention. Plunkett dealt with each one of these in turn. While admitting that the revolutionaries had had some contact with Germany he believed that 'no Irishman whose opinion counts in Ireland would run the risk of Prussian rule (good as a year of it might be for some of us) on the chance of it bringing him his particular brand of home rule'. Hatred of Britain was a much more potent factor in the situation, aggravated by contempt for British statesmanship and utter distrust of British promises. Increased prosperity had done nothing to dampen the fires of nationalism, leading to the conclusion that the problem was political and amenable only to a political solution. The apparent bad faith of the government in withholding the concession of home rule was responsible for the recrudescence of an historic hatred which, by 1914, had almost disappeared. In considering the action of the Catholic Church in resisting conscription two facts had to be taken into account. Firstly, the bishops had not led their flocks on this occasion; the people had called on them to give moral sanction to the resistance they proposed to offer to the government's proposal. Secondly, the bishops believed (and Plunkett backed up their judgement) that if they had held aloof the country would have been plunged into disorder and bloodshed. The government claimed that the Convention had been a failure, yet a larger measure of agreement had been reached upon the principles and details of self-government than had ever before been attained.

He proposed that a bill be introduced in parliament as a war measure based on the report of the Convention. One of the Irish leaders should be invited by the king to form a temporary cabinet along coalition lines, its chief function being to set up an Irish parliament at the earliest possible date and to assist the military authorities in obtaining voluntary enlistment; but 'before that appeal can be made to Irishmen they must be given the freedom for which they are asked to fight'. Prior to this, the temporary cabinet should be responsible to Westminster or the Convention. The middle party formed during the Convention by the southern unionists and moderate nationalists was to be revived and formally constituted. He reiterated his plan for temporary inclusion of Ulster arguing that if her attitude did not change, the British people would have to decide whether or not to acquiesce in this continued challenge to the empire, concluding optimistically that, once the opinion of world democracy was expressed, there would be no need to coerce Ulster or any other part of Ireland. The nationalists would have to agree to the postponement of a decision on the fiscal question until the end of the war; indeed, in the Convention they had already agreed to imperial control of Irish defence, a contribution to the imperial exchequer, and Irish representation at Westminster. The middle party would have the task of persuading nationalists to accept these temporary limitations on the powers of the Irish parliament. 'Give us self-government now that you may save your honour and we our self-respect'. [3]

The Parliamentary Party was now on its last legs and about to be superseded by Sinn Féin. Plunkett had always remained critical of southern nationalism's failure to appreciate the depth of protestant Ulster feeling. The war had imposed further barriers. Nationalist failure to salute Ulster's sacrifice in the Battle of the Somme reflected this lack of comprehension. Attending a mass for Irish soldiers killed in the war, he was horrified to learn that the catholic archbishop of Dublin had refused to allow it be held in any church under his jurisdiction for fear of offending Sinn Féin. [4] AE's moving tribute 'To the Memory of Some I Knew who are Dead and who Loved Ireland' [5] was the only utterance of the time to mourn the deaths both of those who fell in the Easter Rising, and on the Western Front.

Three alternatives presented themselves to Plunkett as Anglo-Irish relationships deteriorated rapidly in mid-1918. He could eschew politics altogether; maintain a low profile but offer tacit support to the moderate wing of Sinn Féin; or attempt to mould moderate opinion into a non-party pressure group which would point a middle way and act as mediator to assist a settlement. One year earlier he had recorded in his diary, 'Fr. Finlay very much annoyed at my touching the Convention. He thinks the co-operative movement the only thing worth fighting for in Ireland at present'. [6] There is little doubt that this was the advice tendered to him by his closest friends, but, all his life Plunkett was lured to politics as a moth to a flame, with consequences which were as regularly fraught with disaster. His tenuous links with unionism were, by now, completely severed. Sinn Féin, which was a movement rather than a political party, had a large moderate wing with whom Plunkett was in close touch. Griffith's emphasis on self-reliance corresponded, largely, with his own, moreover, Griffith envisaged the crown as the link between Ireland and

England, while any proposals for the partition of Ireland were anathema to both men.

But sinn féin policy was becoming progressively anti-imperial and republican, leaving only two alternatives for Ulster, either partition or civil war. Further, although opposed to the idea of Irish conscription, he was fervently in favour of Irishmen playing their part in Europe, and, on the collapse of the Convention, was persuaded to become chairman of the Irish War Aims Committee, issuing propaganda to encourage recruitment. Supported by nationalist MP's such as Hugh Law and Stephen Gwynn, it only got off the ground in August 1918, but its efforts were inevitably confused with conscription, driving a further wedge between Plunkett and Sinn Féin. However the chairman, showing his unerring capacity for evenhandedly offending both sides, invited G. K. Chesterton, in September, to assist the committee. The famous writer regaled a group of dominion journalists visiting Dublin with his opposition to conscription and support for home rule, detecting a teutonic strain in English government of Ireland. Unionists were furious, the Ulster press, comparing the two men to Don Quixote and Sancho Panza, asked who, but Sir Horace Plunkett, could have brought such a mountebank to Ireland?[7]

With the experience of the Recess Committee still uppermost in his mind, Plunkett chose the final of his three options, concentrating on the task of rallying moderate opinion. The dominion possibility he discussed with Smuts who advised the establishment of an Ulster committee in the Irish parliament empowered to summon a joint meeting of the two houses upon bills to which Ulster objected.[8] The Boer general had become an advocate of the commonwealth ideal following Campbell Bannerman's grant, in 1905, of independence to the Transvaal and the Orange Free State. Having joined the war cabinet he urged the prime minister to postpone conscription in Ireland; at the end of June a postponement was agreed until October, but by then the damage had been done. Suspicions of the government's Irish policy were confirmed by the appointment of Field Marshal Lord French, as lord lieutenant, to oversee a quasi-military policy of repression. Returning from London in May, Plunkett recorded that hatred of England was the all pervading passion.[9] The end of the war was now in sight, peace would soon set in, as AE put it, with 'unusual severity', and Ireland would face its winter of discontent.

In November 1918, emphasising the serious economic difficulties which faced the country, he suggested the formation of an

Irish Reconstruction Association which was not to constitute a political party, but would be open to all who accepted self-government within the empire. (The Association was bound to be confused with Dunraven's Irish Reform Association of 1904 but its initials were soon to take on a more military significance). In the general election held one month previously, Sinn Féin, on an abstentionist ticket, had swept the boards everywhere but in the north-east, obliterating the Parliamentary Party in the process. Southern abstention from Westminster combined with Carson's proposed partition would, Plunkett argued, have the effect of confining the benefits of UK reconstruction to the north 'while the most the rest of Ireland can hope for is such crumbs as fall from the Ulster table'.[10] But reconstruction was not the dominant theme of the Ireland of 1918 and his appeal made no impact anywhere.

The sinn féin members elected to Westminster met, instead, in the Mansion House, Dublin and constituted themselves the first Dáil Eireann (Irish Parliament). Subsequently an administration to rival that of Dublin Castle was established by the Dáil but, in September 1919 the Dáil was proscribed, and those members who escaped internment went on the run. In certain areas such as the administration of justice, Sinn Féin had considerable success but other departments, organised under conditions of extreme difficulty, were merely shadows of their Castle counterparts.

Robert Barton was appointed director of agriculture by the first Dáil. In 1916 Barton had resigned his commission in the Dublin Fusiliers to join the republicans and, in 1918, was elected sinn féin MP for Wicklow. He was a enthusiastic co-operator, had served on the IAOS committee since 1910, with a break of one year, and was an old friend of Plunkett's. One of his first moves was to establish a National Land Bank which was affiliated to the IAOS and had the task of redistributing land through the medium of co-operative farming societies. The IAOS was thus immediately given recognition by the fledgling administration.

Friction between the rival administrations was bound to grow, but Barton recognised the home rule veneer which Plunkett, via his scheme of local representation, had given to the DATI. Barton was arrested in 1919 but escaped from Mountjoy Prison, he was rearrested in 1920 and sentenced to three years penal servitude (Plunkett making strenuous efforts to have him released);[11] happily his view of the DATI was inherited by his successor Art O'Connor. The rival departments of agriculture tacitly avoided confrontation,[12] (the work of the 'Castle' department was actually commended by Arthur Griffith in a Dáil debate of June 1919)[13] Sinn Féin remaining content that their overwhelming electoral strength (in May 1920 there were sinn féin majorities on 28 out of the 33 county councils) would give them control of the Council of Agriculture and the Boards of Agriculture and of Technical Instruction. (This strategy was never tested for the Treaty had been signed before it could be given effect).

Differences of opinion arose within the Plunkett House which contained several moderate sinn féiners as well as a group who wished to steer clear of politics. The IAOS committee contained convinced unionists as well as extreme republicans (such as Father Michael O'Flanagan whose activities as acting head of Sinn Féin had led the bishop to deprive him of his curacy in Roscommon) but politics were eschewed in the interests of co-operation and in the summer of 1919 a resolution was passed by IAOS staff that:

Having regard to the existing condition of unrest in Ireland and to the vital importance to our country of the work in which we are engaged, the undersigned senior members of the staff of the IAOS, while claiming our right as citizens to hold, in that capacity, any political or religious views, hereby voluntarily agree to refrain from any active participation in any organisation of a political character, and to concentrate all our efforts in the promotion of our work, which aims at uniting Irishmen and women in a movement for the common welfare.[14]

Although he was firmly opposed to the republicanism now implicit in Sinn Féin's philosophy, Plunkett believed, from his many contacts with the moderate wing of the movement, that Sinn Féin would accept a dominion settlement which embraced the whole island. He had magnanimously patched up his quarrel with Dillon[15] whose political power and parliamentary seat had both vanished. In private the former Irish parliamentary leader was very contrite about his earlier misjudgement of Plunkett[16] who felt that he could count on Dillon's tacit support in an attempt to form a centre party. Stephen Gwynn was another former parliamentarian of the same mind, and Plunkett received further encouragement from the Belfast nationalist MP, Joe Devlin. By January 1919 the Midletonite Unionists had broken with the Irish Unionist Alliance dominated by the diehards to form the Anti-Partition League (APL), and although it had, as one of its objectives, the maintenance of the Union, its members were coming increasingly to the realisation that rule by Sinn Féin promised more peace and stability than could be hoped for from the government. The APL put forward a policy reminiscent of that outlined by Plunkett in *Ireland in the New Century*, indeed one of the MP's, Walter Guinness, urged the House of Commons to recognise that 'Ireland differs from England in race, temperament and social organisation, and that difference must be reflected in the legislation suitable for that country'.[17]

James Douglas, the quaker sinn féiner, came urging Plunkett to abandon his scheme for a dominion party which would lower the Irish demand and incur the wrath of the extremists.[18] But Plunkett, showing his obstinate streak, was not to be deterred and, in June 1919, the Irish Dominion League was launched, supported by a weekly journal the *Irish Statesman*. The paper was edited by Warre B. Wells, an Englishman who had edited the wartime Sunday edition of the *Irish Times*; his assistant editors were George O'Brien (later to become professor of political economy in University College, Dublin) and Cruise O'Brien who had served on the secretariat of the Convention. The first *Irish Statesman* (modelled on its English counterpart) was a high quality paper; besides its political columns, it had a strong literary bias and in the year of its existence carried contributions from Erskine Childers, John Eglinton, Stephen Gwynn, Paul Henry, J. M. Hone, Shane Leslie, Susan Mitchell, P. S. O'Hegarty, Forrest Reid, Lennox Robinson, Bernard Shaw, James Stephens and Jack Yeats.

The first issue carried the manifesto of the League. Irish nationality, unity and self-determination were the three essentials upon which a settlement should be based. Ireland was to be self governing and within the empire; representation at Westminster should cease and Ireland was to be represented in the League of Nations and at imperial conferences. All Irish legislation was to be enacted in Ireland; the Irish parliament should have full control of customs and excise and a free trade agreement was to be concluded with Britain. Naval and military defence of both countries would be under a central authority but conscription could only be imposed in Ireland by the Irish government. The rights of minorities would be constitutionally recognised and the problem of Ulster dealt with as similar problems had been in other parts of the empire. Two points were added by way of explanation. The demand for a republic was turned down on the grounds that it would lead to partition and mean tariffs in Anglo-Irish trade; while the empire, on account of the war, was developing into a commonwealth of free nations. The signatories of the manifesto contained moderate unionists and nationalists but not members of the APL (which however by August 1920 had come out in favour of dominion home rule).

The League was, predictably, attacked from all sides. De Valéra, in a message from America, wired that the move to found the League was inspired by Lloyd George;[19] the prime minister claimed that he had sought repeatedly for 'a single Irishman who has got the authority to speak for his countrymen who would say he would accept dominion home rule';[20] the *Belfast Newsletter* denounced Plunkett as an 'altogether impracticable politician' referring to him picturesquely as 'that miserable weathercock of public man';[21] while Carson took the opportunity afforded him by the orange parades in Ulster on 12 July to dismiss dominion home rule as the 'camouflage of an Irish republic', stating unequivocally that 'we will have nothing to do with dominion home rule or any other home rule — they may call it what they like,' before launching into a vigorous attack on Plunkett punctuated by the enraptured orangemen's laughter and applause.

Some of you in the north of Ireland know what the name of Lundy* means. There are a lot of Lundies knocking about . . . there is a man in Ireland here at the present moment. He is a gentleman whom I have known for many years — I don't know him now — a gentleman named Sir Horace Plunkett. Now Horace Plunkett thinks that his mission in life is to beget leagues. He is not married. Every month or two he forms a new league with a few respectable names of well-known Lundyites, and he has lately formed a Dominion League . . . But who was this Horace Plunkett? He would tell them all about him. Horace Plunkett entered Parliament as a unionist member. He voted for him; what was more he came all the way from the county of Sussex to vote for him when he was a candidate for South Dublin; and he went back by the next boat. It cost him five or six pounds and he was very sorry for it. He got in and made his reputation as a unionist member, and he got office as a unionist member, and then he lost his seat, and he (Sir Edward) was glad that he lost his seat. And then he lost his office, and then he became a home ruler because he lost his office and saw no possibility of getting another one. From that day to this he had gone from bad to worse. At first he was a moderate home ruler; then he was less moderate . . . And now he had got his Dominion League.

He had once a great triumph. He was selected as chairman of the Convention . . . And a nice mess he made of it. Then because the Ulster people would not fall in with his views at the Convention . . . he thought to himself what about another league? And so he formed the Dominion

*A traitor among the defenders at the Siege of Derry.

League. He wanted to know whether they preferred the Union and the king or Sir Horace Plunkett and his last league?[22]

Plunkett had not helped matters with his injudiciously widely circulated 'secret' report of the Convention, and Carson must, by now, have been aware of his trenchant criticisms of the Ulstermen. In the pages of that document Carson's influence was adjudged a negative one, 'we search his speeches in vain for any light upon the dark places of the Irish question'. There was no hint of anything constructive, no mention of the Midleton compromise which, Plunkett believed, had been frustrated solely by Ulster's refusal to consider it, and no attempt at taking up a positive position since the whole of nationalist Ireland had supposedly gone over to Sinn Féin. His one contribution had been to compare the merits of Sinn Féin's proposals with the status quo. 'Whether Ulster's case was helped by this treatment of the Irish problem may be doubted, but there can be no question as to the immense stimulus it gave to Sinn Féin'.[23]

Plunkett ultimately detected a link between Carsonism and capitalism. 'He never was an Ulsterman; he had almost ceased to be an Irishman. He had transferred his law business to London. There he became a great 'corporation lawyer' ... The party of law and order, of property and privilege — the reactionary party ... selected him to stay what they regarded as red revolution'.[24] There was more than a grain of truth in this for, during Gerald Balfour's chief secretaryship, Carson had allied himself with the Irish landlords as an opponent of progressive unionism, while, as Ulster leader he had linked up with the extreme wing of the Tory Party. But their intention had been to use Ulster as a weapon to defeat the liberals while Carson remained an Irish unionist aiming to block any proposals for home rule. James Craig and his supporters formed a third interest group for they were Ulster unionists who cared little for the rest of Ireland, and Carson, who had never sought partition, was trapped by the very momentum of his own campaign.

The Dáil was proclaimed on 13 September 1919, Plunkett protesting that its suppression would lead to 'further transference of moral sanction from the unconstitutional government of the Castle to the unconstitutional government in the Mansion House'.[25] An English proposal for a home rule government of Ireland excluding four of the Ulster counties he dismissed as 'half a parliament for three-quarters of a country'[26] but his London contacts assured him that the coalition cabinet was bent on partition and the ensuing bill contained proposals for separate parliaments linked by a council of Ireland; Irish representation at Westminster; with customs reserved to the imperial parliament.

In October he made his philosophy quite clear in a speech to the National Liberal Club. Stating that he loathed the partition of Ireland in any shape or form, he added that he had no fear of it if unity were fairly tried:

You are governing Ireland with the help of a huge army of occupation, with all the latest engines of destruction which in England are already finding their proper place in museums. This monstrous substitute for statesmanship is superimposed upon the largest police force in proportion to population in the world.

The Convention report had

laid a foundation of Irish agreement unprecedented in history. Upon this foundation the Government proceeded to build an edifice of mingled mistrust, hatred and contempt which characterises the existing situation in Ireland.[27]

A threatening letter advising him not to return, which he received in London, indicated that he was ruffling the feathers of Sinn Féin.[28] Later that month the government issued a proclamation that the hunger strikers in Irish gaols would be allowed to die. Plunkett protested that if this was intended to break the spirit of Sinn Féin it would have exactly the opposite effect and, if some did die, mayhem would reign in Ireland.[29]

His visit to the United States at the end of the year got off to a flying start when he was reported dead by a journalist who pestered him but failed to get a story. The aftermath was amusingly described by Oliver St. John Gogarty:

Sir Horace was disatisfied with his death, of which the press notices were quite unworthy. He had just died in New York, so that his loss would be all the greater in Ireland, which could not compensate itself by a public funeral. But, so inadequate were the obituaries that, without waiting for the Irish mail, he wrote on the fourth day to the newspapers pointing out omissions and misunderstandings, and assuring 'those who worked with him' that the announcement of his death was premature, but that they and his country would have whatever years were left to him, devoted selflessly to their service.[30]

A banquet (to celebrate his resurrection) was organised on his return to Dublin. Plunkett referred to his obituary notices and the fact that one of them deplored his lack of a sense of humour. Meeting its author in London he told him he was delighted that at least one member of the press took his speeches seriously! He used the occasion to attack the government's proposals. The recent home rule bill, the fourth (and worst) to have been prepared, was a bill to confer upon Ireland government with dissent of the governed. Even more disconcerting was the presence on the drafting committee of men who had threatened the empire with civil war should parliament fulfill its pledges to Ireland. The government was not content to give Ulster that measure of autonomy in its own affairs to which all such minorities were entitled; it was making Ulster a virtual mandatory over Ireland without responsibility. He appealed to the Anti-Partition League to support the objects of the IDL. Lord Midleton was the leader of those southerners who had fought to preserve a union now irretrievably broken down; 'the only union to fight for now is that of Ireland'.[31]

A second banquet, to celebrate Plunkett's return, was held a week later. (The first function had been a large affair organised by the moderates and attended by the press). The menu[32] indicates that the second dinner was arranged by friends who were his political opponents. The guest list included Diarmuid Coffey, Douglas Hyde, Erskine Childers, Mrs. Stopford Green, James MacNeill and Col. Maurice Moore making up 'a strange party of revolutionaries manufactured by Lloyd George'.[33] That these two groups by March 1920 were hardly on speaking terms was an ominous portent of things to come.

The *Irish Statesman* ran for just one year, its last issue appearing in June 1920. During its brief existence affairs in Ireland had gone from bad to worse. In the summer of 1919 it was still possible to believe that the situation might be resolved without extensive violence. Twelve months later both sides had settled down to fight it out. Neither was interested in dominion status, for the Dáil it was too little, for the British it was too much. The League made little political headway in Ireland, but the *Statesman* had an impact on that sector of British public opinion, instinctively in favour of a liberal settlement, which was growing restive at the methods used by the authorities to restore order. The paper exhibited an increasing conviction that nothing less than a radical settlement could be of any use. Plunkett felt that it was flirting with Sinn Féin and turned off the financial tap.

The Government of Ireland Bill having passed through Westminster was, predictably, accepted by Ulster and, equally predictably, rejected by Sinn Féin. Plunkett saw little hope for the northern parliament and, approving the nationalist decision to abstain, wrote prophetically:

There will be no opposition in the legislature, but a fierce opposition outside, which can rely upon the sympathy of the whole, and not improbably the co-operation of a part, of the population of the rest of Ireland.[34]

In a letter to *The Times* of November 1920, he blamed the pledges given to Carson by party leaders for government policy acceptable to one-fifth of the Irish people. The prime minister should have foreseen that

this would be regarded as a gross breach of faith by the other four-fifths, that it would arouse the fiercest opposition, that it would create a state of political disorder in which the worst political crimes would inevitably occur, and that his undisguised partiality for the northern extremists would throw all power outside the north-east corner, into the hands of southern extremists ... The new English pale which is now to be set up, with Belfast instead of Dublin as its capital, is justified as a redemption of the pledge that Ulster shall not be coerced ... Can it be denied that the discreditable portion of English government in Ireland today is the direct and inevitable result of making this country, as so often before, a pawn in the English game ... A country must either be governed or govern itself. The tragic demonstration that England cannot govern Ireland is complete.[35]

Although appalled by the increasing violence, ('I would give a lot to get Sinn Féin to spare the police');[36] Plunkett admired the idealism of the 'new leaders of Ireland' who were carrying out their 'carefully planned, methodical and completely effective transfer from the government to Sinn Féin'.[37] To Bryce, in June 1920, he wrote:

the sad thing is that the English have given up arguing about Ireland. The murders of policemen make it easy for the most shameless governmental propaganda I have yet seen in Britain, to justify the usurpation of civil government by the military authorities.[38]

Sinn Féin through its military wing, the Irish Republican Army (IRA), had learned guerrilla warfare. 'But its moral strength is far greater than its physical. In the main it has an unanswerable case against the Government and it is not only more feared but also more respected'.

He hoped that thinking people would realise that the only alternative to a republic (which meant civil war with Ulster) was dominion home rule and that nationalist pressure, particularly from the north, would help to avoid partition. Again he wrote to Bryce:

I have actually been consulted by unionists, who a year ago regarded the dominion solution as extreme, whether they should not for peace sake formally join Sinn Féin and subscribe to the bonds of the Irish Republic. Some have stated that only the murders of police prevent them doing so. [39]

The bluff Canadian Sir Hamar Greenwood ('the most grotesque figure who has ever appeared in the British cabinet')[40] had taken over as chief secretary and, with his blessing, a policy of coercion was continued with renewed vigour. As a convenient means of reprisal for republican atrocities, the police and military (notably the black and tans — an undisciplined paramilitary force recruited to augment the police) started systematically burning creameries in 'rebellious' areas of the country. Beginning on 9 April 1920 with an attack on Rearcross Creamery in Co. Tipperary, over sixty attacks were made on co-operative premises. One society, in Raheen, Co. Clare, was attacked on thirteen different occasions. The value of co-operative property destroyed was put at a quarter of a million pounds and the estimated loss in trade at over a million pounds. In an attack on Ballymacelligot Creamery in Co. Kerry one man was killed and another seriously wounded.[41] Letters from two creamery managers, reprinted in the *Homestead*, give a stark picture of confusion and terror.

We were put completely out of action as nothing is left of either cheese, building or creamery but the walls, and all for the simple reason that a girl's hair was cut who kept company with policemen. It was the military done the damage ... Creamery , was done for at 8.30 p.m., and private houses during the night. We will never forget it as they kept firing until 6.00 o'clock the morning after. They refused us permission to save anything, and fired on the police when they tried to save houses ... To make matters worse the military looted my own house and took everything of use to them ... I don't believe you will ever see a co-operative here again, as we are not able to pay our suppliers owing to the big quantity of cheese destroyed on us.

The second letter ran as follows:

About a week ago constable X came into the shop and in a friendly manner informed me that it was planned, that if any disturbance happened in the district, to burn the creamery and the store. Sergeant Y called today and informed me that he had instructions from the competent military authority to warn us that if anything happened in the district that we would be burned down. I understand that he gave the same warning to a good few houses in the village. [42]

Evidence was produced in court concerning the destruction of the Newport Creamery in Co. Tipperary implicating the forces of the crown, but no police or military witnesses appeared to refute the charges. The same pattern recurred in so many of the other cases that it became clear, in spite of official denials, that the systematic destruction of co-operative premises had been authorised at the highest level. The editor of the *Homestead*, relentlessly exposing the gaps and untruths in the statements of Sir Hamar Greenwood, finally exploded at the 'doctrine of indiscriminate justice':

It is not merely the hard justice of a eye for an eye or a tooth for a tooth exacted from the doer of the deed, but the knocking out of eyes and teeth indiscriminately without concern whether the victims of this policy are guilty or not. What pacific results can follow from this policy? What has followed already from its adoption? Have there not been more killings than ever before? What is to be the end of it? [43]

The IAOS, from the outset, brought the attacks to the notice of government officials in Dublin and London along with indications that available evidence implicated the forces of the crown. In London a deputation of British and Irish co-operators met Greenwood [44] who refused point blank to accept the possibility that the police or military were involved. He declined to set up a enquiry but gave a promise of protection for co-operative property which proved to no avail as the very forces supposed to supply this protection were themselves the assailants. As he explained to the annual meeting of the IAOS, Plunkett himself investigated the burning of Newport Creamery in Co. Tipperary on 23 July:

We implored the government, where the evidence implicated the forces of the crown, to take whatever steps were necessary to have compensation paid not as provided by the malicious injuries acts, by the ratepayers, many of whom would be actual victims, but by the British treasury.

I am bound here to state that we were not fairly met by the authorities, They suggested that the perpetrators of the outrages might be Irish republicans disguised in stolen British uniforms, travelling in stolen British motor-lorries, filled with stolen incendiary material from the arsenals of the preservers of Irish peace. Another suggestion was that the traders of the country towns were taking advantage of the state of the country to wreak their vengeance upon a movement which was interfering with their profits . . . Then it was asserted that the buildings of our societies were occupied by the Irish Republican Army, who fired at the forces of the crown. Now there are only two cases in which, either in public or in private, have we heard the suggestion of any actual firing. The first was the Newport case, which I personally investigated, because the military called upon me to substantiate statements I had made in the press. As the case was about to be brought into court, I asked the military authorities to be represented, to produce their own evidence and cross-examine our witnesses, this they declined to do. The judge, appointed by the crown, and not, remember, a local jury, awarded over twelve thousand pounds damages to the society upon evidence every bit of which consistently proved that the incendiarism was the work of soldiers as a reprisal for the cutting off of a girl's hair, and that not a shot was fired by anyone except the military. [45]

The British co-operators, setting aside all memories of past differences with the Irish movement, played a major role in exposing the hollowness of official explanations and in bringing the true nature of these atrocities before the public. The Central Board of the Co-operative Union on 28 August 1920 deplored the failure of the government to protect the creameries or to bring to justice those responsible for their destruction. [46] The Joint Parliamentary Committee of the Union (whose secretary, A. V. Alexander, later Viscount Alexander of Hillsborough, was tireless in his efforts) on 28 October urged Greenwood to protect the creameries, provide adequate compensation for the damage caused, and to set up an impartial enquiry which might uncover the facts of the matter. [47] Sometime later the Committee reported back to its parent body that none of its recommendations had been acted upon.

These unseemly affairs were subsequently raised at the annual congress of the Co-operative Union held in Scarborough in May 1921. The IAOS was represented by Plunkett and the assistant secretary, H .F. Norman. Firm expressions of support from the British co-operators were offered to the Irish movement in its hour of need; members were urged to bring these matters to the immediate attention of their parliamentary representatives; delegates called for a political solution (including the withdrawal of auxiliary forces from Ireland) to what they perceived to be a political problem; and a resolution was passed underlining the sentiments already expressed by the Central Board proposing the grant of a form of home rule which would be acceptable to the Irish people as a whole. [48]

Attacks on co-operatives abated towards the end of 1920 but

isolated assaults continued in many parts of the country until April 1921. In May, as milk supplies were moving towards their peak, a different tactic was adopted. This was the compulsory closing of creameries by military order, intended as a form of reprisal for 'occurrences' in the area. Sir Nevil Macready, military commander in Ireland, paying scant attention to the facts, discussed these events in his autobiography:

In districts where road cutting was very prevalent the creameries were closed down, a restriction which raised a considerable outcry. As a matter of fact these creameries were in many cases the distributing centres of rebel orders and instructions to the surrounding districts through the agency of the peasants who brought in the milk from the various farms.

According to rebel sympathisers great hardship was inflicted on the peasantry by the closing of the creameries, but from reliable local information this was by no means the case, the poorer peasants who owned one or two cows, being by no means averse to a restriction which enabled them to enjoy the full benefit of their cows instead of the skimmed milk which was returned to them from the creameries. The howl no doubt originated from those who were financially concerned in the success of those establishments, a considerable number of which were afterward burnt by the rebels*. [49]

Over thirty creameries were affected in this way and suffered serious financial loss. It would be difficult to imagine any more successful expedient to ensure the complete alienation of a people's sympathies and drive them to total rebellion. The burning and closing of creameries was raised on over forty separate occasions in the House of Commons, and the notoriety which these outrages attracted was a contributory factor in the British admission of the ungovernability of Ireland leading to the truce of July 1921.

Foxrock, the neighbourhood of Kilteragh, was, in 1921, an area of considerable republican activity. Two IRA men, on 28 March, told the secretary Gerald Heard that they intended to borrow Plunkett's car. He advised Heard to refuse and they left without trouble. That same day the IRA removed the telephone apparatus from Foxrock Post Office. It was restored in the evening. [50] Two days later Plunkett was held up and forced to turn back on a journey into the city [51] and, on a number of occasions, the road outside his gate was trenched. At the end of May, a former garden boy at Kilteragh was shot in his bed; [52] he may have been

---

*Although trade was considerably disrupted, no creameries were, in fact, destroyed during the civil war.

a member of the IRA and local opinion implicated crown forces.

On 21 May the black and tans raided the area around Foxrock, but, although they did not visit Kilteragh, they let locals know that they knew all about Plunkett and that his creameries were 'mere camouflage for murder'. [53] There seems to have been little or no hard evidence to support government claims that the creameries were used for storing arms or as assembly points for the insurgents, but Plunkett had recognised that the organisational ability fostered by the Land League had proved important in the foundation of co-operatives. The co-operative movement always had the support of Sinn Féin, while the ability to organise semi-autonomous groups working in an overall structure, such as the local co-operatives linked to the IAOS, was also the key to efficient guerrilla warfare. It is therefore hardly surprising that counties Limerick, Cork and Tipperary, the heartland of the co-operative dairy industry, were exceptionally rebellious. The parallel breaks down with Clare and Longford, warlike counties with little co-operative organisation also in counties Cavan, Kilkenny and Waterford where there was a strong co-operative movement but little fighting. However, the overall pattern which emerges in the rural districts of nationalist Ireland supports the theory that, where there was a strong co-operative movement, there was more likely to be vigorous resistance to British rule. [54]

As the situation deteriorated further in 1921, Plunkett maintained, both in private, and in letters to the press, a constant stream of criticism of government policy 'apparently so insane and, incidentally, so ghastly in its sacrifice of life and in its moral and material destruction'. [55] The Rising and the anti-conscription campaign conducted by Sinn Féin had alienated the majority of the British people. Had the government in 1919 succeeded in crushing the insurgents in a short, sharp campaign then, in Britain at any rate, its actions would have commanded overwhelming support. But the long drawn out struggle, with its hesitating policy and the reproaches such a policy brought in its train, wearied a nation attempting to recover from a major war; thus, by 1921, opinion had changed sufficiently for one commentator to write:

If, as it appeared, coercion was impotent to end a struggle which to the majority of Englishmen seemed utterly purposeless, then by all means give the Irish their country to govern. But let it be clearly understood that such a experiment must involve no disruption of the empire, nor must Ulster be made to suffer for the sins of the south. [56]

General Smuts' advice at last was heeded and the royal address at the opening of the northern parliament, signalled a change in direction. 'The king has given to the birth of their parliament a dignity which was lamentably lacking in its conception', Plunkett wryly recorded. [57] Sunday papers of 14 August carried a letter from Smuts to de Valéra asking him to accept partition and Lloyd George's offer of full dominion status for the twenty six counties subject to military safeguards. Moderates, such as Monteagle and Dunraven, had come out for partition, as had a section of the Dominion League (so Plunkett wound it up). He felt that the majority of Irishmen would like de Valéra to accept the proffered terms but doubted if he could carry the extremists with him:

Mr. de Valéra will have a hard task in so stating the Irish case as to avoid being charged by his own followers with lowering the Irish demand, on the one hand, and appearing intransigent to British and American observers on the other. [58]

Plunkett maintained his contact with Erskine Childers, who, on the completion of his war service, returned totally committed to Ireland's struggle for independence; though they now viewed the situation from quite different angles. Owing to the arrest of the leaders, as well as to Erskine's patent ability and unswerving dedication, his rise in the Sinn Féin organisation had been meteoric. With Molly in July he pressed Plunkett to come out in favour of de Valéra, but, to Plunkett's way of thinking, Childers was exerting a malevolent influence upon the Irish leader, preventing the compromise 'which the Irish increasingly want'. [59] A month later they met again. 'Lunched with the Childers pair. Fortunately Bob Barton was there and I talked IAOS with him. The two Childers were intensely bitter and I feel they hate me because I won't hate England. But Bob Barton is a simple honest fellow'. [60] To James Bryce, Plunkett described Childers as 'fanatical and in the inner counsels of the republicans; he is also honest and is probably one of the most dangerous men in Ireland today', [61] while, when the Treaty negotiations were underway, he wrote, 'Erskine Childers is said to be the most arcane stickler for independence and de Valéra to be largely in his hands'. [62]

Following the publication of Smuts' letter Plunkett wrote to de Valéra. Donegal, Cavan and Monaghan, of the nine Ulster counties, had such large nationalist majorities that they would have to come under a home rule parliament. Tyrone and Fermanagh had smaller nationalist majorities and he urged de Valéra to insist on their inclusion in the south, leaving the unionists with a barely viable area. De Valéra's reply was friendly but emphasised that a unified Ireland was essential, indicating to Plunkett, who was just as opposed to partition, that he had missed the point.[63] As he put it to James Bryce:

the only thing that puzzles me about the attitude of the new rulers in Ireland (for they are steadily taking over the whole government) is the little attention paid to the Ulster difficulty. I think they think Tyrone and Fermanagh will have to be given up and that the rest of the problem will solve itself.[64]

Once the truce had come into effect on 11 July, it was unlikely that hostilities would be resumed. Plunkett knew that Ireland longed for peace and his English contacts informed him that Lloyd George's position would be desperate if he failed to get a settlement.*[65] But any proposals which were being considered should be put to the people; the British were in the dark as to what was happening in Ireland, 'Do they not want to hear other minorities than that of NE Ulster?'[66]

While the preliminaries between Lloyd George and de Valéra were going through a sticky patch, Plunkett wrote, 'I still think an Irish — or rather Anglo-Irish settlement will be reached without further bloodshed. The Ulster-Irish conflict is in another category. I don't think we are near a settlement there'.[67] He believed that agreement would ultimately come about through the sacrifice of Ulster on the altar of British political expediency, and it was difficult to envisage how negotiation could surmount that particular obstacle. But Lloyd George's wizardry proved equal to the task of obtaining tory acquiescence to the dismemberment of the Union, and persuading the Irish delegation, led by Collins and Griffith, to accept partition in the belief that the findings of the Boundary Commission† would make Ulster's position untenable. One leading unionist remained unimpressed by this feat of political dexterity for Carson launched a blistering attack on the Treaty in the House of Lords‡

*The coalition government collapsed and Lloyd George was ousted from the premiership less than a year after the signing of the Treaty.
†Established on foot of the Treaty to determine the boundary between north and south.
‡Carson having refused the premiership of Northern Ireland had become a Lord of Appeal.

describing Lloyd George, sometime later, as 'a mass of corruption'.

When the Treaty terms were published on 7 December, Plunkett felt that they were in substance the Dominion League's policy, and that the moral coercion of Ulster was cunningly camouflaged therein. Regarding partition as an unfortunate, if temporary, inevitability he issued the following approval:

The peace-makers at Downing Street have done all that was possible. They have ensured Anglo-Irish accord and have given to the Irish people a proud place along the nations who have won their freedom in the British Commonwealth. They have laid the foundation upon which Irish unity can surely be built. The representatives of forty millions of British people have treated as equals the representatives of less than four millions of Irish people. In that spirit the majority in Ireland must now deal generously with the dissentient minority and the Irish question, as we have known it, will trouble the world no more. [68]

But de Valéra and his followers took a different view, vigorously opposing the the terms obtained by Collins and Giffith, and the Treaty was only ratified by 64 Dáil votes to 57. In America at the date of ratification Plunkett's impression was that anti-Treaty feeling in Irish-America was negligible. [69] During the early part of 1922 he urged Irish-Americans to invest in the new Irish State. To a capacity audience in New York's Town Hall he gave his version of the Anglo-Irish war, emphasising that Ireland had, for too long, been a pawn in the Westminster game; when asked by a heckler what was the difference between Sir Roger Casement and Sir Edward Carson, Plunkett brought the house down with his reply: 'Casement was hung, Carson was made a judge!'. [70]

XI

Partition and Civil War

News of ratification of the Treaty by the Dáil reached Plunkett at Battle Creek Sanitarium, Michigan in January 1922. The people, he felt, would accept the Treaty, but the narrowness of the majority was an indication 'that the Anglo-Irish pact may be followed by a terrible Irish row'.[1]

Subsequent division crystallised around allegiance to the crown rather than that other stumbling block — the future of Ulster. Ireland's internecine struggle followed a pattern familiar in the decolonisation process; national forces of every hue, having united to eject their colonial masters, split immediately this aim had been achieved and the opposition which cemented them had disappeared. In Ireland's case the opposing groups consisted of free staters, who believed with Collins and Griffith that their country, though partitioned, had won its freedom to achieve freedom; and republicans who aimed to prolong the struggle to get better terms. The people as a whole were weary of warfare in which the country had been embroiled, in one form or other, for the past seven years. Those who, like Plunkett, saw the overriding need for economic reconstruction plumped for the Treaty but men of equal integrity, including Childers, took the opposite view.

By April the IAOS account had been transferred to the National Bank 'to get into official touch with the new regime'.[2] Ernest Blythe, the provisional government's minister of finance was co-opted to the IAOS committee, while James MacNeill (later to become governor general) was a director of the National Land Bank. MacNeill was another moderate sinn féiner with co-operative connections. Co-operative legislation had been introduced in India in 1903 during his period in the Indian civil service, and MacNeill had made an extensive tour of the Irish co-operative movement when home on leave in 1901-2. Consequently Plunkett was asked to advise the Indian co-operators,

197

and MacNeill's support for the movement, and his admiration for
Plunkett are borne out by his writing in 1931 as governor-general
of the Free State, 'I have never wavered in the belief that I
accepted from you thirty years ago to my astonishing personal
advantage'.[3]

Plunkett, appreciating the desperate need to rebuild Ireland's
shattered economy, threw in his lot, without hesitation, with the
provisional government. He had frequent meetings with
members of the cabinet and his offer to drum up support from his
Irish-American friends was gratefully accepted. Cosgrave,
Griffith, Collins, and later O'Higgins and McGilligan all
impressed him but it was the response from Patrick Hogan, the
young minister of agriculture, which delighted Plunkett and
provided a lifeline for the IAOS, which, after the depredations of
the previous three years, was on the verge of financial collapse.

As the enmity between the pro- and anti-treaty factions
sharpened into civil war, the task of the provisional government,
barricaded into its Dublin offices, was made so much more difficult by the death of its leader, Arthur Griffith, due to a heart
attack resulting from overstrain. On 12 August Plunkett
recorded, 'A. Griffith died this morning. A terrible loss as he was
not a gunman'.[4] A week later he met Collins at Kilteragh:

Lady Lavery brought Michael Collins to supper. This was my first talk to
the commander in chief of the army of the provisional government. He
is an interesting personality. Too fat, but virile, 32 years old, forcible,
direct, simple and yet cunning. A bit crude (perhaps due to shyness) in
the expression of his views. I got in my economic (agricultural) ideas
and, I think, at last got the unprotected condition of the district attended
to ... He took a risk in coming here without a escort. I fear he is too
careless of his life. His car was bombed only yesterday when, luckily, he
was not in it.[5]

Four days later he, too, was dead having been ambushed not
far from his home in Co. Cork. Collins, the dynamo driving the
military machine in the guerrilla warfare against crown forces,
and the most impressive member of Ireland's treaty delegation
had intended to devote his energies to economic regeneration.
His ideas would have dovetailed neatly with Plunkett's as this
hastily written sketch of Ireland's future shows:

The development of industry in the new Ireland should be on lines
which exclude monopoly profits. The product of industry would thus be
left sufficiently free to supply good wages to those employed in it. The
system should be on co-operative lines rather than on the old commercial

capitalistic lines of the huge joint stock companies. At the same time I think we shall safely avoid state socialism, which has nothing to commend it in a country like Ireland, and, in any case, is a monopoly of another kind.[6]

The impact which Collins made upon Plunkett comes over very clearly in a letter to House:

The death of Michael Collins is a calamity of the first magnitude. I have made it a rule not to obtrude my presence upon the younger men whom Lloyd George has placed in power. But on the Saturday before he was killed he came here to have a talk with me. It was very frank and free, and he made a most favourable impression upon me![7]

Foxrock had seen plenty of action during the Anglo-Irish conflict, and now a small but determined band of anti-treaty or republican forces was making life difficult in the vicinity of Kilteragh. They regularly disrupted communications between Dublin and the south-east by blowing up the track or damaging the telegraph at the railway station a few hundred yards from the house. Kilteragh itself was secluded, surrounded by a plantation of pine trees, and the domestic staff were not unsympathetic; so the republicans, who were constantly on the run from government troops, occasionally used the house or its environs as a temporary billet.[8] Plunkett had plenty of evidence of the fighting. In October he wrote to an Irish-American supporter:

the moral result of long continued contempt for the law and resistance to constituted authority was fraught with disastrous consequences which will remain long after the cessation of the tyranny;[9]

while a few days later he recorded, 'The republicans, are I fear, much stronger in the country than is generally imagined. The provisional government troops are hopelessly indisciplined. I don't see how order is to be restored'.[10]

Besides trying to obtain protection for Kilteragh and Foxrock, another problem haunted him. As an extreme measure, the government had introduced the death penalty for anyone arrested carrying arms. Plunkett approached Kevin O'Higgins, minister for justice, urging that Childers and de Valéra should be deported rather than executed if they were caught.[11]

The X-ray burns on his stomach kept him in constant pain necessitating the regular use of morphia. This interfered with his work, but dreadful insomnia was the result if he abstained. Worn out both physically and mentally in November 1922, Plunkett went for a mediterranean cruise with Lennox Robinson as companion. At sea the news came through that Childers had been captured[12] and when they reached Gibraltar it was reported that he had been shot.[13] Plunkett was deeply moved. It was a tragic ending for the man whom he described as 'the worst political doctrinaire I have ever met, but personal friends we remained'.[14] A few days later he wrote to Lady Fingall:

Erskine Childers execution was, I suppose, unavoidable. Had I been in the government, I should have offered him his life if he would undertake to leave Ireland absolutely alone. He would probably have refused ... Beyond all question he was sincere in his insane hatred of imperialism. His bravery, ability and industry were all of a very high order. If only he had taken a sound line he would have been far the ablest man in Irish affairs. It was a tragedy if ever there was one.[15]

In the early hours of the morning of his execution, Childers had written a last letter to his beloved Molly, containing a message for his co-operative friends. She transmitted the letter to Plunkett with a covering note, 'I send this to you and join my message of love with his. Always there will be this bond between us'. The letter ran:

Will you send my affectionate farewells to the following from me, all on the other side, but all dear! Horace; Mary Spring Rice; Lord Monteagle; AE; RA; James Douglas; Normans ... Horace's face has often appeared before me tonight, I hardly know why, except that he has the heroic quality that you have, and he is so deeply connected — and in an inspiring way — with our first big push for Ireland.[16]

Kilteragh, which had been partially closed since August 1914, and had never fully re-opened, was now too big for Plunkett and he had decided to build a smaller residence in the grounds. Use of the adjoining 90 acres as a model farm had been discontinued during the war (although Wibberley continued to propagate his gospel of continuous cropping for winter feed as director of agricultural education at Queen's University, Belfast). The republicans were wreaking considerable havoc in and around Foxrock. On a number of occasions in 1922 Plunkett's car was commandeered,[17] and the republicans, on one occasion, made off with a taxi which had been ordered to transport guests from Kilteragh to the Horse Show.[18]

Besides the owner and his domestic staff there were two other residents regularly at Kilteragh in 1922-23. Henry Fitzgerald Heard acted as Plunkett's secretary. He was a northern Irishman possessed of that strange power common to many evangelists, but his crusade was in the cause of scientific humanism. With striking blue grey eyes set in a pointed face, a remarkable fund of knowledge and a deep interest in the para-normal, he exercised a hypnotic power on many of his generation.[19] Plunkett had fallen under his spell and he must have cut a striking figure in the conservative surburb of Foxrock, for he dressed outlandishly and was openly homosexual. Although an author with a considerable reputation, his brilliance was more apparent in the spoken than in the written word, leading John Betjeman (who for a brief period in 1929 worked as secretary to Plunkett in the Crest House) to describe him as 'Gerald Heard but not understood'.[20] Lennox Robinson, nicknamed 'the Lynx', a more orthodox, but nonetheless distinguished, member of the Kilteragh establishment resided in one of the gate lodges. He was at the time organising Carnegie libraries up and down the country (Plunkett was Irish trustee of the Carnegie Foundation). Prior to this he had been manager of the Abbey Theatre and had already achieved considerable distinction as a playwright.

President Cosgrave who succeeded Griffith, nominated Plunkett, among a group of ex-unionists, to the Senate of the Free State. They had been deliberately chosen for their disinterested efforts on their country's behalf, and Plunkett was well aware that he, or his house, might now become a target for republicans. In June Heard had been threatened,[21] and a month later he had exchanged shots with an intruder attempting to enter by the drawing room window,[22] while in August some shots were fired at the house from the plantation during a more determined attack on a neighbour.[23] Plunkett was not deterred. Early in the year he had spoken vigorously to the Dublin Chamber of Commerce about the resolute steps required of the provisional government to combat the militarists who were determined 'to out Cromwell, Cromwell'. 'But', he reflected beforehand, 'I shall have to speak and may have my house burned!'[24]

In his maiden speech on 20 December 1922 shortly before embarking for America, Plunkett received Senate approval for two enquiries he intended to make in the United States. He wished to examine the working of the Legislative Reference Library set up by his friend Charles McCarthy (who had just died) to assist the legislators in the State of Wisconsin (which had already been used as the model for the Co-operative Reference Library in the Plunkett House) with a view to establishing a similar library in the Irish parliament; he also intended to get up to date with developments in American agricultural policy.[25] Before he left he visited Cosgrave, then he and Oliver St. John

Gogarty paid their respects to the governor general, Tim Healy, an old friend of his parliamentary days, now installed in the vice-regal lodge in the Phoenix Park. They had a long talk, Healy gave him letters of introduction to all and sundry in America, and nobody, Plunkett felt, could have been kinder.[26] Finally there was a sad meeting with Molly Childers, for 'Erskine really liked me and I liked him'.[27]

Although on his arrival in the United States he had been unable to visit the Free State's consular office, which had been established in New York and was under siege by republicans,[28] he was gratified to find much support among Irish-Americans for the provisional government.[29] A case in point was that of the influential Judge Cohalan, whose position, according to information from a third party, was 'the anti-Treatyites have no case. Free State now, Republic later', and he shrewdly observed, 'Horace Plunkett is a good man but always three laps behind.'[30]

On 30 January Plunkett went to the state capital of Madison, Wisconsin to deliver an address commemorating the work of Charles McCarthy. Before the lecture he was confronted by a reporter with the news that Kilteragh had been destroyed by republicans. Plunkett went ahead with his lecture and later received a confirmatory telegram from Heard, 'Smouldering by mine, important wait letter'.[31] The next day a second telegram arrived 'Extinct January thirty first, no person injured'.[32]

An order had gone forth from republican headquarters that, in a desperate attempt to bring the government to its knees, the houses of senators were to be destroyed. On the night of 29 January, nine attacks were made on the properties of government supporters in Dublin. The first battalion of the south-Dublin brigade of the anti-Treaty forces was active in an area which included Foxrock, stretching from Ballsbridge south to Monkstown and then west to Glencree. Units of this battalion had used Kilteragh as a billet and since it still might be of use in this capacity it was decided that the house should not be totally destroyed.[33] The republicans arrived, ordered out Heard and the chauffeur Murray, who were the only occupants of the house and set off a bomb in the main hall. Guards who were on duty at nearby Foxrock railway station rushed to the scene, but the raiding party had escaped. They found considerable structural damage, doors and windows were blown out, one side wall was down, other walls were cracked, ceilings had fallen in, wood panelling was smashed, the landing was unstable, and every-where was covered with dust and debris. Yet a china cabinet close to the explosion remained intact and the art treasures, and the library, had virtually escaped unscathed.

Next day workmen were called in to sheet up the premises and insert beams to support the upper floors. The guards and military stood by to discourage looters who were already starting to congregate. The workmen left at nightfall, a guard remained on duty until 2 a.m. When the guard went off duty another raiding party arrived armed with petrol. Heard was alone in the house as his quarters were still habitable; he had gone to bed having taken a sleeping draught. He was not wakened by the raiders, or the fire, which was spotted by the farm steward's son, who, with his father, only succeeded in waking Heard by throwing a stone through his window. [34] Heard was able to escape but by this time the mahogany panels in the library were ablaze, the telephone lines had been cut and it was impossible to call a fire brigade. By dawn the house and any of its contents which had not been removed the previous day were completely gutted. The pictures, including thirty of AE's best paintings, some by Jack Yeats and a few old masters, along with Plunkett's private papers had perished in the fire.

Two eye witness accounts of these events have been left for posterity. Lennox Robinson's story is contained in his autobiography:

After Christmas he [Plunkett] went to America. Gerald remained alone in the big house. He dismissed all the servants. One night he hammered at my door and begged me to come up and try to save the house. The Republicans had got into it and set off a bomb in the big central hall. There was a smell of fire but he hoped no serious damage had been done. We ran back. It was a grim sight; the explosion had burst every window and the winter wind blew right through the house. The burning was only a fused electric wire and we quickly quenched it. I begged Gerald to come back with me but he wouldn't leave the house. Next morning he went into Dublin to try to get from the military protection for the house but they could not afford to spare any men. It was republican policy to burn senators' houses and, in spite of all Sir Horace had done for Ireland in his organization of agriculture, no exception was going to be made in his case. [35] When I got back from Dublin about six o'clock that evening I tried to see Gerald and knocked and rang but could get no reply. Next morning at eight there was a feeble knock at my front door. Gerald was sunk on the step. 'They've done it.'

It was only too true. They had come back and this time had succeeded. No bombs, just petrol, and no attempt to warn Gerald who was fast asleep. A gardener living in an upper lodge saw the flames, rushed down and got him out and between them they saved a few bits of furniture but the place was entirely gutted. Sir Horace when he went to America — he went nearly every year — liked to leave behind him a telegraphic code. A farseeing man, he had visualized this, and as I put Gerald to bed he muttered, 'The word is 'extinct'. Please send it off.'[36]

Heard's story of the second of the two days was given to Lady Fingall and is contained in her reminiscences.[37] Lady Fingall's autobiography also contains an account, which she got from Lennox Robinson,[38] which has a number of discrepancies with that given above. In this version he makes it clear that a friend was staying with him in the gate lodge on the first of the two nights, who accompanied him and Heard to inspect the damaged house. Also he talks of land mines having exploded in the house rather than a single device. A mystery surrounds the Kilteragh affair. In the first place it seems strange that Robinson and his friend, living about 100 yards or so from Kilteragh, did not hear the explosion (or explosions) of the first night which must have rocked the countryside. The second problem concerns the identity of those who came to burn Kilteragh on the second evening. The author was assured by George Gilmore,[39] who commanded the republican raiding party which mined Kilteragh, that neither he, nor any of his men, were involved on the second evening. In a letter to Lady Fingall early in 1923,[40] Heard reported that a Kilteragh employee, whose republican activities during the civil war were well known, had been shot in a lane near Milltown station close by. His comrades may have believed that information from Kilteragh had been passed to the authorities which led to his murder, and the burning of the house on the second night may possibly have been a reprisal for this. There was no evidence of looting and the action seems to have been premeditated, for the raiding party systematically destroyed the Foxrock telephone exchange before proceeding to Kilteragh.

The third part of the mystery concerns Gerald Heard. It seems most unusual that a writer like Heard left no autobiographical account of what must have been the two most traumatic nights of his life. The only account to survive is that contained in a letter to Lady Fingall. It is also strange that none of the paintings or none of Plunkett's papers were moved to safety either during the day or at the start of the fire, particularly as Plunkett's diaries, stretching back to 1881, somehow came through the ordeal absolutely unscathed. These diaries contain many frank comments on his acquaintances and on members of his family. They would have to have been kept in Kilteragh; if there was a safe they could well have been inside. But there seems to be no record of a safe surviving the fire; it would also have contained other personal papers, and Plunkett makes many references to the fact that all his private papers were incinerated.[41] Heard did manage to salvage the Kilteragh visitors' book and the *Encyclopaedia Britannica*, but he must also have preserved the forty two separate (fairly bulky) diaries spanning the period 1881-1922, for the complete set of Plunkett's diaries came into Heard's possession (as sole executor*) after Plunkett's death, and he, in turn, passed them on to the Plunkett Foundation.

Lady Fingall recalled 'that booklined room where we had talked of Ireland, the dining room with its table of boundless hospitality, set beneath AE's fairy sands and seas; the hall where AE's magic again had looked down on our musical evenings and where Lord Shaftesbury had sung his Irish songs from the Ulster glens.'[42] Now the burnt out shell at Foxrock marked Plunkett's rejection by the new Ireland. Despite his premonitions, he was shattered by the blow, pouring out his feelings to Anderson from aboard ship as he returned from America:

Upon Kilteragh I don't care to write. Its loss will deprive me of half of my physical, and if my records are not saved, of most of my mental efficiency. No place was I so fit — not even at sea. But the priceless service of the house was the friends of Ireland it brought together — surely for the good of us all. If I were younger I might go on with my work and take my chances of assassination, or what I should hate worse, of kidnapping. But to go about with an armed escort would be as disgusting as it would be mad to go undefended. It would have been much easier to protect a stationary residence than a wandering senator![43]

The destruction of Kilteragh provoked an outburst of feeling, of sympathy for Plunkett and of revulsion at the deed. 'Ireland is being humbled before the eyes of mankind', lamented the *Irish Times*, 'and the pity of it is that her own children are the authors of her sorrow'.[44] To Susan Mitchell (AE's assistant in the Plunkett House) it seemed a peculiarly 'ugly manifestation of the Irish character . . . Everything good and bad . . . has boiled up . . . we are under no illusions now; our vanity is punctured; we have seen our ugly faces in the glass.'[45] AE, who appealed to republicans, through the columns of the *Irish Homestead*, urging them to halt their campaign of destruction, felt that Ireland's supporters overseas would now recognise the mentality of a

---

*Heard was also the main beneficiary of Plunkett's estate. He moved to California with Auden and Isherwood and died there in 1975.

group which had descended to such a level. He contented himself with the thought that, in a dozen years, Ireland would be
ready to show herself a brilliant country, 'for the moment', he
wrote drily, she was 'rather dull ... from oversensation'.[46]

A strange postscript to this unhappy saga came in a letter to
Margaret Digby after the publication of her biography of
Plunkett. The writer, Mr. Eoin O'Keefe, chairman of the Dublin
Sinn Féin Peace Committee of 1922-3, which made strenuous
efforts to end the civil war, described a meeting with Plunkett in
September:

In 1922 in the height of the Civil War I was asked to call on him to ask for
a subscription to the Republican Prisoners' Dependents Fund, and
accordingly Mr. Seán O'hUadhaigh solicitor; Mr. J. W. O'Sullivan,
MRIAI; and myself waited on him. He received us politely and on being
assured that it was charitable help we were seeking and that we made no
distinction between the political opinions of the dependents he gave us
what was the handsome sum of ten pounds. With the gift however he
enjoined us that we must keep the name secret as he feared it might be
used for 'propaganda' purposes. We kept our word. Then came the
tragedy of the burning of his house, and the sardonic aspect of the matter
was that I am sure that if we had allowed his generosity to be known
Kilteragh would have been untouched.[47]

However, the strength of republican feelings against Plunkett at
the time, may be gauged by a letter from George Gilmore (who
commanded the bombing party of the first evening) to the
author:

I do not want you to think that I — or we — had any friendly feelings
towards Plunkett. He was one of the most determined enemies of the
independence movement and was close to the British government in its
efforts to destroy it.

Plunkett continued on his American tour with the loss of
Kilteragh preying on his mind, 'but all day the loss of all my
implements of usefulness, all ties with my past life except the few
survivors and my poor memory'.[49] Overwhelming feelings of
loss and rejection were countered with reserves of idealism and
courage. He had one last major contribution to make to political
and cultural life in Ireland and the remainder of his time in the
United States was devoted to raising money for a revival of the
Irish Statesman. In this he was successful and his spirits had risen
sufficiently in March after his return to England (he couldn't
bring himself to revisit Ireland for another two years) to write
optimistically to *The Times* that the civil war would soon be over;

that the present chaotic situation had its origins in the previous decade of British rule; that Irish agriculture under a native government was poised to make a great leap forward; ending with an appeal to Britain to take a generous view of the financial settlement between the two countries. [50]

The revived *Irish Statesman* ran from 1923 to 1930. Besides Plunkett, James Douglas, Lionel Smith-Gordon, W. B. Yeats and George O'Brien were directors (he had checked with President Cosgrave before appointing them). The editorship was originally offered to Robert Lynd, [51] a journalist from Belfast with nationalist sympathies then based in London, but Lynd's asking price proved to be too high. Ultimately, and with considerable reluctance, AE was persuaded to take the post and the *Irish Homestead* (which he had edited since 1905 and which was taking a strong pro-Treaty line) was incorporated into the new *Irish Statesman*. J. W. Good, a Dublin journalist and percipient critic of Irish unionism, plus Susan Mitchell became his assistants.

The aims of the new *Irish Statesman* were set out in a letter from Plunkett to one of his most generous Irish-American supporters:

The paper will stand for the faithful observance of the Treaty (with such amendments as may be agreed to by the parties thereto) and a constitution framed in accordance with its terms. It will promote the principles of justice and liberty, will advocate a persistent endeavour by the state to improve the condition of every section of the Irish people, will seek to maintain in the national economy a just balance between the several interests more particularly between those of the rural and urban communities — and uphold the belief that these objects can best be attained by constitutional means and not by violence, no man being deprived of his property otherwise than by due process of law and on fair compensation. The unity of Ireland will be sought by demonstrating its advantages to every part of the country and by fostering the mutual regard and conciliation between the majority, to whom the integrity of their country is essential to national progress, and the minority who have claimed and won from the British parliament a separate political existence. [52]

The intellectual blossoming, so marked at the turn century, had been, to a large extent, the product of an invigorating clash between the ideas of Anglo-Ireland and of emerging nationalism. After partition a reaction set in and the nineteen twenties were, in social and cultural terms, 'a dispiriting decade', through which the light from the *Irish Statesman* shone like a civilising beacon. [53] The contributors were as varied and distinguished as in the first series. The first volume contained Thomas Bodkin, Austin

Clarke, Padraic Colum, Edmund Curtis, Robin Flower, Alice Stopford Green, Oliver St. John Gogarty, Denis Gwynn, F. R. Higgins, Douglas Hyde, Michael MacLiammoir, Seán O'Casey, Liam O'Flaherty, Forrest Reid, Lennox Robinson, Bernard Shaw, Walter Starkie and James Stephens. Under AE's spirited leadership the *Statesman* proved to be one of the finest journals of modern Ireland — humane, politically engaged and broadly literate. From the outset AE opposed any signs of exclusivism or cultural xenophobia, determined that Ireland should encompass the Anglo-Irish and the Gael, while remaining open to diverse influences from abroad:

We say we cannot merely out of Irish traditions find solutions to all our modern problems. It is no use reading Wolfe Tone or John Mitchel or Thomas Davis in the belief that they had a clairvoyance which pierced into our times with their complexities, or that by going back to Gaelic Ireland we shall find images upon which we can build anew. We shall find much inspiration and beauty in our own past but we have to ransack world literature, world history, world science and study our national contemporaries and graft what we learn into our own national tradition, if we are not to fade out of the list of civilized nations. [54]

The paper folded when the funds ran out in 1930 and its last days were marked by a libel action over a harsh review of a book of Irish songs. In the final issue, Patrick Hogan, the minister of agriculture, reflecting government feeling, described the *Statesman* as 'the outstanding moral influence in Irish journalism' which had 'done more that any other journal to dissipate the ... confusion with which we have been struggling'. [55]

The Crest House, in the exclusive neighbourhood of St. George's Hill, near Weybridge, in Surrey was discovered by Lady Fingall to be a smaller replica of Kilteragh. Plunkett settled there with Gerald Heard as his amanuensis, and many distinguished names were added to the Kilteragh guest book which had, somehow, survived the fire. He resigned from the Senate in October 1923 when he had decided to live in England, but maintained his connection with the IAOS, of which he remained president until his death.

After partition the IAOS went through a most difficult time. The subsidy from the British government, which had been paid through the Development Commissioners, ceased in March 1922. Due to the unsettled state of the country, the societies, in many cases, were not in a position to contribute to the funds of the central body. Many of them in the south were still attempting to recover from the ravages of the black and tans. The whole structure would have undoubtedly collapsed, were it not for generous support from the United States, and Plunkett's acceptance of the Society's overdraft as a personal liability.[56] At the earliest opportunity an application was made to the provisional government in Dublin for a grant on a similar basis to that given by the Development Commissioners. The sense of relief was immense when it was learned that the application had been successful, and that the government intended to support the co-operative movement; however, a condition of the grant was that the money must be spent inside the new state.

Under Hogan's guidance the government of the Free State threw its weight behind the co-operative movement by giving it, at a critical time in 1926, an annual grant of £10,000 with an additional endowment of £8,500 for the next four years, on condition that its work was satisfactory to the Department of Lands and Agriculture. Faculties of agriculture (incorporating the Albert College), and of dairy science (incorporating the model farm), were established in the University Colleges at Dublin and Cork. Last but not least, a pension fund was set up by the government for the long suffering staff of the IAOS. Plunkett was delighted at these developments. His relationship with Hogan (whom he described as the 'best agricultural minister in Europe')[57] was most cordial. Hogan, who himself had been secretary of a co-operative society, while his father was the president of another, obtained a vote from the Dáil of four hundred thousand pounds, to buy out the proprietary creameries, and to turn them into co-operatives, writing thus to Plunkett:

The brightest side of the whole thing is that now that it is done, it can't be undone. The state is definitely committed to agricultural organisation . . . a full right turn has been taken and cannot be retraced. I don't care what government is elected again, it must travel along the new road. I think I have a fair idea of what our policy means and of its value, but I have a just idea also of the amount of spadework that was done by you in the IAOS in the past. The fact is that you sowed the seed, watched its growth during stormy times, took all the opposition and hard knocks, and when I appeared on the scene the fruit was ripe and practically dropped into my hands.[58]

Owing to the dependence of the central organisation on government subsidy, partition of the co-operative movement, although anathema to Plunkett, had become inevitable after the passing of the Government of Ireland Act in 1921, and the establishment of separate administrations for the two parts of

Ireland. Ulster's regional identity in co-operative matters had been recognized as early as 1904 when a re-organisation of the IAOS led to provincial representation. The situation in Ulster was different from that in other parts of the country by virtue of the existence of a powerful consumer-based co-operative movement with headquarters in Belfast. The Belfast Co-operative Society founded in 1889 (the year in which Plunkett had embarked on his co-operative crusade) had a turnover of one million pounds twenty years later. This society paid a token subscription to the IAOS but its roots lay in the British movement. Flax co-operatives were another Ulster phenomenon. These regional distinctions led to some grumbling by northern co-operators that they were not getting a fair crack of the whip from Dublin. The IAOS, they complained, was orientated towards the dairy industry in Munster;* this made society subscriptions to the central body particularly hard to collect in Ulster.

Plunkett had outlined the intricacies of the northern situation to Erskine Childers in May 1912:

I cannot expect you to understand my obligations to Sinclair, Andrews and other influential Ulster unionists who, by breaking away from Saunderson and joining the Recess Committee, enabled me to take the second step in the policy I set before me three and twenty years ago; nor would it be possible for you to realise the immense injury it would do the working out of home rule, and conceivably also to the working for home rule, if the remarkable record of harmonious co-operation between thousands of Irishmen, mostly nationalist were suddenly broken by the formation of an Ulster unionist section of the IAOS.[59]

In 1914 a partial decentralisation was effected, aimed at strengthening rather than weakening co-operation, with the establishment of a provincial office at Dunmurry on the outskirts of Belfast. But the problem raised its head again as partition loomed nearer and, in 1921, Plunkett wrote to Lady Betty Balfour that

the Ulster societies in the Carson area, always the most difficult to get to bear their proper share of the general upkeep of the movement, are of course talking about secession and indeed would have seceded long ago only they get so much more from us than they give to us.[60]

The Ulster provincial committee of the IAOS led by Harold Barbour approached the northern government at the time of the

---

*A considerable number of co-operative creameries had, in fact, been established in the dairying districts of Ulster.

IAOS discussions with the provisional government in Dublin. E.M. Archdale, the minister of agriculture, had formerly been president of the Ballinamallard Co-operative Society in Co. Fermanagh, while the minister of finance was Milne Barbour — Harold's brother. But there was opposition at civil service and cabinet levels from traders and other interests and a long correspondence ensued. Plunkett gave strong support to the application and eventually a grant of £900 for 1922/23 was agreed, with the possibility of a further £300 on a pound-for-pound basis on subscriptions in excess of £900.

Thus, against the sentiment of many of its members, the Irish co-operative movement was forced to split,* and a letter, signed by the president, Horace Plunkett, and the vice-president, Fr. Finlay, was sent by the IAOS to the chairman of each affiliated society on 16 October 1922:

> The provisional government in Dublin, and the northern government in Belfast, having both recognized the principle of state aid for the organisation of agriculture, through the IAOS, and it being a condition precedent to the carrying out of any such scheme involving expenditure, that any grants in aid of the work in the twenty-six counties and the six counties respectively, shall be spent within the respective areas.
>
> The committee of the IAOS ... were forced to the conclusion that the most effective course, in the circumstances, was the formation of a autonomous and separately registered society for Northern Ireland ...
>
> We wish for the Ulster Agricultural Organisation Society, which we are glad to know will be presided over by our old friend and colleague, Mr. Harold Barbour, a prosperous career and we most sincerely hope that the new central body will receive the active and cordial support of every society within the area. [61]

The subsequent history of the UAOS provided a stark contrast to that of its southern counterpart. Relations with the northern ministry of agriculture soon showed signs of strain, culminating in the withdrawal of the grant in 1924, on the grounds that the organisational work could be adequately carried on by the ministry itself. Suspicions were aroused that the non-sectarian nature of the co-operative movement was not favoured by some of the unionist diehards whose maxim was divide and rule. Knowledge of the southern government's generous support for co-operation only added fuel to the fire; further, some of the senior civil servants in the northern ministry had transferred

---

*The Irish Agricultural Wholesale Society (IAWS) was not partioned and remains an all-Ireland body.

from the DATI in Dublin carrying their prejudices against co-operation with them. Happily, the UAOS, thanks to the generosity of Harold Barbour and to the dedication of its few officials, soldiered on to overcome all obstacles. Though with less state support than that afforded to the movement in the south, it continues to play a vital role in the agricultural life of Northern Ireland.

His departure to England in 1923 led, inevitably, to a lessening of Plunkett's influence in Ireland. He remained as president of the IAOS until his death with Father Finlay as vice-president; but Anderson, who had lost two sons in the war (a blow from which he had never really recovered) moved to take charge of the IAWS, and was succeeded as secretary of the IAOS by Henry Kennedy. Never the sort of person to be satisfied with nominal, but not actual control of the organisation which he had founded, Plunkett was soon unhappy. Kennedy, who concentrated on Better Business to the exclusion of the other two thirds of Plunkett's slogan, was materialising the movement rather than spiritualising it, and, in 1925, Plunkett reflected upon the failure of his ideals to take real root:

A material bias was given to the movement, the old idealism and enthusiasm melted away; the co-operative spirit, which ensures the essential loyalty of members to their societies and which the deeper thinkers among us know was, even from an economic point of view, of more vital importance than the practical work our organisers had to concentrate upon, was very insufficiently cultivated. That is the weak spot of the movement; by the restoration of the co-operative spirit can it alone be saved for the great work which lies before it. [62]

Kennedy had been faced with a crisis stemming partly from the depression. A mathematician and economist, he perceived that co-operative strength depended on the dairy industry, that Ireland's real economic potential lay in her grasslands, thus the development of the dairy sector must be the means of bolstering up the whole movement. With the assistance of his brother-in-law, Patrick Hogan, minister of agriculture, proprietary creameries were bought out and made co-operative with funds provided by the state; and it was his constant emphasis on the farmers lack of capital which led to the formation of the Agricultural Credit Corporation, of which Robert Barton was chairman for twenty years.

The old order was passing. Plunkett spoke for the last time at an IAOS annual meeting on 1 May 1929. The meeting was badly attended and poorly reported, but one important ingredient was not missing for 'Father Finlay followed me with a marvellous exhibition of his quality after 81 years of life'. [63]

Plunkett was now an elderly man, in failing health, settled in England, living with his memories but haunted by the destruction of Kilteragh. In typical fashion he pulled himself together, turning his attention to the agricultural problems of England and the empire, although his heart remained in Ireland. To the rising generation he seemed a lonely old man, a figure out of his time, while his obsession with co-operation had made him something of a bore.

The Co-operative Reference Library was transferred across the Irish Sea after a skirmish between Lennox Robinson and the Church in 1924. Thirteen years before Robinson had written a story which had been praised but rejected (on the grounds that it might give offence) by the editor of an English magazine. Some years later it was published in America, then he sent it to a somewhat audacious journal in Dublin (which only lasted two issues). [64] The rest of the story is told in Plunkett's own words.

He had written a story in a rag of an anti-clerical magazine called 'The Madonna of Slieve Dun'. The heroine was raped after fainting in the struggle by a drunken ruffian. She had been very devout, had imagined that Christ would be born again at Xmas, and her baby was so born! Thereupon Father Finlay writes to Provost Bernard, Chairman of the Carnegie UK Trust Irish Advisory Committee on which he serves and says he can't even meet the blasphemous Lennox again and resigns his membership. LR was a fool but he was doing good work, spreading libraries in the most difficult counties of Ireland. [65]

Robinson refused to resign, the affair became a cause célèbre, and he was eventually dismissed. The Carnegie Trustees took the opportunity to wind down their Irish operation by shifting its headquarters back to Scotland. The staff of the Co-operative Reference Library had been paid for by Carnegie and a condition of the continuation of his support was that the Library should be moved from Ireland.*

In 1919 Plunkett had created the Horace Plunkett Foundation[†] with an endowment of £20,000 which he later augmented with a further £15,000 to continue his life's work. Sir Daniel Hall (formerly a development commissioner and a leading authority on UK agriculture), Prof. W.G.S. Adams (now in Oxford),

*The Carnegie Trust's subvention to the Library ceased within three years of its move to England.
†Restyled the Plunkett Foundation in 1959.

Dermod O'Brien (the distinguished painter who was a supporter of Plunkett and a nephew of Lord Monteagle), Lionel Smith-Gordon (chairman of the National Land Bank in Dublin), and Harold Barbour (now a member of the Northern Ireland Senate) were trustees. The two institutions were happily married, first in London and then in Oxford, and the Foundation's worldwide propagation of Plunkett's slogan: Better Farming, Better Business, Better Living, is backed up by the finest collection of co-operative publications in existence.

Plunkett's attempts to influence agricultural policy in the United Kingdom made little headway, either with the farmers, or with the government. Nearing the end of his life he wrote:

In my view England has no agricultural policy. Ireland when my life began was politically and economically part of England. Now 26 counties of the 32 of Ireland manage their own affairs which are as predominantly agricultural as England's affairs are predominantly non-agricultural. The Irish Free State is gradually working out an agricultural policy of its own based on the principles which I believe are wholly in accord with the needs of agricultural England. [66]

His ideas made more impact in other parts of the world, and to his great delight, the principles to which he had dedicated his life's work were summarised in a resolution passed at a conference on agricultural co-operation in the British empire, in 1924:

That agricultural prosperity depends fundamentally upon the fulfillment of three conditions:
1. the application of scientific knowledge, under the guidance of the state, to the farming industry;
2. the voluntary organisation of farmers for business purposes along co-operative lines; and
3. a reconstruction of social life in the country with a view to removing the disparity between the respective attractions of the town and country. [67]

It was July 1925, just two and a half years after the destruction of Kilteragh, before Plunkett could bring himself to revisit Ireland. [68] His impression was, on the whole, favourable. He had a number of interviews with government ministers to whom he expounded his agricultural policy: President Cosgrave, Ernest Blythe (finance), Eoin MacNeill (education), Kevin O'Higgins (justice), Patrick Hogan (agriculture), Desmond Fitzgerald (external affairs), and Patrick McGilligan (industry and commerce). The breadth of vision which lay behind the hydro-electric Shannon scheme, involving the construction of a huge dam at

Ardnacrusha, delighted Plunkett, as did the responsible
minister, Patrick McGilligan, whom he described as 'possibly the
best constructive mind, and, as the Shannon scheme shows, by
far the finest constructive imagination, in the Free State government'. [69] On his next visit in 1927 he saw Hogan, McGilligan and
Thomas McLaughlin, the Irish engineer responsible for the
works at Ardnacrusha, 'a stupendous operation — the mind
boggles' he wrote having inspected the scheme. [70]

In October 1928 he paid his final visit to Belfast, his primary
purpose being to encourage the struggling UAOS. He also visited
the northern parliament. It could hardly have been expected to
impress him:

The bewigged and begartered speaker and bewigged clerk at the table
lent the dignity. But, oh what a dull chill farce. Big business, with the
pope as an ever present helper in time of trouble, has a sure majority. [71]

Although Plunkett's health was failing he still retained an
adventurous spirit. The Crest House, Weybridge, lay adjacent to
Brooklands with its race-track and aerodrome. Having been a
pioneer of the motor car in Ireland, predictably but improbably,
he signed on at Brooklands flying school, learning to fly at the age
of 75. (To his reproving friends he pointed out that he had
reached the age at which a man could afford to live dangerously!). Grasping at once the immense potentialities of air travel,
on his next visit to Ireland he flew with Oliver Gogarty and
Colonel Russell, the head of civil aviation in Ireland, from the
airport at Baldonnel. To Russell he preached 'the opportunity of
making Ireland the landing and jumping off place between the
old and new worlds' [72] (an opportunity soon to be translated into
reality with the development of Shannon Airport), and followed
up in a half-hour discussion with Cosgrave on a future Irish air
policy. [73]

His disappointment with the failure of the revived *Irish
Statesman* (through lack of readership) was more than counter-
balanced by state support for his co-operative movement:

It was the greatest happiness of my life when the policy for which my
fellow-workers had been laboriously laying the foundations for some
five and thirty years was definitely adopted by the government with the
approval of every part of the legislature. [74]

Plunkett had been a fervent supporter of the Cosgrave
administration. The balance began to swing as de Valéra's
supporters, having overcome their scruples concerning the oath

of allegiance, entered the Dáil in 1927. The general election of February 1932 returned Fianna Fáil as the largest party (though without an overall majority), and de Valéra prepared to form his administration. The maturity of the young state was displayed as power was transferred in a manner befitting a democracy. Plunkett's news from Ireland came mainly from co-operative sources: 'they were as much in the dark as de Valéra is himself as to the policy he will advocate when he becomes president of the "Republic" '.[75] Thus, ten years after the foundation of the state, in whose gestation and birth he had played a not insignificant part, came the first change of government. It was the end of an era in more ways than one, for Plunkett died in Weybridge on Good Friday 1932. The inscription on his gravestone in the churchyard of St. Mary, Byfleet reads, 'Behold, the sower went forth to sow'.

XII

Retrospect

Politics are to me silly and wicked. Of all shoddy makebelieves, politics, as understood by the ordinary candidate and constituency is the most egregious. I know because I have had to be a politician.

Thus ran Plunkett's somewhat rueful verdict, delivered at the very end of his career, on the profession which had proved such a fatal distraction to his work for rural reform.

'But', he explained, 'I have forgiven myself because I fulfilled my sole purpose which was to get England to give Ireland the education the farmer just had to have. And this when the Manchester School* was at the height of its power and educating farmers for the business of their lives was a monstrous interference with the business of the people!!'[1]

At the head of a powerful apolitical movement (although he afterwards gave himself as a hostage to politics) Plunkett posed a threat to the party organisations; by crossing the old tribal boundaries he soon incurred the wrath of the extremists. He had compared himself to a dog on a tennis court, but his opponents, including both constitutional and physical-force unionists and nationalists, clearly regarded him as a more dangerous carnivore, for he was:

1. deprived of his parliamentary seat in 1900 by the unionists;
2. driven from office in 1907 by the nationalists;
3. denounced for espousing dominion home rule in 1919 by Edward Carson; and
4. burnt out of Kilteragh in 1923 by the republicans.

Even in an embittered Ireland this constitutes a unique, if undesirable, record!

Such a fate would have been unthinkable at the commencement of his career; indeed omens for the moderates in the ten

*The leading advocates of free trade and non-intervention by the government in the economy.

years from 1895 could, at first sight, hardly have been more favourable. Both political parties were seriously divided; Gerald Balfour was in charge from 1895, and Balfourian policy was carried on at an increasing tempo by George Wyndham after 1900. In the cabinet Arthur Balfour was powerful enough to resist the protestations of reactionary Irish unionists, and it seemed (although the nationalists by 1900 had re-united under John Redmond) that continuation along the same lines might see the the formation of a middle ground solid enough to support the foundations of the new Irish administration.

But appearances were to prove deceptive. Individual moderates, apart from Dunraven and William O'Brien, never managed to join forces to work together. The cabinet balance of power changed after the tarrif reform split in 1903, and Balfour was unable to stave off unionist reaction to the Dunraven devolution scheme of the following year. Finally, the Anglo-Irish, as the one group with a foot in both camps, with a perception of English misunderstandings and misrule as well as an appreciation of the justice (and inevitable resurgence) of Irish claims for nationhood, failed to give worthwhile support to those who were struggling for compromise.

Although Plunkett's eight years at Westminster culminated in the establishment of the DATI, his involvement in party politics, despite one signal triumph, was ultimately to prove a grave embarrassment. If his initial acceptance of a unionist nomination was a mistake, his attempt to regain a seat in the Galway by-election was another. Attacks on the RDS unnecessarily increased the opposition to his movement, while publication of *Ireland in the New Century* fanned the embers of controversy over his retention of public office without a parliamentary seat, besides alienating many of his catholic supporters. Plunkett's declaration for home rule some years later estranged his liberal unionist friends, while the formation of the Irish Dominion League, in 1919, effectively put the dominior. solution out of bounds to the moderate wing of Sinn Féin. All these incidents reveal, besides political naiveté and misjudgement, his engaging but unpolitical habit of speaking his mind. ('Why not let sleeping dogs lie?' he was once asked on a matter of controversy. 'Certainly', came the reply, 'but I will not let lying dogs sleep!'). In fact, Plunkett's private views, as evinced by his diaries and correspondence, were, in general, remarkably close to his public pronouncements. Such honesty may have been the best policy but was hardly the best politics!

This quality alone makes him a worthwhile study. There is no doubt, for example, that *Ireland in the New Century* expressed his own deeply held convictions. It was a novel theme to propagate, in 1904, that the Irish question was neither political, nor economic nor religious, but primarily a problem of character. Indeed, the task of developing a true spirit of self-reliance faces all colonial or post-colonial peoples. His underlying theme, that social and economic development should precede, rather than follow, constitutional change, may have been heresy to the nationalists, but fifty years of stagnation after independence lend retrospective weight to his view, while a number of the defects which he noted in the Irish make-up seem to have diminished but little under a native administration. Unflattering comments on catholicism served only to increase his unpopularity. Plunkett had uncovered a raw nerve in catholic nationalism which continued to reverberate long after his death. Ireland was not mature enough in 1904, nor (as this excerpt from the *Catholic Bulletin* for 1935 shows), for some time afterwards, to benefit from such constructive self-criticism:

This wealthy person Plunkett, exploited his IAOS officials over a whole generation in aid of his political ambitions and schemes. That he was a political agent of the English crown. Plunkett himself has, with gratuitous folly and garrulity, set out in his ... (secret) report to the English king and cabinet. [2]

His continuing desire to form a centre party, his contacts with the literary and language movements, plus his rejection of the philosophies of the two major parties, all combined after 1907 to move him closer to the moderate wing of Sinn Féin. The last link fitted into the chain with the arrival of Erskine Childers at Kilteragh. It was *The Framework of Home Rule* which convinced Plunkett that Ireland must have control over her financial affairs (a rock on which the Convention was to perish a few years later), while he tried to distil for Childers the essence of Ulster's objection to an Irish parliament. Their relationship was all the more remarkable in that the two men found so much in common when they first met, then came to differ over an issue of fundamental importance, yet managed to remain friends. Ironically too, Childers' bitter anti-English feelings helped to push Plunkett away from Sinn Féin and towards the foundation of the Irish Dominion League. Civil war completed the antithesis: Childers was executed because he had gone too far; Plunkett was driven out because he had not gone far enough.

Appreciating the fact generally ignored by separatists, that the damage inflicted upon the nation in the struggle for independence, might render that independence hardly worth having, Plunkett strove manfully to resolve the constitutional impasse by peaceful means. His failure to bring the Convention to a successful conclusion may, in the circumstances, have been inevitable, but acceptance of home rule by the influential group of southern unionists led by Lord Midleton was to prove of utmost importance to the emerging southern state. In the aftermath only the dominion alternative held out any hope of avoiding partition; but emotions were taking over, the hour of reason was past. Again he made a serious political misjudgement in pinning his colours to the dominion mast. It was not the time for publicly rallying moderate opinion, but for privately working with his many contacts among the moderates on both sides. Allied to those who already recognised the dangers inherent in the straight jacket of a republic, Plunkett's influence would have been considerable; instead his action gave de Valéra, Carson and Lloyd George, a heaven-sent opportunity to repudiate the dominion plan. Later, de Valéra (with Childers at his elbow) differentiated between 'dominion status' and the 'status of a dominion':

'Dominion status' for Ireland, everyone who understands the conditions, knows to be illusory. The freedom which the British dominions enjoy is not so much the result of legal enactments or of treaties, as of the immense distances which separate them from Britain and have made interference by her impracticable. The most explicit guarantees, including the dominions' acknowledged right to secede, would be necessary to secure for Ireland an equal degree of freedom.[3]

But Smuts, who, prior to the Treaty negotiations acted as a contact between Lloyd George and de Valéra, pointed out that any British encroachment on the de facto status of an Irish dominion, would be strenuously resisted by the other dominions for reasons of self interest.[4] Subsequent experience vindicated Smuts' view; the Irish Free State playing a leading part in the discussions between the United Kingdom and the dominions, which culminated in the Statute of Westminster in 1931, making her *de facto* status *de jure*.

During the agonising period, scarred by reprisals and counter reprisals, prior to the about turn in government policy midway through 1921, Plunkett's campaign, in a stream of letters to the press, and through his contacts with those of influence in

Westminster, proved an important factor in enlightening British opinion as to the regime of 'Prussian militarism' in Ireland. 'It is hard to realise', he wrote, 'how wrong England has been fundamentally. Ireland is so wrong superficially.'[5] 'Never again must a British military force be employed for the establishment or support of any political system in any part of Ireland'.[6]

Then with the signing of the Treaty the Irish question became the Ulster question; more than half a century later it still remains unresolved. The decay of the Anglo-Irish, severing of links between the north and south of Ireland, obsessively introspective attitudes in both parts of the country, and Britain's disregard of her obligations towards her former kingdom, have contributed to the continued misunderstanding between the people of both islands. As a consequence of continued political reluctance to grasp the Ulster nettle, violence has still to run its course; with the burning of the giant York Street store of the Belfast Co-operative Society by the IRA in 1972,[7] the co-operative movement has again become the victim of civil strife. As the old divisions appear in ever sharper perspective, the reconciling power of a movement such as Plunkett's, marks it out as an important stabilising agent in modern Ireland.

* * *

Someone of Plunkett's background, with so many interests, such a remarkable range of contacts and of such varied experience was bound to be a complex personality, so it was not really surprising that even his friends found him difficult to understand. He was a medley of strange paradoxes. A combination of the man of business with the idealist; a man of strong family affections who never married; a sociable man, yet one who was always ready to sacrifice the pleasures of friendship to the demands of work; an aristocrat of great charm possessing exquisite manners, who could nonetheless be quite ruthless in pursuit of his objectives; a man who drove his subordinates hard, yet inspired in many a life-long devotion; above all, a man whose hold on life was always precarious, but whose zest for living was inexhaustible. But beneath these superficial contradictions were attributes of courage, strength of character, and a desire to serve. Above all, he had a concept of Ireland that was essentially constructive, that was both national and international. In Lady Fingall's words, 'Ireland had laid her burden upon him'; it was a true saying for his was a dedicated life.

He suffered more pain and physical torture than most men, yet possessed an incurable optimism and, in the face of the most grievous disappointments retained a certain sad serenity. Although a poor public speaker, he had, in private conversation, a talent for drawing people out, a wonderful tenacity in argument, never giving up his point but handling it in such a way that the person he disagreed with felt almost flattered. Notoriously lacking in aesthetic sensibility, he had no ear for music, was unable to tell one flower from another, and left no reference to the awe-inspiring scenery of Wyoming; yet he revelled in the company of writers and artists counting them among his closest friends.

His most sympathetic portraits, such as those left by Lady Fingall or by Oliver Gogarty, reveal that Plunkett was sometimes regarded, even by those who took his ideas most seriously, with a slight air of amusement. After a continental holiday he imported Swiss goats to the congested districts. Livelier than their Irish counterparts and considerably more destructive they ate everything before them, hedges, gardens, bark of trees and the clothes on the clothes line. The experiment was called to a halt only after the goats had discovered the thatch on Irish cottages to be a new and even rarer delicacy! Another experiment involved an attempt to harvest apples in the Boyne Valley with the object of producing cider. 'Bottle of the Boyne' was the slogan dreamed up by Father Finlay, but the Boyne Valley proved unsuitable, the orchards reverted to pasture, and the owners to their 'lotus eating occupation of opening and shutting gates'.

The fashionable landlord argument, in the final decades of the nineteenth century, that a change in the system of land tenure would be disastrous for Irish agriculture, was as wide of the mark as the boast of the tenant representatives, that unbounded prosperity would follow the transfer of ownership. Plunkett was one of the first to recognise the fallacy in both of these arguments, the agnostic streak in his nature prompting a more measured view. His attempt to establish an agricultural co-operative movement, and then, before it had had time to sink deep roots, to graft onto this somewhat tender plant the apparatus of government, met vigorous political opposition from the nationalists, and could, with justification, have been criticised on administrative grounds. But the desperate need to modernise Irish agriculture combined with an urge to strike while the iron was hot impelled Plunkett to create his opportunity via the Recess Committee, and then to seize it brilliantly while the

Above left: Edward Martyn, by Sarah Purser (HLMG). Above right: The Hon. Emily Lawless. Below left: T. W. Rolleston, by John Butler Yeats, collection Michael B. Yeats. Below right: Susan Mitchell, c. 1902, by John B. Yeats (NGI).

Above: Michael Davitt speaking in Parliament, 1889, (detail), and John Dillon leaving Parliament, by Sydney Prior Hall (NGI). Below left: Sir Horace Plunkett makes a Presentation to Cathleen ni Hoolihan, a cartoon by Grace Gifford/Plunkett. Below right: A Mixed Card. Coercion *v.* Conciliation in Ireland. Sir Hamar Greenwood and Sir Horace Plunkett. From *Punch*, 15 October 1924.

Above: a traditional milk delivery to a co-operative creamery. Below: Horace Plunkett driving an early tractor. Two photographs from *Survey*, 26 November 1921.

Above: a creamery destroyed by the Black and Tans. Below: the opening of a co-operative creamery. Two photographs from *Survey*, 26 November 1921.

Balfours remained in office.

The remarkable achievement of the Recess Committee ensured that legislation establishing the DATI, rather than slavishly following the British model, should be directed at specific Irish needs and conditions. This innovative approach of the first vice-president was not, however, matched by his successors. Russell and Gill were not the men to direct the modernization of Irish agriculture, and the stamp which Plunkett had set upon the new Department was soon obliterated. His brave attempt, through the Council of Agriculture, to involve local authorities in formation of policy, disappeared in 1922. More serious was the failure to recognize, as he had done so clearly, that education was the DATI's primary and most vital task. His challenge to his new Department to provide 'practical instruction to young and old, in schools, upon the farms, and at meetings, lectures, experiments and demonstrations'[8] was conveniently forgotten. Lack of awareness of the need for an expanded and integrated system of agricultural education (which continued after independence) is, perhaps, the principal reason for the Irish farmers' failure to make the most of their opportunities since then. Recent innovations have, ironically, been prompted by the extension system in American universities, whose work was influenced by Plunkett and where a gospel is propounded similar to that which he preached in Ireland more than three quarters of a century ago.

He was not, himself, a great original thinker; his strength lay in his appreciation of the use to which new inventions could be put, and in the practical application of current social thinking. The Scandinavian invention of the steam-powered cream separator, he instantly realised to be the key to modernisation of the dairy industry. Wibberley's system of catch cropping and silage making, as demonstrated at Kilteragh, solved the problem of producing winter milk. The *Daily Express*, during the brief period of Plunkett's control, pioneered the use of wireless as an adjunct to journalism, and, as he forecast, this invention of Marconi's was to prove a powerful agent in the brightening up of rural life. The establishment of the Council of Agriculture was a brave experiment in the democratisation of administration. His vision of the role of the state, supplementing, but not supplanting, local effort, plus his acute awareness of the need to revivify rural culture and to revitalise rural life, show that, as a practical social philosopher, Plunkett was well in advance of his time.

He was at his best when the ideas which he germinated were fleshed out, and put into practice, by an able second-in-command.

R. A. Anderson acted in this capacity in the IAOS, AE and Father Finlay helped to develop a philosophical basis for his work, besides giving invaluable advice on all practical problems, while T. P. Gill smoothed his political path in the Recess Committee. Gill's assistance and political wisdom proved invaluable,[9] but his about turn in 1907 showed that Plunkett had misjudged his man. He remained at his post until 1921. After his death, ten years later, Plunkett attempted this assessment:

As politicians go he was no worse than the next man. He helped me greatly in my parliamentary days as he knew the tricks of the trade but he helped himself more ... When I was ousted he was in with Redmond, T. P. O'Connor and Co ... How can I judge such a man?[10]

Plunkett's youthful attachment to an oppressively fundamental anglicanism dwindled to an agnosticism which pervaded his political as well as his religious beliefs. But there was, he often emphasised, a moral dimension to his movement. It might have been that, had the pioneers concentrated on a less ambitious but more remunerative programme, the farmers among whom they worked would have been financially better off:

Personally I doubt this and am glad we took the longer view ... Moreover had Mr. Anderson, Lord Monteagle and I, the earliest survivors among the founders of our movement, restricted our aim to better business methods for the farmer we should not have secured and kept such invaluable helpers as Father Finlay and George Russell.[11]

AE* and Father Finlay were great men. The philosophy in whose evolution they played a major part, established individual self-reliance as the foundation upon which to build the character of the nation. Equal in stature to Plunkett, attracted to the movement by their leader's enthusiasm, idealism and integrity, they helped to raise the economic struggle to a level from which vistas might be glimpsed 'elsewhere obscured by the darkness of materialism'. Monteagle, Anderson, Barbour, and the rest formed a solid phalanx of talented supporters whose involvement depended on a commitment to Plunkett as much as to their belief in the ideals which he set before them.

The fact that leadership in the Irish co-operative movement did not come initially from among those who were its main beneficiaries, stood in marked contrast to Rochdale, or to

---

*Twin busts of AE were erected, in 1985, opposite the Plunkett House in Merrion Square, Dublin and at his birthplace in Lurgan, Co. Armagh.

Denmark where it had sprung from among the farmers themselves. Thus for Plunkett to call his movement a self-help movement was, in a certain sense, a contradiction in terms. The IAOS
was never more than partially financed by the affiliation fees of
member societies and, until support was forthcoming from the
DATI, and then the Development Commissioners, the Society
depended, to a large extent, on contributions from its wealthier
supporters. All this was acknowledged by its founder, who
argued that, ideally, co-operation should emerge as a natural by-
product of a sound system of public education, but since this was
such a rare commodity in Ireland, those who had the privileges
and the skills must point the way. [12]

His appeal to the gentry in *Noblesse Oblige* was rejected by all but
an important minority, for there was an influential group of
nationally minded people who supported him and provided an
enlightened leadership for the fledgling co-operative movement:
Robert Barton of Wicklow, Mary Spring-Rice, daughter of Lord
Monteagle, Col. Gerald Dease of Kildare, Sir Joceyln Gore-Booth
of Sligo, Arthur Lough of Cavan, Count Arthur Moore from
Tipperary and Sir Nugent Everard of Meath were members of
this group. Enlightened members of the clergy of every
denomination such as Canon Hannay of Westport, Dean Barry of
Kilkenny, Fr. Michael O'Flanagan an ardent sinn féiner, Rev. E.
F. Campbell, an equally ardent orange man, and, of course,
Father Finlay, all gave devoted service to the movement.

These members of the landlord class, or of the clergy, who
provided the early co-operative leadership made up minorities
within their respective groups. They had to be prepared to face
ridicule, if not outright hostility, for their co-operative
involvement but this was a testimony to their strength of
character and independence of mind. Such leadership required
self-sacrifice in terms of time, effort and, in most cases, money, as
well as a belief in the co-operative ideal. Its withdrawal, before
members had absorbed the principles of co-operation, generally
meant that if the movement continued, it would do so simply
according to commercial criteria.

R. A. Anderson died on Christmas day 1942. He was the last of
the pioneers. AE had died in exile in Bournemouth in 1935,
Harold Barbour in 1938 and Father Finlay (aged 92) in 1940. The
changes which were taking place may be adequately gauged from
the annual reports of the IAOS. From 1894 to 1923, for the first
thirty years of the Organisation Society's existence, these were
fascinating social documents with full reports of meetings,

transcripts of the main addresses, numerous maps, tables and appendices outlining co-operative progress. Rarely did either Plunkett or Father Finlay fail, on these occasions, to restate the movement's ideals and objectives. No reports were published for six years, from 1924 to 1930 after Plunkett left Ireland, and when publication was resumed in 1931, the reports became bare records of minutes and statistics; even the founder's death in the following year received but perfunctory mention.

With the departure of the pioneers, there was no one left at the top who could inspire those further down the line with the co-operative spirit. [13] The process of co-operative education had not gone far enough and little social thinking was carried on inside the movement. The loss of the *Irish Homestead*, absorbed into the *Irish Statesman* in 1923, was a grievous blow, while the departure of the Co-operative Reference Library from the Plunkett House one year later, cut off many of the Irish movement's links with co-operators abroad. Subsequent failure to appreciate the importance of the role to be played by research and education has had an inhibiting effect upon Irish co-operative development.

Economic opportunities afforded by the co-operative system clearly held more appeal for Irish farmers than the moral uplift associated with the movement. Plunkett, Father Finlay, AE and the pioneers have been criticised for emphasising the necessity to develop a co-operative spirit, rather than simply treat co-operation as a convenient way of doing business. But great cultural or social movements generally rely upon a moral stimulus, the Gaelic League and Father Mathew's temperance crusade being two Irish examples. Farther afield, British co-operative philosophy was influenced by non-conformist ideals and christian socialism, while co-operative endeavours in Antigonish (Canada) and Mondragon (Spain) form impressive outgrowths of catholic social teaching. A self-help movement worthy of the name demands self-discipline and self-sacrifice; the question is not whether it functions commercially, which it must in order to survive, but whether it operates according to true co-operative criteria.

The movement in Ireland, as has happened elsewhere, sometimes fails this test. [14] Irish agricultural co-operatives which, in 1983, employed twenty thousand people with a turnover of almost three billion pounds have satisfied the commercial criteria. Development has been essential if farmers are to compete in a market place increasingly dominated by multi-national combines while the co-operativisation of agricultural commerce has ensured that control of farming and food-processing remains firmly in Irish hands. But big is not always beautiful; growth induces its own problems; the challenge which faces co-operators in Ireland, as elsewhere[15], is to remain competitive and yet adhere to the movement's original philosophy and purpose. The full potential of the co-operative system has yet to be exploited but its basic principles remain unchanged since they were laid down by the Rochdale pioneers. If the movement looses its roots in the community which it serves, it no longer deserves the title co-operative and must be categorised differently.

Plunkett was soon forgotten as a politician.[16] Of more consequence to his native land was the fact that his ideals and philosophy were equally neglected. For many years he, and his work, were better known outside Ireland. If he was indebted to America for the opening up of new horizons, the debt was repaid one-hundred fold through his efforts with Roosevelt and Pinchot, to initiate the Country Life Commission, and to inspire the rural reform movement in the United States. His reputation, well known in the British Commonwealth, soon spread to the developing world. W. G. S. Adams recalled how, on a visit to China in 1931, students in Shantung, Nanking and Canton frequently referred to the rural philosophy of the Irish co-operator, Horace Plunkett.[17]

Happily, the recent past has seen a change and a reassessment. The fiftieth anniversary of Plunkett's death was marked by co-operators all over Ireland. The credit union movement (a successor to Plunkett's Raiffeisen-inspired land banks) has swept the country. Producer co-operatives in industries other than agriculture are emerging in many areas. A Centre for Co-operative Studies has been established, with the help of one of the major banks, in University College, Cork. Plunkett's writings are now required reading in the university faculties of agriculture. A new edition of *Ireland in the New Century* has recently been published as part of a programme to put the co-operative classics back into print;[18] Patrick Bolger's splendid history of the Irish co-operative movement having appeared in 1977. The co-operative movement itself, realising that economic strength, though an essential, is not the only criterion by which it may be judged, is seeking to re-interpret the ideals of its founders in a modern idiom. Happily too, new links are being forged between the IAOS (now the Irish Co-operative Organisation Society, ICOS) and the UAOS, to give practical expression to AE's sentiments at the parting of the ways:

There is no quarrel, no unfriendliness, no separation of ideals. Our old colleagues who have worked so steadily and enthusiastically in the past when Ireland was a political unit, will continue their labours for the democratic and co-operative ideals which are common to the movement north and south. Hence forward it will be a friendly rivalry as to which area will develop the most co-operative spirit and the most efficient organisation.[19]

Internationally, Plunkett takes his place in the ranks of the great rural reformers alongside Grundtvig and Raiffeisen; in his own country he is the pioneer of modernisation in Ireland's principal industry. He showed, both in his work and through his movement, how men of differing parties and opposing creeds could work together, believing that through mutual effort, Irishmen would learn to respect those whose backgrounds and opinions differed from their own.

At the commencement of his vice-presidency of the DATI, Plunkett underlined his faith in the bond uniting Irishmen:

Our success depends upon the growth of the sentiment of common interest and this will never be fully developed unless the north learns its lesson from the south and the south its lesson from the north. We down here, have got to emulate those sterling qualities which have gained for the industrial life of the north its world-wide renown. You, in the north, must learn to understand our southern ideals. In this coming together there may be a softening of the north and a hardening of the south. Neither will suffer in the process. But come together we must if we aspire to see our country mend its fortunes in our time.[20]

Later, from the vantage point of the Irish Dominion League, he recalled this period, stressing the central tenet of his political faith:

During seven years of my official life, I worked as hard to make the Department, for which I was responsible, subserve the interests of the northern industrialists, as I did when I was working for my own friends among the farmers of the south. Then I learned what a united Ireland meant.[21]

Perhaps more than any other major figure, without conceding the separatist case, Plunkett appreciated the strength of Ulster's objections to an Irish parliament and the depth of northern feeling against home rule. He may well have been correct in his belief that, in the prevailing circumstances, dominion home rule was the only form of administration which could have sheltered a united Ireland. That this approach was never adopted had as much to do with the struggle between the main English parties as it had with the divisions inside Ireland. As for nationalist criticism that he was dragging a red-herring across the path of home rule, nothing could have been further from the truth. Plunkett may have, unwittingly, dragged a red herring across the path of the Parliamentary Party (which it found impossible to resist), but his achievement was to establish a form of home rule in both the administration of Irish agriculture (via the DATI), and in its practice (through the co-operative movement), with the support of a large body of Irish unionists, equally acceptable to the north and to the south. As a fact of co-operation in its widest sense, this stands unequalled in a divided Ireland.

One fine Easter afternoon on a last visit, Lennox Robinson took him south to the countryside just outside Dublin.

We drove to Bray, up to Windy Gap, and walked a little. He took my arm because he was very feeble. We got to the brow of the hill looking down on Greystones and the mountains beyond. The prospect was utterly lovely. His clutch on my arm tightened, trembled, 'Oh Lynx, what wouldn't a man do for a country like this?' [22]

APPENDIX[1]

OMAHA. When Sir Horace Plunkett was a cowboy in Western Nebraska and Eastern Wyoming, he had an amusing experience with the famous old scout and frontiersman, Jim Bridger,[2] in which Bridger, telling the truth in describing the wonders of Yellowstone National Park, was voted a bigger liar than Sir Horace, who was rehashing the world's champion lies as told by Baron Munchausen.

The 'jury' was a bunch of wild cowboys who had never heard of the immortal Munchausen. And at that time Yellowstone was almost an unknown region and had been visited by few white men. The stories were told while sitting around a camp fire at night, after the 'night herd' riders had been posted, supper over and the big herd 'put to bed'. Then, as the cowboys sat around the fire, smoking and joking, stirring tales of the early West, which never found their way into print were told, tales of the old Bozeman Trail, Powder River tales, tales of old, tales of gold, tales of '49.

In Omaha, where he owned several hundred thousand dollars worth of real estate, Sir Horace Plunkett was 'somebody'. In London, Sir Horace was more than a mere 'somebody'. But out on the great Wyoming cattle range he was just 'Hod' Plunkett, just as good as anybody else and not one whit better. He held up his end of the 'stick,'* could ride a horse, throw a lariat, shoot a gun with the other cowboys. And he knew Baron Munchausen, which the other cowboys did not.

The story-telling game started one night when old Jim was telling about Yellowstone Park. He was skirting a lake of very cold water, he said, when he saw some big trout in the shallows. Then, in picturesque language which cannot be reduced to 'dictionary words,' nor spelled with any known combination of letters, the old Indian trader went on with his tale.

'I took my ramrod for a fish pole, rolled some fiber into an Injun

*He pulled his weight.

231

fish line, got out a fish hook I always carried, baited it with a piece of bacon and dropped it among the fish. One big fellow grabbed it. I jerked. It was hard pulling, and when that trout came out, the spring of the ramrod threw it clear over my head. It fell into a hole of hot water which happened to be right behind me, and in a few minutes I had a fine boiled trout for dinner.'

'Yah,' laughed a cowboy. 'Yes, you did.'

'Well,' said Hod Plunkett. 'One time I was out hunting. I saw a fine buck. But I had run out of bullets. I had been eating some cherries and I loaded my gun with cherry seed and shot at the buck. I thought I had missed. The buck bounded away. Five years later I was in that same forest. I saw a cherry tree about 10 feet high. When I walked up to it, the tree suddenly jumped up and ran away. Then I saw it was growing on the back of a big buck deer. I found the cherry stones I had shot had taken root in the back of the buck and had grown.'

'Tell another, Jim,' bantered a cowboy. 'Tell another.'

'The night after I had that boiled trout for my dinner,' the old plainsman told, 'I made camp down close to a little stream. I had shot an antelope. When I went to dress the meat I found that stream so hot I couldn't bear my hand in it. I rolled up my blanket and went to sleep. Long towards midnight I hear a roar like a thunderstorm coming from upstream and the water started rising. And getting hotter. Soon that little brook was a raging river. And the water was boiling, too. I had to move camp three times in that night, getting to higher ground. At daylight, I started out to find what all that noise was about. Upstream aways I found a big hole, big as a house, in the mountain side, just shooting out boiling water, full size. While I watched it the roaring ceased, the boiling water stopped running out, and in a while that river was just a little brook again.'

'How about you, Hod?' called one of the boys. 'Hod' was equal to the call.

'One time in Siberia night overtook me, and while my map showed a town at this point, there was no town there. The snow was deep. By the side of the road was a large cross protruding from the snow. I hitched my horse to the cross, rolled up in my big cloak, and went to sleep in the snow. The next morning, when I woke up, I was in the centre of a town and the snow had all melted. I looked around for my horse and finally found him hanging by the bridle from the cross on the church steeple. Investigation disclosed the snow had been so deep it had covered the entire town. What I thought was a cross on the ground was the cross on the church steeple. A warm wind had thawed the snow during the night. We got the horse down and I continued my journey.'

'Can you beat that Jim?' somebody laughed. 'I don't believe what that English fellow tells,' replied Jim, 'but I know I'm telling the gospel truth.'

'Well, sir, for about two weeks I wandered around in a sort of fairyland. I came to a river down in a deep gulch. The river was wide and deep. I wanted to get across but I couldn't find any way. After a while I came to a broad stone bridge made out of a single rock that spanned the canyon, and I walked across to the other side on this. Later that day I followed deer tracks through the forest. I was so busy tracking that deer that I wasn't watching other things. Suddenly I found myself in a forest that had turned to stone. Everything was petrified. The big trees were all standing just as if they were alive, except that they didn't have any leaves. Next I came to a mountain of glass. You couldn't see through it because it was black glass. But it was bright and shiny. There wasn't any tree, nor grass, nor bushes on it. It was just a high mountain of black glass. And then . . .'

'Hold on there, Jim,' a cowboy called out. 'Covering a lot of ground. ain't you? Give Hod a chance.' 'Hod' took his opportunity.

'On that same trip to Siberia,' said Hod, 'my horse went lame and I had to hire another horse and a sleigh. In the midst of a dark, dismal forest a big timber wolf chased us. My horse was doing his best, but he couldn't outrun that wolf. The beast overtook us and sprang at me. I dropped to the bottom of the sleigh and the wolf struck the hindquarters of the horse and started tearing and eating the horse, which kept on running. Finally, when the horse was almost devoured, I took my whip and gave that wolf a cut. It bounded forward just as the horse died and dropped out of the harness. The harness dropped on the wolf. I grabbed the reins and by liberal use of the whip kept the wolf going forward, and soon drove right up to an inn in a town. Here the wolf was killed. I secured another horse and continued my journey.'

'Jim, you've got to go some to beat that one,' said the foreman. But Jim was ready.

'After I got away from that glass mountain,' Jim told the cowboys, 'I went along by the river. The water was about a mile down in a canyon. It looked like a silver ribbon down there, it was so far away. And there were spires of rock about 100 feet high down there. And on top of each one of these spires an eagle had built its nest. And the eagles were flying around about as tame as a flock of pigeons. And then I came to a valley of about 50 acres. Long before I got to it I saw white steam rising, I didn't know what it was. But I came over the top of a little mountain and down there was the strangest sight I ever saw. There were about a thousand little volcanoes, each about a couple of feet high, and out of every one hot steam was pouring. The ground was all white and I thought at first it was snow. But it was some sort of mineral. I walked out among the little volcanoes and the ground shook just like a bowl of jelly. I was afraid my foot would break through, so I tiptoed off that place and got out on solid ground. But the queerest thing ...'

'Wait a minute, Jim,' suggested the foreman. 'You'll get so far ahead of Hod he'll never catch up.'

'After I got back from that Siberian trip I had to go down into Africa on business,' broke in Hod Plunkett. 'While down there I went hunting. After I had shot away all my shells I met a lion. There was a high bluff on one side and a deep swift river on the other. I turned to run and there right behind me was a crocodile, the biggest thing I ever saw. The crocodile opened its great jaws to swallow me just as the lion leaped from the other side. I ducked and the lion went right over my head and into the jaws of the crocodile. He came with such force that his head stuck in the croc's mouth so that the big alligator couldn't swallow the lion and couldn't spit him out either. The lion started eating away on the other's innards and I saw the greatest fight you ever heard of. The lion was getting the best of it. So I took out my hunting knife and cut the lion's head off, leaving it in the crocodile's mouth. That choked the crocodile to death. After it was dead I measured it and found it was 100 feet long. Then I skinned the dead lion and took the skin back to London with me, and had a rug made of it. That rug is in my house over there now to prove the story.'

'Can you beat that, Jim?' asked the foreman. 'I ain't trying to beat nothing,' replied Jim. 'All I know is what I saw.'

'Now as to that queer thing I started to tell you about. Me and my horse were riding along kinder quiet like when all of a sudden there was a roar like 40 cannon and right up out of the ground about 50 feet away busted up a column of water about as big around as a hogshead that reached just about to the clouds. I could see from the steam that it was boiling, too. When it got to the clouds it started falling like rain. Me and my horse took a running jump and got far enough away so that that hot water wouldn't fall on us, and then we stopped to watch it. Well, sir, that thing spouted along there for about 10 minutes and then it stopped just as sudden as it started. I went back to investigate and there was a hole about as big as a barrel or little bigger. I hung around for about an hour, and damned if it didn't go off again! And the same big column of boiling water busted out just as it did before. Well, I camped close there that night, and, bing me, if about every hour, as regular as my old watch run, that thing broke out. It woke me up every time and I got to reckoning the hour by that blamed thing!'

Old Jim got lots of applause on that story, which no one believed, of course, but which the old fellow insisted was the gospel truth. Then Hod Plunkett started again.

'Once I was on a boat crossing the Mediterranean Sea when there was a big storm and our boat was wrecked. I was a good swimmer and I struck out for land, about 10 miles away. But before I reached shore I was overtaken by a big fish and was swallowed. When I got down into that fish's belly I found there was lots of room and I decided to make that animal sick and maybe he would eject me. And I was right. After I had danced around a while and played some games, that fish got awfully sick. He tried so hard to eject me that he stood straight up, with his head and shoulders out of water. Some sailors in another boat saw him and harpooned him and dragged him on board. They started cutting him up for food, and when there was a hole in his belly I called to them to hurry, that I wanted to get out. They got scared and started to throw the remains overboard. But I worked fast from the inside and managed to get out, feeling rather hungry, but none the worse for my queer experience.'

'Say,' spoke up Powder River Pete. 'Are you that fellow that was swallowed by a whale? I always thought there was something fishy about that story, and I'm glad to hear the truth about it at last. Down to Cheyenne one evening I didn't have anything else to do, and I stopped on the street and heard a preacher talk. He told us all about that experience of yours, while the name he used didn't sound just like your name he probably got mixed up a little. Anyway, I'm glad to hear the story first hand. And that proves all you've been saying is true, too, because that's the strangest story you told.'

'Whose the biggest liar of these two fellows?' asked the foreman. 'Suppose we take a vote.' 'There's nothing to it,' announced Pete. 'Hod there's been telling the truth and Jim Bridger's just an old liar all the way through. How about it boys?'

Unanimously Bridger, who had been telling the exact truth, was voted a bigger liar than Sir Horace Plunkett, who had been telling some of the choicest of Baron Munchausen's adventures.

This incident was told by the late F. G. S. Hesse[3] of Buffalo, Wyoming. In 1919 when Sir Horace was in Omaha looking over his investments, Col. Hesse came from his Wyoming home to see the Irish baronet and to talk over old times. Whenever Sir Horace came to America, he and Col. Hesse always spent a few days together, going over 'Powder River Days' as they expressed it.

Sir Horace came to America when a young man, seeking health. He first went to Denver, and then northward into Wyoming, where he made big investments in cattle and ranches and mines. At the time of his death a few weeks ago his investments in Wyoming were more than $1,000,000.[4]

'I saw Hod Plunkett the first day he arrived in the Powder River country.' Col. Hesse said. 'He was sitting on the tongue of a bull wagon and he had come all the way from Denver, 400 or 500 miles, either walking or riding that wagon tongue, in search of health. He was ragged and dirty. Hadn't had a bath since the last rain or the last river. And both are scarce in that part of Wyoming. He and I bunked together for six or seven years.

'Hod dropped all this 'Sir'[5] business while in Wyoming. He was just like the rest of us. He used to go back to London every winter, and over there he was 'Sir'. But when he would get back to Wyoming in the spring, he was just plain 'Hod' again. He got to be the best horseman on the range. But when he tried to ride a steer one day, you would have thought the animal was his long lost brother from the way he hugged its neck. Last thing I saw of that critter he was going across the plains, head and tail up, while Hod Plunkett was on the ground, searching for the breath he lost when that critter shook him off.

'Not very dignified for a British lord, but all right for old Hod Plunkett!'

NOTES

Abbreviations

HC	House of Commons
IH	The *Irish Homestead*
IS	The *Irish Statesman*
NLI	National Library of Ireland
NLS	National Library of Scotland
NRAS	National Register of Archives (Scotland)
NYPL	New York Public Library
PD	Plunkett Diaries
PF	Plunkett Foundation
PRI	Public Record Office of Ireland
PRONI	Public Record Office of Northern Ireland
TCD	Trinity College Dublin

I.   MEATH AND WYOMING

1   PD, 16 May 1881.
2   *Irish World* (New York), 11 September, 18 September 1880.
3   *Omaha Daily Bee*, 18 May 1881.
4   PD, 19 May 1881.
5   He turned down an offer of a directorship of the Bank of Ireland in order to devote himself entirely to his co-operative campaign. PD, 25 January 1891.
6   E.F.Schumacher, *Small is Beautiful: a Study of Economics as if People Mattered* (London, 1974) p.198.
7   *IS*, 1st series, 5 June 1920.
8   *The Gael* (New York), March 1902, p.81.
9   *The Union* (Dublin), 17 March 1888.
10 *Ibid.*, 17 March 1888.
11 PD, 3 February 1885.
12 PD, 8 September 1885.
13 PD, 22 November 1881.
14 PD, 23 May 1883.
15 PD, 19 May 1883.
16 PD, 27 July 1888.
17 PD, 25 May 1884.
18 PD, 20 August 1884.
19 PD, 4 July 1884.

20   PD, 12 June 1883.
21   PD, 23 September 1881.
22   PD, 3 June 1881.
23   Horace Plunkett, *The Rural Life Problem of the United States:Notes of an Irish Observer* (New York, 1910) p.110.
24   PD, 15 May 1884.
25   PD, 26 August 1881.
26   PD, 11 October 1881.
27   PD, 6 November 1881.
28   *Cheyenne Leader*, 5 November 1889.
29   PD, 2 November 1887.
30   PD, 19 October 1887.
31   *Report of the British Association for the Advancement of Science*,1908, p.797.
32   Elizabeth Countess of Fingall, *Seventy Years Young: Memories (told to Pamela Hinkson)* (London, 1937) p.149.
33   PD, 2 April 1891.
34   PD, 10 June 1891.
35   PD, year end 1892.
36   Bernard Shaw to Margaret Digby, 16 June 1948 (PF SHA 37).
37   Horace Plunkett, *Ireland in the New Century* (London, 1904) p.19.
38   *Ibid.*, p.23.
39   W.E.H.Lecky, *Clerical Influences, an Essay on Irish Sectarianism and English Government* (Dublin, 1911; first published in 1861) pp.45-6.
40   Emily Lawless, *Ireland* (London, 1923) p.300.
41   George Berkeley, *The Querist* (published anonymously Dublin and London, 1735-7).

II.   THE CO-OPERATIVE MOVEMENT AND THE IAOS

1   E.T.Craig, *An Irish Commune: the History of Ralahine* (Dublin, undated).
2   *Daily Express* (Dublin), 21 March 1900.
3   L.P.Curtis, *Coercion and Conciliation in Ireland, 1880-1892:a Study in Constructive Unionism* (Princeton, 1963) p.336.
4   PD, 7 February 1886; *Fortnightly Review*, new series,55 (1894) p.278.
5   *The Nineteenth Century*, 24 (1888) pp.410-418.
6   Horace Plunkett, *Co-operation for Ireland: Self-help by Mutual Help* (Manchester, undated c. 1890) p.3.
7   L. Smith-Gordon and L.C.Staples, *Rural Reconstruction in Ireland: a Record of Co-operative Organisation* (London, 1917) pp. 38-9.
8   PD, 1 October; 14 December 1888.
9   Smith-Gordon and Staples, *Rural Reconstruction in Ireland*, p.39.
10   PD, 30 November 1888.
11   PD, 9-12 June 1889.
12   *The Times*, 28 December 1926 (obituary notice for Lord Monteagle); PD, 28 December 1926.
13   Horace Plunkett, *Co-operation for Ireland: Self-help by Mutual Help*, p.6.
14   To remedy this weakness Plunkett engaged E.P.M. Marum (a nationalist MP from Kilkenny) in September 1890 to speak at co-operative meetings. Marum started his work with great verve and enthusiasm but died suddenly ten days later.

15 J.E.Wrench, *Struggle, 1914-1920* (London, 1935) p.432.
16 M.J.Bonn, *Wandering Scholar* (London,1949) p.84.
17 Monteagle's daughter, Mary Spring Rice (1880-1924), a nationalist,Gaelic Leaguer and 'a kind of parish providence' was enthusiastically involved in every endeavour of the local community.
18 R.A.Anderson, *With Horace Plunkett in Ireland* (London,1935) pp.2-3.
19 *A Page of Irish History: Story of University College, Dublin 1883-1900* (Dublin, 1930) pp.246-57.
20 *Ibid.*, pp.251-2.
21 N.F.S. Grundtvig (1783-1872) titular bishop of Zealand, poet, philosopher, theologian, inspired the Danish folk high schools to educate for life. Ironically it was Patrick Pearse, in Scoil Eanna ('Pearse's academy of Irish — and rebellion', PD, 13 May 1916) who most faithfully followed Grundtvig's educational precepts.
22 *Third Report of the Royal Commission on University Education in Ireland; Evidence*, 1902, Cd.1229, xxxii, p.237.
23 Horace Plunkett, *A Suggested Solution to the Rural Problem* (Dublin,1913) p.19.
24 Horace Plunkett, *Co-operation for Ireland: Self-help by Mutual Help*, p.8.
25 Lady Gregory ed., *Ideals in Ireland* (London, 1901) editor's note p.10.
26 *Studies*, 29 (1940) p.35.
27 Horace Plunkett, *Ireland in the New Century*, p.182.
28 Horace Plunkett, *Co-operation for Ireland: Self-help by Mutual Help*, p.8.
29 *Ibid.*, p.9.
30 Horace Plunkett, *Co-operation in Ireland: the Best Means of Promoting both Distributive and Productive Co-operation in the Rural Districts of Ireland* (Manchester, 1890) p.7.
31 R.A.Anderson, *With Horace Plunkett in Ireland*, pp.47-8.
32 Robert Dennis, *Industrial Ireland: a Practical and Non-political View of 'Ireland for the Irish'* (London, 1887) p.36.
33 Patrick Bolger, *The Irish Co-operative Movement: its History and Development* (Dublin, 1977) p.65.
34 *Ibid.*, p.66.
35 Quoted in Plunkett, *Ireland in the New Century*, p.190.
36 Arthur Balfour spent less than six months of his four and a half years as chief secretary in Ireland. He could never be accused of 'going green' like his sister-in-law, Lady Betty, or his successor George Wyndham.
37 *The Nineteenth Century*, 48 (1900) p.893.
38 PD, 5 January 1891.
39 T. de V. White, *The Story of the Royal Dublin Society* (Tralee, 1955) pp.166-171; James Meenan, Desmond Clarke (eds.) *The Royal Dublin Society 1731-1981* (Dublin, 1981) p.96; Minutes of RDS Agricultural Committee, 22 January, 19 February, 19 March 1891.
40 'The United Irish League's policy of land agitation in the west of Ireland may be too strong for social and economic reform', Plunkett commented in 1900, PD, 5 December 1900.
41 Horace Plunkett, *The Trend of Co-operation in Great Britain and Ireland* (Dublin, c. 1902) p.8.
42 Horace Plunkett, *Oxford and the Rural Problem* (Oxford, 1921) p.9.
43 *Cork Herald*, 19 March 1896.
44 PD, 31 July 1891; Plunkett to T.P.Gill, 13 October 1891(NLI Ms 13,493(1)).
45 Horace Plunkett, *The Unsettlement of the Irish Land Question* (Dublin,1909) p.20.

46 *Freeman's Journal*, 9 July 1891.
47 PD, 30 June 1891.
48 C.C.Riddall, *Agricultural Co-operation in Ireland: the Story of a Struggle* (Dublin, 1950) p.25.
49 Margaret Digby, *Horace Plunkett, an Anglo-American-Irishman* (Oxford, 1949) p.63.
50 Riddall, *Agricultural Co-operation in Ireland*, p.14.
51 *Ibid.*, p.15.
52 James Musgrave (1829-1904) after whom the Musgrave Channel in Belfast Harbour is named, director of a major engineering firm in Belfast and a benevolent landlord of a large estate in Glencolumbkille, Co. Donegal.
53 F.W.Raiffeisen (1818-88) German economist and co-operator established his first people's bank near Coblenz in 1865 to free the local farmers from usury. He lived to see his movement spread to Austria, Switzerland and Italy.
54 Smith-Gordon and Staples, *Rural Reconstruction in Ireland* (appendices).

III. PARLIAMENT AND THE RECESS COMMITTEE

1 F.S.L.Lyons, 'The Economic Ideas of Parnell', in *Historical Studies* ii (ed. Michael Roberts) (London, 1959) pp.64-5.
2 *Ibid.*, p.70; *The Times*, 20 April 1891.
3 *Ibid.*, p.73.
4 *IAOS Annual Report* 1907, p.63.
5 Plunkett to T.P.Gill, 20 June 1891 (NLI Ms 13,493(1)).
6 Plunkett to T.P.Gill, 12 July 1891 (NLI Ms 13,493(1)).
7 Horace Plunkett, *Oxford and the Rural Problem*, p.8.
8 PD, 26 June 1891.
9 Elizabeth Malcolm, 'The Catholic Church and the Irish Temperance Movement, 1838-1901', *Irish Historical Studies*, xxiii (1982) pp.1-16.
10 PD, 31 October 1891.
11 PD, year end 1891.
12 *Hansard*, H.C., 4th series v. 2, cols. 1396-99, 21 March 1892.
13 PD, 3 February 1893.
14 Hansard, H.C., 4th series v. 11, cols. 697,702,706, 19 April 1893.
15 Winston Churchill (collected works). *A History of the English Speaking Peoples IV: The Great Democracies* (London, 1976) p.285.
16 W.B.Wells, *An Irish Apologia: Some Thoughts on Anglo-Irish Relations and the War* (Dublin, 1917) p.3.
17 PD, 9 August 1893.
18 PD, 1 May 1894.
19 Michael Davitt, *Leaves from a Prision Diary; or, Lectures to a 'Solitary' Audience* (London, 1885).
20 PD, 24 June 1892.
21 PD, 27 May 1895.
22 PD, 12 June 1895.
23 PD, 19 June 1895.
24 Horace Plunkett, *The Evolution of Ireland's Agricultural Policy, a Retrospect and a Prospect* (London, 1925) p.8.
25 *Irish Textile Journal*, 15 January 1897.

26 J.Coolahan, *Irish Education: its History and Structure* (Dublin, 1981) p.88.
27 J.R.Fisher, *The Ulster Liberal Unionist Association: a Sketch of its History* (Belfast, 1914) p.99.
28 *Irish Textile Journal*, 15 February 1893.
29 *Ibid.*, 15 June 1893.
30 J.Larmor (ed.), *The Scientific Writings of the late George Francis Fitzgerald* (Dublin, 1902) pp.393-404.
31 *Irish Times*, 28 August 1895; *Belfast Newsletter*, 29 August 1895.
32 Horace Plunkett, *Ireland in the New Century*, p.216.
33 R.J.Lucas, *Colonel Saunderson MP* (London, 1908) p.240-3.
34 *Belfast Newsletter*, 29 August 1895; *Northern Whig*, 29 August 1895; *Irish Textile Journal*, 15 September 1895.
35 PD, 20 December 1895.
36 T. Sinclair to Plunkett, quoted in *IH*, 11 January 1896.
37 *Report of the Recess Committee* (Dublin, 1896) p.3.
38 *Belfast Newsletter*, 6 August 1896; *Northern Whig*, 6 August 1896.
39 *New Review*, 31 October 1896.
40 *Freeman's Journal*, 4 August 1896.
41 Minute Book of the Recess Committee (T.P.Gill papers NLI Ms. 4532).
42 *Fortnightly Review*, new series, 55 (1894) p.283.
43 *Observations on the References in the Recess Committee's Report to the Royal Dublin Society, its Work and Position in Ireland* (Dublin, 1896), p.14.
44 *New Ireland Review*, 6 (1897) pp.328-336.
45 *IH*, 2 January 1897.
46 The complex tactical reasons for the withdrawal of the first agriculture and industries bill are detailed by Andrew Gailey,'Unionist Rhetoric and Irish Local Government, 1895-9'. *Irish Historical Studies,*xxiv (1984) pp.52-68.
47 *Hansard H.C.* 4th series v. 37, col. 481, 17 February 1896.
48 R.J. Lucas, *Colonel Saunderson MP*, p.246.
49 *Ibid.*, p.248; Col. Saunderson letter to *The Times*, 9 March 1896; Plunkett letter to *The Times*, 12 March 1896.
50 Lord Ardilaun to C.L.Falkiner, 14 December 1896 (T. P. Gill papers NLI Ms 13,509(6)).
51 *Hansard HC*, 4th series v.41, cols. 677,679, 8 June 1896.
52 *Irish Times*, 7 January 1897.
53 R.J.Lucas, *Colonel Saunderson MP*, p.262.
54 *Hansard HC*, 4th series v.48, cols. 171-7, 30 March 1897.
55 *IH*, 10 April 1897.
56 *Ibid.*, 1 May 1897; Minute Book of the Recess Committee (T.P.Gill papers NLI Ms. 4532).
57 *Irish Textile Journal*, 15 December 1897.
58 *Ibid.*, 15 December 1897.
59 *IH*, 12 February 1898.
60 *Hansard HC*, 4th series v.53, col. 196, 9 February 1898.
61 PD, 18 May 1897.
62 Plunkett to T.P.Gill, 11 August 1899 (NLI Ms 13,494(8)).
63 T.Sinclair to G.Balfour, 21 January 1900 (Balfour papers NRAS TD 85/97/4/274).
64 Plunkett to T. P. Gill, 9 February, 19 February, 20 February 1900. (NLI Ms 13,495(1)(2)).
65 PD, 21 February 1900.
66 PD, 4 January 1894.
67 *Irish Times*, 5 December 1899.

68 *Daily Express* (Dublin), 31 May 1900.
69 PD, 12 June 1900.
70 *Daily Express*, 25 August 1900.
71 PD, 22 May 1900.
72 *The Nineteenth Century*, 49 (1900) p.898.
73 *Ibid.*, p.891.
74 *Daily Express*, 2 October 1900.
75 *Irish Times*, 9 October 1900.
76 *Northern Whig*, 11 October 1900.
77 *Ibid.*, 26 September 1900.
78 *Irish Times*, 9 October 1900.
79 PD, 31 October 1900.
80 PD, 22 March 1901.
81 PD, 29 January 1901.
82 PD, 15 November, 21 November 1901. Plunkett received strong support during the campaign from Michael Cusack, founder of the Gaelic Athletic Association. *Freeman's Journal*, 27 November 1901.
83 The election was unusual in another sense for Lynch, an Irish-Australian who never appeared in the constituency, had fought for the Boers in South Africa. On arrival at Westminster to claim his seat, he was promptly arrested and tried for high treason (a capital offence). Carson was counsel for the prosecution and Lynch was sentenced to death; this was commuted to life imprisonment; he was released having served only a few months of his sentence and in 1907 procured a free pardon. He subsequently sat as a nationalist MP for West Clare from 1909 to 1918, advocated a more vigorous prosecution of the war against Germany (winning Carson's warm commendation) and was given a commission to conduct a recruiting campaign in Ireland. Arthur Lynch, *Ireland, Vital Hour* (London, 1915).
84 H.G.Smith to Lady Fingall, 1 February 1938 (PF miscellaneous correspondence).
85 PD, 11, 12 March 1901.
86 Edward Carson to the Provost of TCD with a copy to Plunkett, 20 June 1915 (PF CARS 3/1, 3/2).

IV.   IRELAND IN THE NEW CENTURY

1   PD, 9 April 1901.
2   Plunkett to T.P.Gill, 27 June 1896 (NLI Ms 13,509(2)).
3   Daniel Hoctor, *The Department's Story: a History of the Department of Agriculture* (Dublin, 1974) pp.66-7.
4   *Irish Textile Journal*, 15 December 1901.
5   *DATI Journal* 1901-2, p.692.
6   R.Meyer (secretary of the Northern Subcommittee of the Recess Committee) to C. L. Falkiner, 24 July 1896 (T.P.Gill papers NLI Ms 13,509(4)).
7   T.Sinclair to T.P.Gill, 25 July 1896 (NLI Ms 13,509(4)).
8   Plunkett to Lady Betty Balfour, 21 December 1899 (PF BAL 55).
9   J.Coolahan, *Irish Education*, p.88, Archbishop Walsh to Plunkett, 25 August 1896, (T. P. Gill papers NLI Ms 13,509(5)).
10 *Report of the Departmental Committee of Enquiry into the Provisions of the Agricultural and Technical Instruction (Ireland) Act 1899, Minutes of Evidence*; 1907, Cd. 3574,xviii, pp.179-80,207-8.

11 PD, 7 November 1900.
12 PD, 24 October 1900.
13 PD, 18 February 1901.
14 *Third Report of the Royal Commission on University Education in Ireland, Minutes of Evidence*; 1902, Cd. 1229, xxxii, p.232.
15 *Ibid.*, p.236.
16 Horace Plunkett, *Ireland in the New Century* (popular edition with epilogue, London, 1905) pp.322-4,329-31.
17 Secretary of the Lurgan Technical Schools to Plunkett,29 October 1901 (PRI DATI papers Box L).
18 Plunkett's speech at the opening of the Newtownards Technical School,3 February 1903 (PRI DATI papers Box N).
19 Standish O'Grady's son was turned down for a DATI post on the grounds that, while his qualifications were suitable, he lacked practical experience. O'Grady went on the attack in the columns of the *All Ireland Review*, and Plunkett commented, 'Standish O'Grady is the only man in the world who could with absolute sincerity write a leading article in his own newspaper advocating his son's pre-eminence for a government post in the public interest'.Standish O'Grady file, particularly Plunkett to T. W. Rolleston, 9 October 1905, (PRI DATI papers Box O).
20 Plunkett to Hugh A. Law, 16 March 1905 (PRI DATI papers Box L).
21 Douglas Hyde to Plunkett, 28 October 1904; Plunkett to Douglas Hyde, 17 November 1904 (PRI DATI papers Box G - Gaelic League).
22 Ardilaun to Plunkett, 28 May 1904; Plunkett to Ardilaun, 16 May, 17 May 1904 (PRI DATI papers Box A).
23 Shan Bullock, *After Sixty Years* (London, 1931) p.v.
24 PD, 11 November 1900.
25 Plunkett to T.P.Gill, 27 February 1903 (NLI Ms 13,496(4)).
26 Horace Plunkett, *Ireland in the New Century*, p.vii.
27 *Ibid.*, p.2.
28 *Ibid.*, p.10.
29 *Ibid.*, p.64.
30 *Ibid.*, pp.66-7.
31 *Ibid.*, pp.67-8.
32 *Ibid.*, p.79.
33 *Ibid.*, p.83.
34 *Ibid.*, pp.86-7.
35 Plunkett to T.P.Gill, 11 July 1901 (NLI Ms 13,495(9)).
36 W.G.Neely, *Kilcooley: Land and People in Tipperary* (Belfast, 1983) p.117.
37 Plunkett to the Bishop of Winchester, 14 May 1913 (PF WINC 4).
38 Horace Plunkett, *Ireland in the New Century*, pp.120-121.
39 Plunkett had put his finger on the tendency for architects of Irish churches to use poor quality imported stained glass, statuary and metal work at a time of renewal of these crafts in Ireland. The interior of St. Brendan's Cathedral, Loughrea (influenced by Edward Martyn and by Fr. Jeremiah O'Donovan, another co-operative enthusiast) is a remarkable tribute to the skill of Irish craftsmen and women of the period. (*Ireland in the New Century*, p.108n).
40 Joseph Lee, *The Modernisation of Irish Society 1884-1918* (Dublin, 1973), chapter 1.
41 Horace Plunkett, *Ireland in the New Century*, p.138.
42 *Ibid.*, p.291.
43 *Northern Whig*, 24 February, 27 February 1904; *All Ireland Review*, 9 April 1904.

44 *Freeman's Journal*, 5 March 1904.
45 *Ibid.*, 7 March 1904.
46 M.O'Riordan, *Catholicity and Progress in Ireland* (London, 1905).
47 *Hansard* HC 4th series v. 136, cols. 1015-1060, 1067-1087,23 June 1904.
48 Alphonse Désjardins to Plunkett, 31 January 1907 (PRI DATI papers Box D).
49 Dr.S.Welch to Plunkett, 20 April 1904 (PRI DATI papers Box W).
50 P.J.Hannon, assistant secretary of the IAOS, was at the time visiting the USA and the adverse publicity which the book received largely negatived his fundraising attempts among Irish-Americans. Starting life as a railway signalman in Co. Sligo, Hannon was promoted to the main junction at Mullingar. The directors arrived in a special train to open a new branch line. In his excitement he pulled the wrong lever and, instead of steaming out onto the main line, the special crashed into the buffers at the end of the siding. Hannon was transferred to a level crossing where he found plenty of time to read between trains. Some articles he wrote on the Recess Committee's report came to Plunkett's notice, he was appointed assistant secretary of the IAOS and became a successful organiser in the west of Ireland. A request for assistance from the Cape Colony government led to him working in South Africa. He returned a convinced imperialist, joined Chamberlain's campaign for tarrif reform, became a tory MP for Birmingham for 21 years, was a director of many midland companies and received a knighthood. (P.J. Hannon papers, House of Lords).
51 Horace Plunkett, *Ireland in the New Century* (popular edition with epilogue, London, 1905) p.310.
52 Elizabeth Fingall, *Seventy Years Young*, p.329.
53 *Hansard* HC 4th series v. 155, cols. 370-1, 3 April 1906. Plunkett was well aware of the real motive for he wrote, 'The Committee of Inquiry was all a blind ... Bryce kept me on simply to save the Department from wreck in Dillon's hands'. Plunkett to Gerald Balfour, 28 April 1907 (Balfour papers NRAS TD 85/97/2/113).
54 Patrick Bolger, *The Irish Co-operative Movement*, p.97.
55 R.A.Anderson, *With Horace Plunkett in Ireland*, pp.130-1.
56 *Hansard* HC 4th series v.170, cols. 876-884, 6 March 1907.
57 *Ibid.*, 4th series v.173, cols. 136-176, 24 April 1907.
58 *IH*, 20 April 1907.
59 *Irish Textile Journal*, 15 May 1907.
60 *Hansard* HC 4th series v.173, cols. 149-154, 24 April 1907.
61 Plunkett letter to *The Times*, 16 January 1912; John Dillon letter to *The Times*, 17 January 1912.
62 PD, 18 August 1891.
63 *Report of the Departmental Committee of Enquiry into the Provisions of the Agricultural and Technical Instruction (Ireland) Act, 1899*; 1907, Cd 3574, xviii p.501.
64 *Ibid.*, p.12.
65 *DATI Journal*, VII (1907) p.626.
66 T.W.Russell, *Ireland and the Empire: a Review, 1800-1900*, p.96.
67 T.W.Rolleston to Douglas Hyde (undated) quoted in C.H.Rolleston, *Portrait of an Irishman; a Biographical Sketch of T.W.Rolleston* (London, 1939) p.51.
68 *Freeman's Journal*, 20 January 1908.
69 *IH*, 25 January 1908.
70 Russell, who in 1897-8 had chaired a House of Commons select committee on money lending which had reported in favour of the agricultural banks, in 1910, decided that the whole system was 'rotten and indefensible', and the Departmental subvention to the banks linked to the IAOS was then withdrawn.
71 *Northern Whig*, 25 June 1910.

72 Sinn Féin, 25 November 1911.
73 IH, 20 August 1910, 12 November 1910, 13 June 1912; IAOS Annual Report, 1910 p.42.
74 IH, 23 September 1916.
75 Plunkett received strong backing in his application to the Commissioners from Lord Carrington, president of the British Board of Agriculture and Fisheries. (Addresses delivered at the Meetings of the Council of Agriculture during the First Vice-Presidency, 1900-1907 (Dublin, 1907) p.106).

V. NOBLESSE OBLIGE

1   Shane Leslie, The Irish Issue in its American Aspect (London 1918) p.97.
2   Emily Lawless, With the Wild Geese (London, 1902).
3   IH, 6 July 1918.
4   Lady Gregory's Diary, 21 March 1897 (Berg collection, NYPL).
5   PD, 10 September 1897.
6   Lady Gregory's Diary, autumn 1897.
7   Plunkett to T. P. Gill, 19 May 1898 (NLI Ms 13,494(1)).
8   Daily Express, 27 August 1898.
9   Evening Mail, 20 July 1898; Daily Express, 21 July 1898.
10 Lady Gregory's Diary, 21 February 1898.
11 Ibid., 19 February 1899.
12 Ibid., 4 February 1900.
13 Yeats spoke at a dinner for co-operators during the annual meeting of the IAOS in 1897, Lady Gregory comparing the effect to that of a 'rose-leaf falling among a lot of agricultural implements'. He addressed meetings of co-operators on at least two other occasions: the Beagh and Kiltartan Societies at Gort, Co. Galway in 1898; and a Galway conference in 1899. IH, 6 November, 1897; 24 September 1898; 28 October 1899; Lady Gregory's Diary c. November 1897.
14 Ibid., 3 May 1900.
15 PD, 22 February 1899.
16 Daily Express, 12 May 1899.
17 W.B.Yeats, Autobiographies (London, 1980) p.424.
18 George Moore, Hail and Farewell,3 vols., (London, 1911).
19 Plunkett to Alice Balfour, 20 February 1901 (Balfour papers NRAS TD 85/118/3/213).
20 Correspondence between Plunkett and Lady Betty Balfour (PF).
21 IH, 27 February 1897.
22 John P. Frayne (ed.), Uncollected Prose by W. B. Yeats (London, 1970),ii, p.162.
23 Daily Express, 29 January 1900.
24 Horace Plunkett, Ireland in the New Century, p.150.
25 Ibid., p.153.
26 IH, 3 August 1901.
27 IH, 22 October 1904.
28 Plunkett to Douglas Hyde, 22 March 1904 (PRI DATI papers Box G-Gaelic League).
29 Bancanna Tíre (IAOS pamphlet no. 2a, Dublin, undated).
30 Douglas Hyde, Ms. account of the Gaelic League Convention at Dundalk in 1915 (Archive of the Folklore Commission, Dublin).
31 Standish O'Grady to Plunkett, undated (PF O'G1).
32 J.O.Hannay to H. de F. Montgomery, 29 May 1907, (PRONI T1089/324).

33 AE (George W. Russell) *The National Being: Some Thoughts on an Irish Polity* (Dublin, 1916) p.172.
34 J.E.Wrench, *Struggle, 1914-1920* (London, 1935) p.431.
35 Elizabeth Fingall, *Seventy Years Young*, pp.313-5.
36 *Ibid.*, pp.313-5.
37 Wibberly observed that the most enthusiastic students in the agricultural classes which he ran as instructor with the DATI were invariably Gaelic Leaguers (Thomas Wibberly, *Profitable Tillage*, IAOS pamplet, new series, Dublin, undated).
38 *IAOS Annual Report* 1914, p.65.
39 E.E.Lysaght, *Sir Horace Plunkett and his Place in the Irish Nation* (Dublin, 1916) pp.85-6.
40 J.H. Kellogg, medical superintendent of the Sanitarium, was a distinguished surgeon and a health propagandist advocating vegetarianism and abstinence from alcohol, tea or coffee (a regime which Plunkett generally followed). With his brother W.K. he founded the cereal company of that name.
   The wheel turned full circle in 1953 when the Irish Countrywoman's Association (formerly the United Irishwomen) were presented with their magnificent headquarters, An Grianán, (the sunny place) at Termonfechin, Co. Louth by the Kellogg Foundation for the 'health, recreation and welfare of the people of Ireland.'
41 PD, 22 July 1903.
42 PD, 22 July 1903.
43 H.G.Smith to Lady Fingall,1 February 1938 (PF miscellaneous correspondence).
44 *Year Book of Agricultural Co-operation, 1939*, p.16.
45 The previous headquarters of the IAOS in Lincoln Place adjoined the Dublin Dental Hospital where visitors and staff were regularly disturbed by the howls of demented patients.
46 *Fortnightly Review*, new series, 47 (1890) pp.656-669.
47 *IAOS Annual Report* 1910, p.45.
48 Simon Goodenough, *Jam and Jerusalem, a Pictorial History of Britain's Greatest Woman Movement* (Glasgow, 1977) p.14.
49 Horace Plunkett, *Noblesse Oblige* (Dublin, 1908) p.7.
50 *Ibid.*, p.26.
51 *Ibid.*, p.37.
52 Standish O'Grady had written in 1900, 'Aristocracies come and go like the waves of the sea; and some fall nobly and others ignobly. As I write, this protestant Anglo-Irish aristocracy which once owned all Ireland from the centre to the sea, is rotting from the land ... without one brave deed, one brave word!' (*Selected Essays and Passages* (London, undated) p.180). He had expressed his earlier forebodings in *The crisis in Ireland* (Dublin,1882) and *All Ireland* (Dublin, 1898) chap. IV.

VI. ULSTER AND THE FRAMWORK OF HOME RULE

1 *Irish Textile Journal*, 15 December 1891.
2 *Ibid.*, 15 September 1892.
3 *Ibid.*, 15 May 1894.

4 *Belfast Newsletter*, 27 September 1895.
5 *Tyrone Constitution*, 15 November 1895.
6 *Belfast Evening Telegraph*, 18 November 1895.
7 *Coleraine Constitution*, 23 November 1895.
8 *Ibid.*, 30 November 1895.
9 *Northern Whig*, 20 December 1895.
10 PD, 31 March 1891.
11 PD, 1 April 1891.
12 Horace Plunkett, *Plain Talks to Irish Farmers* (Dublin, 1910) p.17.
13 *IH*, 7 August 1920.
14 Patrick Bolger, *The Irish Co-operative Movement*, p.147.
15 PD, 18 December 1901; correspondence between Plunkett and M.J.Magee
    (PRI DATI papers Box M).
16 *IH*, 10 March 1917.
17 *IH*, 16 March 1922.
18 Horace Plunkett, *Ireland in the New Century*, p.208.
19 PD, 26 January 1888.
20 PD, 23 March 1888.
21 Plunkett to Charles Gavan Duffy, 4 October 1892 (NLI autograph letter
    collection).
22 PD, 22 March 1893.
23 PD, 12 March 1905.
24 Plunkett to Arthur Balfour, 7 March 1905 (A. Balfour papers, British Library
    Add. Ms. 49792); Plunkett to Gerald Balfour, 7 March 1905 (Balfour papers
    NRAS TD/85/97/2/113).
25 PD, 20 November 1883.
26 PD, 20 October 1896.
27 *Irish Times*, 12 January 1903.
28 Plunkett to the *New Liberal Review*, 3 February 1903 (PRI DATI papers Box N).
29 Plunkett to Lady Gregory, 26 September 1902 (Berg collection NYPL).
30 PD, 20 September 1913.
31 Plunkett to Erskine Childers, 8 April 1914 (TCD Ms 7850/1003).
32 PD, 9 July 1906.
33 PD, 9 April 1923.
34 PD, 28 February 1923, 24 August 1924.
35 PD, 28 December 1926; *The Times*, 28 December 1926.
36 Anita Leslie, *Mr. Frewen of England* (London, 1966) p.51.
37 Elizabeth Fingall, *Seventy Years Young*, p. 267.
38 AE (G.W.Russell), *Co-operation and Nationality* (Dublin, 1912) p.30.
39 Plunkett to Lawrence Lowell, 23 December 1913 (PF LOW 11).
40 PD, 29 January 1908.
41 PD, 8 March 1922.
42 Arthur Griffith, *The Resurrection of Hungary: a Parallel for Ireland* (Dublin,
    1904).
43 John Sweetman to George Gavan Duffy, 27 October 1909, quoted in Seán O
    Lúing, *Art O Gríofa* (Dublin, 1953) p.185.
44 *Sinn Féin*, daily edition, 28 August 1909.
45 PD, 19 July 1912, 13 May 1916.
46 *Northern Whig*, 25 January 1908.
47 PD, 19 November 1908.
48 PD, year end 1909.
49 PD, 14 February 1910.

50 Plunkett to Monteagle, 27 August 1911 (NLI Ms 13,414).
51 PD, 19 August 1911.
52 PD, year end 1911.
53 Plunkett to Richmond Noble, 22 October 1911 (PF NOB 2).
54 Plunkett to Erskine Childers, 22 November 1911 (TCD Ms 7850/973).
55 AE to Erskine Childers, undated c. November 1911 (TCD Ms 7851/1158).
56 PD, 9 April 1908.
57 PD, 4 October 1908.
58 PD, 17 March 1911.
59 PD, 19 August 1911.
60 PD, 13 September 1911.
61 Erskine Childers, *The Framework of Home Rule* (London, 1911) p.64.
62 *Ibid.*, p.151.
63 *Ibid.*, p.215.
64 Plunkett to Erskine Childers, 27 April 1911. (TCD Ms 7850/965).
65 Plunkett to Erskine Childers, 18 January 1912 (TCD Ms 7850/975).
66 Horace Plunkett, *The Irish Situation in America, at Westminister and in Ireland* (Dublin, 1920) p.22.
67 S.Rosenbaum (ed.) *Against Home Rule; the Case for the Union* (London,1912).
68 PD, 10 March 1912.
69 PD, 5 May 1912.
70 PD, 1 April 1912.
71 PD, 11 April 1912.
72 PD, 25 April 1912.
73 PD, 29 June 1912.
74 PD, 24 September 1912.
75 PD, 8 November 1912.
76 PD, 25 June 1912.
77 Alec Wilson, *A Protestant Protest* (Ballymoney, 1913).
78 See chapter X, p. 184.
79 PD, 16 May 1894.
80 PD, 13 July 1892.
81 PD, 16 January 1914.
82 Plunkett to Carson, 2 February 1914 (PRONI D/1507/1/1914/4).
83 PD, 19 January 1914.
84 PD, 23 January 1914.
85 PD, 1 February 1914.
86 PD, 6 February 1914.
87 Plunkett to F.S.Oliver, 9 February 1914 (NLS Ms Acc 7726/88,8).
88 PD, 26 February 1914.
89 PD, 8 May 1914.
90 Childers had been introduced to Mary Spring Rice in the unlikely setting of an agricultural fair in Westminster Hall, London by Paddy the Cope (Patrick Gallagher, *My Story by Paddy the Cope*, Dungloe undated, p.138).
91 PD, 9 August 1914.
92 *The Times*, 10 February 1914.
93 Horace Plunkett, *A Better Way: an Appeal to Ulster not to Desert Ireland* (Dublin, 1914) p.5.
94 *Ibid.*, p.11.
95 *Ibid.*, p.13.
96 *Ibid.*, p. 16.
97 *Ibid.*, p.16.

98   *Ibid.*, p.18.
99   *Ibid.*, p.20.
100 *Ibid.*, p.25.

VII.   AMERICA AND THE WAR

1   PD, 27 November 1895.
2   PD, 23 December 1901.
3   Horace Plunkett, *The Rural Life Problem of the United States*, p.68.
4   Pinchot later became governor of Pennsylvania. His missionary temperament was unsuited to politics and although a great conservationist he was an unsuccessful politician.
5   Roosevelt to Plunkett, 3 July 1906 (PF ROO 5/1).
6   Plunkett to Noel Buxton, 31 July 1928 (PF BUX 2).
7   US Senate, *Report of the Country Life Commission*, 60th Congress, document no.705, 9 February 1909, p.4.
8   *IH*, 29 May 1909.
9   PD, 22 March 1919; Plunkett to Charles McCarthy, 15 June 1918 (PF MacC 136).
10 Gifford Pinchot to Plunkett, 29 May 1908 (PF PIN 1).
11 *North American Review*, 166 (1898) p.120.
12 Shane Leslie to John Dillon, 1 January 1917 (NLI Ms 22,853).
13 Horace Plunkett, *Ireland in the New Century*, p.74.
14 Plunkett to Lady Betty Balfour, 2 January 1901 (PF BAL 64).
15 PD, 24 December 1904.
16 Plunkett to Lady Betty Balfour, 2 January 1901 (PF BAL 64).
17 Roosevelt to T.P.Gill, 17 January 1911. E. Morrison et. al. ed., *The Letters of Theodore Roosevelt* (Cambridge, 1954) vol. vii, p.209.
18 PD, 19 June 1913.
19 PD, 7 December 1914.
20 PD, 20 December 1914; F. M. Carroll, *American Opinion and the Irish Question, 1910-23: a Study in Opinion and Policy* (Dublin, 1978) pp. 40, 44.
21 F.M.Carroll, *American Opinion and the Irish Question*, p.29.
22 PD, 16 January 1915.
23 PD, 6 February 1915.
24 Plunkett to E.M.House, 8 June 1915 (PF HOU 12).
25 The Treaty of Versailles, more an instrument of retribution than a foundation for peace, led to instability in post-war Germany thus contributing to the rise of Hitler.
26 PD, 3 December 1915.
27 Arthur Balfour memorandum (PF BALF.A 19/1).
28 Horace Plunkett, Memorandum on the Anglo-American Situation, Feburary 1916 (PF BALF.A 19/2).
29 Plunkett to House, 7 June 1916 (PF HOU 66).
30 Plunkett to House, 2 November 1916 (PF HOU 74).
31 Plunkett to House, 2 November 1916 (PF HOU 74).
32 E.M.House, *Intimate Papers: Arranged by Charles Seymour* (London, 1926-28) v. 2, p.400.
33 *Ibid.*, p.409.
34 PD, 3 April 1917.
35 F.M.Carroll, *American Opinion and the Irish Question*, pp.95-7.

36 Plunkett to T.A.Spring Rice, 18 June 1917, (PF SPR 13).
37 PD, year end 1916.
38 House cable to Plunkett, 29 April 1917 (PF HOU 86).

VIII. 1916

1 *Irish Times*, 7 October 1913.Two months later Plunkett referred to this as AE's'glorious indiscretion'. 'To attack the Dublin employers,the Castle, the police, the National MP's, the Ancient Order of Hibernians, the Roman Catholic Church over the condition of the Dublin slums was a magnificent exhibition of moral courage — so magnificent that I can forgive all his recklessness of consequence to my own little schemes'. Plunkett to F.S.Oliver, 18 December 1913 (NLS Ms Acc 7726/88).
2 *Co-operative News*, 4 October, 27 December 1913.
3 Plunkett to Lord Salisbury, 24 December 1913 (PF SAL 3).
4 Plunkett to John Redmond, 12 August 1914 (NLI Ms 15,221).
5 Plunkett to John Redmond, 9 August 1914 (NLI Ms 15,221).
6 Shane Leslie, *The Irish Issue in its American Aspect*, p.101.
7 W.Fitzgerald (ed), *The Voice of Ireland* (London, 1924) pp.125-128; Philip Magnus, *Kitchener: Portrait of an Imperialist* (London, 1968) pp.357-8; Lady Fingall, *Seventy Years Young* p.348; Speech by Lloyd George,*Hansard* HC, 5th series v.86, cols. 645-6, 18 October 1916.
8 PD, 23 April 1916.
9 Plunkett to James Byrne, 14 June 1916 (PF BYR.J 63).
10 Charles McCarthy to Plunkett, 10 May 1916 (PF MacC 104).
11 Lawrence Lowell to Plunkett, 5 July 1916 (PF LOW 22).
12 Theodore Roosevelt to Plunkett, 9 July 1916 (PF ROO 21).
13 Plunkett to Lawrence Lowell, 29 September 1914 (PF LOW 15). .
14 George Dangerfield, *The Damnable Question: a Study in Anglo-Irish Relations* (London, 1976) pp.159-161.
15 PD, 15 May 1916.
16 PD, 12 May 1916.
17 Thomson and Hall, in their secret service capacity, had also been responsible for concocting a number of wartime scares concerning German conspiracy in Ireland designed to pressurise Dublin Castle into taking a harder line with Sinn Féin. Thomson's career as head of the special branch was a failure. He became obsessed with the activities of the left in Britain, regarding the Labour Party as simply the tip of a Bolshevik iceberg, and erratic conduct led to his sacking by Lloyd George in 1921.The final humiliation came five years later with a conviction for indecent behaviour in a public park. (Eunan O'Halpin, 'Sir Warren Fisher and the Coalition, 1912-22'. *The Historical Journal*, 24, 4(1981) pp.907-27).
18 B.H.Thomson to Plunkett, 1 June 1916 (PF THO 2).
19 Plunkett to B.H.Thompson, 8 June 1916 (PF THO 3).
20 PD, 17 May 1916; Plunkett to Asquith, 22 May 1916 (PF ASQ 4).
21 Plunkett to Asquith, 22 May 1916 (PF ASQ 4).
22 Plunkett to Charles McCarthy, 18 May 1916 (PF MacC 105).
23 Plunkett to House, 25 May 1916 (PF HOU 62).
24 *The Irish Convention; Confidential Report to HM the King by the Chairman* (sine loco, 1918) p.3.
25 James Connolly, *The Reconquest of Ireland* (Dublin, 1917) p.315.

26 *Ibid.,* pp.315-316.
27 Plunkett to James Byrne, 14 June 1916 (PF BYR.J 63); R.F.Tobin to Plunkett, 11 May 1916 (PF TOB 1/2).

IX. THE CONVENTION

1 T.G.Moorhead to Margaret Digby, 6 February 1950 (PF miscellaneous correspondence).
2 Quoted in Dangerfield, *The Damnable Question,* p.50.
3 Lloyd George to Carson quoted in D.G.Boyce, 'How to Settle the Irish Question', in *Lloyd George* (A.J.P.Taylor ed.) (London, 1971) pp.137-64.
4 Plunkett to T.W.Rolleston, 23 May 1911 (PF ROL 19).
5 Plunkett to W.G.S.Adams, 22 May 1917 (PF ADA 26).
6 PD, 21 May 1917.
7 PD, 7 June 1917.
8 Edward MacLysaght, *Changing Times, Ireland since 1891* (Gerrards Cross, 1978) p.74.
9 *Observer,* 15 July 1917.
10 Andrew Boyle, *The Riddle of Erskine Childers* (London, 1977) p.235.
11 T.A.Spring Rice to W.G.S.Adams, 1 June, 4 June 1917 (Lloyd George Papers, House of Lords Record Office F/66/1/15, F/66/1/18).
12 B.L.Reid, *The Man from New York* (New York, 1968) p.331.
13 AE (G.W. Russell), *Thoughts for a Convention* (Dublin, 1917) pp.11-12.
14 Horace Plunkett, *A Defence of the Convention* (Dublin, 1917) pp.9-10.
15 *Ibid.,* p.11.
16 *Ibid.,* p.12.
17 Adam Duffin to Plunkett, 7 June, 16 June, 20 June 1917 (PF DUF 1, DUF 3, DUF 5).
18 *Irish Times,* 13 July 1917.
19 William O'Brien to Plunkett, 29 June 1917 (PF O'B 1).
20 PD, 30 June 1917, 3 July 1917.
21 PD, 11 July 1917.
22 Adam Duffin to his wife, 18 November 1917 (PRONI MIC 127/26).
23 Earl of Midleton, *Ireland — Dupe or Heroine* (London, 1933) pp.114-5.
24 PD, 26 July 1917.
25 Coffey had been a crew-member of the *Kelpie,* skippered by Conor O'Brien, a step-brother of Dermod O'Brien, which accompanied Childers and the *Asgard* on their voyage and landed its cargo of guns at Kilcoole, Co. Wicklow.
26 Diarmuid Coffey papers (in the possession of his daughter).
27 *Northern Whig,* 26 July 1917.
28 PD, 15, 16 August 1917.
29 PD, 26, 28, 29 September 1917.
30 PD, 17 October 1917.
31 Plunkett to Morley, 10 November 1917 (PF MORL 3).
32 Quoted in D.G.Boyce, British Public Opinion and Government Policy in Ireland, 1918-1922, Ph.D. Thesis (Queen's University of Belfast, 1969) p.146.
33 J.R.Fisher, 'Ulster and the Irish angle', *The Nineteenth Century and after,* lxxxii (January-June 1918) p.1088.
34 PD, 18 July 1917.
35 Bernard Shaw to Plunkett, 16 April 1918 (PF SHA 32).
36 Plunkett to H.E.Duke, 24 August 1917 (PF DUK 5).

37　Earl of Midleton, *Ireland - Dupe or Heroine*, p.115.
38　*The Irish Convention: Confidential Report*, p.43.
39　*Hansard HC*, 5th series v.91, cols. 459-466, 7 March 1917.
40　PD, 11 January 1918.
41　Lloyd George to Bonar Law, January 1918 (Bonar Law papers 82/8/4, House of Lords).
42　John Turner, *Lloyd George's Secretariat* (Cambridge, 1980) p.107.
43　*Irish Times*, 4 December 1918.
44　*The Irish Convention; Confidential Report*, p.61.
45　*Ibid.*, p.61.
46　*Ibid.*, p.62.
47　R.B.McDowell, *The Irish Convention, 1917-18* (London, 1970) p.151.
48　*The Irish Convention; Confidential Report*, p.66.
49　Earl of Midleton, *Records and Reactions: 1856-1939* (London, 1939) p.242.
50　*The Irish Convention; Confidential Report*, p.73.
52　Plunkett to AE, 2 February 1918 (PF RUSS 5).
53　AE to Plunkett, 3 February 1918 (PF RUSS 6).
54　*The Irish Convention; Confidential Report*, p.87.
55　*Ibid.*, p.94.
56　*Ibid.*, p.89.
57　*Ibid.*, p.123.
58　*Ibid.*, p.130.
59　*Irish Times*, 6 May 1918.
60　*The Irish Convention; Confidential Report*, p.132.

X.　DOMINION STATUS

1　Horace Plunkett, *The Irish Situation in America, at Westminister and in Ireland* (Dublin, 1920) p.38.
2　*Irish Times*, 2 May 1918.
3　Horace Plunkett, *Home Rule and Conscription* (Dublin, 1918) p.31.
4　PD, 11 November 1919.
5　Henry Summerfield, *That Myriad-Minded Man: a Biography of George William Russell 'AE', 1867-1935* (Gerrards Cross, 1975) pp.186-7.
6　PD, 16 July 1917.
7　*Northern Whig*, 27 September 1918; *Belfast Telegraph*, 26 September 1918.
8　PD, 30 April 1918.
9　PD, 1 May 1918.
10　*Irish Times*, 23 November 1918.
11　Plunkett to Erskine Childers, 22 June 1920 (TCD Ms 7850/1017).
12　Daniel Hoctor, *The Department's Story: a History of the Department of Agriculture* (Dublin, 1971) pp.118-121.
13　Dáil Eireann, Miontuairisc an Chéad Dhála (*Report of the First Dáil*), 1919-21, 19 June 1919, p.129.
14　*IH*, 26 July 1918.
15　PD, 16 April, 17 April 1922; letters from Plunkett to Dillon quoted in Elizabeth Fingall, *Seventy Years Young* pp.404-12. Plunkett received affirmative answers to the following questions which he put to Dillon: Did he and Redmond advise Asquith not to arrest Carson between 1912 and 1914? Did Lloyd George give differing impressions of the future of Ulster to Redmond and Carson in their attempt to reach a settlement?

16 H.F.Norman papers (NLI Ms 8824 p.28).
17 *Hansard* HC, 5th series v.114, col. 123, 24 March 1919.
18 PD, 5 June 1919.
19 *Irish Times*, 15 August 1919.
20 *The Times*, 11 October 1920.
21 *Belfast Newsletter*, 29 June, 14 July 1919.
22 *Irish Times*, 14 July 1919.
23 *The Irish Convention; Confidential Report*, pp.79-80.
24 Plunkett to W.T.Green, 8 December 1920 (PF GRE 1).
25 *The Times*, 15 September 1919 (letter to the editor).
26 PD, 22 October 1919.
27 *IS*, 1st series, supplement 5 November 1919.
28 PD, 5 November 1919.
29 *The Times*, 28 November 1919.
30 Oliver St. John. Gogarty, *As I was Walking down Sackville Street: a Fantasy in Fact* (London, 1980) p.108.
31 *IS*, 1st series, supplement 5 November 1919.
32 Diarmuid Coffey papers (in possession of his daughter).
33 PD, 12 March 1920.
34 *The Times*, 11 May 1921.
35 *The Times*, 17 November 1920.
36 PD, 3 June 1920.
37 Plunkett to James Bryce, 17 June 1920 (PF BRY 55).
38 Plunkett to James Bryce, 11 June 1920 (PF BRY 53).
39 Plunkett to James Bryce, 17 June 1920 (PF BRY 55).
40 PD, 15 July 1920.
41 Patrick Bolger, *The Irish Co-operative Movement*, p.210.
42 *IH*, 11 September, 2 October 1920.
43 *IH*, 2 October 1920.
44 *IAOS Annual Report*, 1920 pp.29-31.
45 *IAOS Annual Report*, 1920 p.47.
46 *Report of the 53rd Annual Congress of the Co-operative Union, Scarborough*, 1921, p.163.
47 *Ibid.*, pp.60-1.
48 *Ibid.*, p,166.
49 Sir Nevil Macready, *Annals of an Active Life* (London, 1924) p.525.
50 PD, 28 March 1921.
51 PD, 30 March 1921.
52 PD, 30 May 1921.
53 PD, 21 May 1921.
54 E.Rumpf and A.C.Hepburn, *Nationalism and Socialism in Twentieth Century Ireland* (Liverpool, 1977) p.49.
55 *The Times*, 11 May 1921 (letter to the editor).
56 C.J.C.Street, *Ireland in 1921* (London, 1922) p.123.
57 *Saturday Review*, 2 July 1921 (unsigned article by Plunkett entitled 'The Move Towards Irish Peace'); PD, 28 June 1921.
58 *Ibid.*
59 PD, 3 July 1921.
60 PD, 27 August 1921.
61 Plunkett to James Bryce, 9 June 1921 (PF BRY 72).
62 Plunkett to James Bryce, 4 November 1921 (PF BRY 76).
63 PD, 14 August, 29 August 1921.

64 Plunkett to James Bryce, 27 October 1921 (NLI Ms 11,016 (10)).
65 PD, 21 July 1921.
66 PD, 4 September 1921.
67 PD, 19 September 1921.
68 *Irish Times*, 8 December 1921.
69 PD, 3 February 1922.
70 PD, 13 February 1922.

XI.   PARTITION AND CIVIL WAR

1   PD, 7 January 1922.
2   PD, 1 April 1922.
3   James MacNeill to Plunkett, 24 November 1931 (PF McN 10).
4   PD, 12 August 1922.
5   PD, 19 August 1922.
6   Michael Collins, *The Path to Freedom* (Dublin, 1922) p.133.
7   Plunkett to House, dated (incorrectly) 29 July 1922, (E.M.House papers, Yale).
8   PD, 16 December 1922.
9   Plunkett to J.S.Cullinan, 9 October 1922 (PF IRS 3).
10 PD, 17 October 1922.
11 PD, 1 December 1922 describing a conversation with Kevin O'Higgins of 10 November 1922.
12 PD, 19 November 1922.
13 PD, 26 November 1922.
14 PD, 28 November 1922.
15 Elizabeth Fingall, *Seventy Years Young*, p.413.
16 Molly Childers to Plunkett, 24 November 1922 (PF CHI 36).
17 PD, 10 July, 18 August 1922.
18 PD, 13 August 1922.
19 P.N.Furbank, *E.M.Forster: a Life* (Oxford, 1979) p.136.
20 Prof. J.E.Bowle (who also worked as secretary to Plunkett at the Crest House) in conversation with the author.
21 PD, 8 June 1922.
22 PD, 29 July 1922.
23 PD, 22 August 1922.
24 PD, 22 April, 25 April 1922.
25 *Seanad Eireann, Díosbóireachtaí Parlaiminte, Tuairisc Oifigiúil (Irish Senate, Parlimentary Debates, Official Report)* v.1, cols. 82-4, 20 December 1922.
26 PD, 21 December 1922.
27 PD, 22 December 1922.
28 PD, 3 January 1923.
29 PD, 12 January, 29 January 1923.
30 PD, 12 January 1923.
31 H.F.Heard cable to Plunkett, 30 January 1923 (PF HEA 15).
32 H.F.Heard cable to Plunkett, 31 January 1923 (PF HEA 24/25).
33 George Gilmore, officer in command of the first battalion of the South Dublin brigade of the anti-Treaty forces, in an interview with the author.
34 Mr.J.Ogilvie (son of the farm steward at Kilteragh) in conversation with the author.
35 Anti-Treaty supporters, under considerable pressure from government

troops and devoting their whole attention to the question of political autonomy, paid little heed to social or economic problems (C.S.Andrews, *Man of No Property* (Cork, 1982) p.57).

36 Lennox Robinson, *Curtain Up* (London, 1942) pp.133-4.
37 Elizabeth Fingall, *Seventy Years Young*, pp.417-8.
38 *Ibid.*, pp.418-9.
39 George Gilmore in conversation with the author.
40 Gerald Heard to Lady Fingall, 1 January 1923, quoted in Elizabeth Fingall, *Seventy Years Young*, p.416.
41 Plunkett to John Dillon, 27 February 1924, quoted in Elizabeth Fingall, *Seventy Years Young* pp.426-7; Plunkett to Lewis Palen, 16 January 1931 (PF PAL 11).
42 Elizabeth Fingall, *Seventy Years Young*, pp.419-20.
43 Plunkett to R.A.Anderson, 15 February 1923 (PF AND 8).
44 *Irish Times*, 31 January 1923.
45 B.L.Reid, *The Man from New York*, p.583.
46 *Ibid.*, p.583.
47 Eoin O'Keefe to Margaret Digby, 14 April 1950, (PF miscellaneous correspondence).
48 George Gilmore to the author, 25 July 1979.
49 PD, 1 February 1923.
50 *The Times*, 20 March 1923.
51 PD, 20 February 1923.
52 Plunkett to J.S.Cullinan, 8 September 1922 (Gogarty letters, Bucknell University).
53 Terence Brown, *Ireland: a Social and Cultural History, 1922-79* (London, 1981).
54 *IS*, 2nd series, 3 November 1923.
55 *Ibid.*, 12 April 1930.
56 C.C.Riddall, *Agricultural Co-operation in Ireland: the Story of a Struggle* (Dublin, 1950) pp.41-3.
57 PD, year end 1928.
58 Patrick Hogan to Plunkett, undated (PF HOGA 13).
59 Plunkett to Erskine Childers, 31 May 1912 (TCD Ms 7850/979).
60 Plunkett to Lady Betty Balfour, 30 August 1921 (PF BAL 97).
61 James Johnston, *Agricultural Co-operation in Northern Ireland: a History of the Ulster Agricultural Organisation Society, the First Forty Years* (London, 1965) pp.4-5.
62 Horace Plunkett, *The Evolution of Ireland's Agricultural Policy, a Retrospect and a Prospect* (London, 1925) p.14.
63 PD, 1 May 1929.
64 *Tomorrow* (Dublin, 1924). Lennox Robinson's story appeared in the first of two issues which also contained Yeats' erotic poem 'Leda and the Swan'.
65 PD, 12 October 1924.
66 Plunkett Notebook (undated PF).
67 *Agricultural Co-operation in the British Empire* (London, 1925) p.9.
68 PD, 5 July 1925.
69 PD, 10 September 1925.
70 PD, 4 July, 5 July 1927.
71 PD, 17 October 1928.
72 PD, 19 November 1929.
73 PD, 20 November 1929.
74 *Irish Times*, 24 October 1928.
75 PD, 24 February 1932.

XII. RETROSPECT

1 Undated manuscript PF.
2 *Catholic Bulletin*, 25 (1935) p.56.
3 De Valéra to Lloyd George, 10 August 1921 in *Thomas Jones, Whitehall Diary, vol.III, Ireland 1918-25*, Keith Middlemas ed.,(Oxford, 1971) pp.93-5.
4 Smuts memorandum to de Valéra, 4 August 1921 in Jean van der Poel (ed), *Selections from Smuts' Papers*, vol.5 (Cambridge, 1973) pp.100-105.
5 PD, 17 July 1921.
6 Horace Plunkett, *The Irish Situation in America, at Westminster and in Ireland*, p.38.
7 *Irish Times*, 20 April, 2 August 1974; a wing of Killeen Castle, former home of Lady Fingall, was burnt by republicans during the H-block protest in 1981 (*Irish Times*, 18 May 1981).
8 Horace Plunkett, *The Rural Life Problem of the United States*, p.14.
9 The voluminous correspondence between the two men shows how much,in the decade prior to 1900, Plunkett relied on Gill's political acumen (T.P.Gill papers NLI).
10 PD, 19 January 1931.
11 *IAOS Annual Report* 1920, pp.42-3.
12 Plunkett memorandum to Walter Long (chief secretary for Ireland) 1905, quoted by Andrew Gailey in *Plunkett and Co-operatives: Past,Present and Future* (Carla Keating ed. Cork, 1983) p.89.
13 This spirit was kept alive by individuals such as Paddy the Cope and Sandy Mc Guckian. Patrick Gallagher, an emigrant from the Rosses in Co. Donegal, encountered co-operation in the mining towns of Lanarkshire, and determined, on his return to Ireland, to establish a similar system in his native parish. Able, perceptive and a natural leader of men, his struggle against the combined opposition of publicans, traders and gombeenmen and his triumph over all adversity is recorded in the great folktale of co-operation: Patrick Gallagher, *My Story by Paddy the Cope* (Dungloe, undated).
   A. A. McGuckian, from Cloughmills, Co.Antrim, a nationalist internee from 1922-24, so developed his family farm that he became an authority on pig husbandry and grassland management, an inspiration to his fellow farmers and a devotee of co-operation. The expertise accumulated at Cloughmills has since been used by his family with dramatic success to adapt and transfer agricultural technology to the Middle East. (A.E.Muskett (ed.) *A.A.McGuckian: a Memorial Volume*, Belfast, 1956).
14 A report by the distinguished American co-operator J.G.Knapp (*An Appraisemant of Agricultural Co-operation in Ireland*, Dublin, 1964) recommended a major programme of research and education plus increased government subvention to the IAOS. While saluting the considerable progress made by Irish agricultural co-operatives in the face of many obstacles, Dr. Knapp raised the following pertinent questions:— How well do the co-operatives act as co-operative institutions? Are they really member-owned and member-controlled? Are they democratically organized and operated? Do they provide agricultural leadership? Do they make the maximum contribution to farm prosperity? Are they pace-setting organisations?
15 The problems of scale encountered by Irish co-operators have had to be faced by the co-operative movement in other developed countries. Perhaps the co-operative ideal applies, in its purest form to a developing economy. John Empson, 'A Review of Producer Co-operative Development in the Dairy

Industry', *Year Book of Agricultural Co-operation, 1985* (Oxford, 1985); J.C. Moody and G.C. Fite, *The Credit Union Movement: Origins and Development* (Lincoln, Nebraska, 1971).

16 His centenary was marked by the *Irish Times* in a series of 6 articles by F.S.L. Lyons commencing on 20 October 1954 and by the *Irish Press* in an essay by Lennox Robinson on 20 October 1954.

17 Margaret Digby, *Horace Plunkett, an Anglo-American Irishman*, p.viii.

18 The Society for Co-operative Studies in Ireland, in conjunction with the Irish Academic Press have reissued (sometimes under different titles): AE, *Co-operation and Nationality,* and *The National Being* (1982); Plunkett, *Ireland in the New Century* (1982); Anderson, *With Horace Plunkett in Ireland* (1983); Craig, *An Irish Commune: the History of Ralahine* (1983) and *The United Irishwomen, their Place, Work and Ideals* (1986).

19 *IH*, 4 November 1922.

20 *Daily Express*, 21 March 1900.

21 Horace Plunkett, *The Irish Situation in America, at Westminster and in Ireland*, p.31.

22 *Irish Press*, 20 October 1954.

APPENDIX

1 *Boston Sunday Globe*, 10 July 1932.

2 Jim Bridger (1804-1881) a famous western explorer, fur-trapper, guide and one of the first white men to visit the Yellowstone had retired to Kansas by 1868 and it is almost certain that Plunkett, who arrived in the West in the spring of 1879, did not encounter him there. Thus this is an apocryphal tale probably based on another evening of story telling around a campfire.

3 F.G.S. (Fred) Hesse was an Englishman who worked as a foreman for both Frewen and Plunkett, survived the Johnson County cattle war (he had been one of the 'invaders') and became a major Wyoming figure.

4 Plunkett's considerable American investments were not accounted for in his estate which was valued at £45,000 in 1932.

5 Plunkett was 'Honourable' as son of a baron. He did not receive a knighthood until 1903, fourteen years after he had left Wyoming.

A HORACE PLUNKETT BIBLIOGRAPHY

Plunkett's diaries (from 1881 to 1932) and his correspondence (from the office of the IAOS) are lodged in the Plunkett Foundation, Oxford and are available on microfilm. Further Plunkett papers are contained in the DATI files (from 1900 to 1907) in the Irish Public Record Office, and in the T. P. Gill papers in the National Library of Ireland.

His published work is listed below excluding articles, or letters, or reports of speeches which appeared in the press. A number of his speeches or memoranda which were published in the *IAOS Annual Reports*, the *DATI Journal* (1900-1907), or the *Reports of the Annual Co-operative Congresses*, or his evidence given to royal commissions are listed without title.

1888
'Co-operative Stores for Ireland', *Nineteenth Century*, v.24, pp. 410-8.

1889
Report of 21st Annual Co-operative Congress, Ipswich, pp.91-2.

1890
Co-operation for Ireland: Self-Help by Mutual Help (Manchester, undated) 13p.
Co-operative Dairying: an Address to the Farmers of the Dairy Districts of Ireland (Manchester) 8p.
'The Working of Woman Suffrage in Wyoming', *Fortnightly Review*, new series, v.47, pp.656-69.
Co-operation in Ireland: the Best Means of Promoting both Distributive and Productive Co-operation in the Rural Districts of Ireland (Manchester) 12p.
Report of 22nd Annual Co-operative Congress, Glasgow, pp.19, 92, 96-9, 101.

1891
Report of 23rd Annual Co-operative Congress, Lincoln, pp.97-8, 100.

1892
Report of 24th Annual Co-operative Congress, Rochdale, pp.8-9, 111.
Third Report of the Royal Commission on Crofters, Cottars and Colonisation, Cd. 6693, xxvii, pp.351 - 63.

1893
Report of 25th Annual Co-operative Congress, Bristol, p.121.

Report of Congested Districts Board, Cd.6908, lxxi, pp.569-79.

1894
'Agricultural Organisation', *New Ireland Review*, June, pp.197-205.
'Ireland Today and Tomorrow', *Fortnightly Review*, new series, v.55, pp.277-93.
The Irish Agricultural Organisation Society and its Aims (Dublin, undated) 4p.

1895
'Co-operation in Ireland', in J.A.Hobson (ed.), *Co-operative Labour upon the Land* (London and New York) pp.35-46.
Report of 27th Annual Co-operative Congress, Huddersfield, pp.15, 139, 142-3.
'Agricultural Co-operation', *IH*, 5 October.
IAOS Annual Report, pp.17-18.
'Agricultural Co-operation in Ireland', *Humanitarian*, v.vii, new series, pp.321-7.

1896
Report of the Recess Committee on the Establishment of a Department of Agriculture and Industries for Ireland (Dublin, Belfast, London) viii, 419p.
'The Recess Committee's Report', *New Ireland Review*, v.5, pp.329-38.
IAOS Annual Report, pp.23-4.

1897
IAOS Annual Report, pp.34-6, 53-5.
'The New Irish Policy', supplement to *IH*, 19 June.
'How to make an Industrial Population', *IH*, 14 August.
'The Apologia of the Royal Dublin Society', *New Ireland Review*, v.6, pp.328-36.
Memorandum of the Recess Committee on the Agriculture and Industries (Ireland) Bill (Dublin) 15p.

1898
IAOS Annual Report, pp.46-9, 61-2, 86-8, 96-101.
The Irish Agricultural Organisation Society and its Aims, (Dublin) 2p.
Help for Self-Help in Ireland, (Dublin) 15p.
'The Irish Question in a New Light', *North American Review*, v.166, pp.107-20.
'The Relationship between Organised State Aid and Self-Help in Ireland', *North American Review*, v.167, pp.497-8.
'The New Movement in Ireland', *IH*, 5 November.
Report of Select Committee on Money Lending, Cd. 260, x, 101, pp.99-109.

1899
IAOS Annual Report, pp.88-90.
Address at Queen's College, Belfast, *IH*, 4 February.
'Bankers and Farmers in Ireland', *IH*, 11 November.

1900

'Bankers and farmers in Ireland', *Journal of the Institute of Bankers in Ireland*, v.ii part 1, pp.18-27.

IAOS Annual Report, pp.105-7,111-113,134-6.

DATI Journal, v.i, pp.4-14.

'Balfourian Amelioration in Ireland', *The Nineteenth Century and After*, v.48, pp.891-904.

L'Enseignment Technique en Irlande, Congrès Internationale de l'Enseignment des Sciences Sociales, (Paris).

1901

Cumh na dToghthóir i gCathair na Gaillimhe [To the Electors in Galway City] (Dublin) 1p.

Memorandum on Agricultural Education in Ireland (Dublin) 24p.

Address to the Ballymena Agricultural Association, *IH*, 29 June.

President's Address to the National Co-operative Festival, Crystal Palace, *IH*, 17 August, and 31 August.

DATI Journal, v.ii, pp.4-14, 18-41, 691-6, 704-5.

1902

Memorandum on Agricultural Education in Ireland,*Royal Commission on University Education in Ireland, appendix to second report*, Cd 900, xxxi, pp.237-44.

Royal Commission on University Education in Ireland, appendix to third report, Cd. 1229, xxxii, pp.231-41.

The Trend of Co-operation in Great Britain and Ireland,(Dublin) 18p.

1903

IAOS Annual Report, pp.155-8.

DATI Journal, v.iii, pp.103-8, 254-60, 478-89, 523-31, 655-62.

The Progress of Economic Thought and Work in Ireland: Four Addresses to the first Council of Agriculture (1900-1903) (Dublin) 56 p.

1904

Ireland in the New Century (1st edition, London) xvii, 300 p.

Foreword to *The Spirit of Greece; the Spirit of a University*. Address by S.H.Butcher, 20 January, on the occasion of a farewell dinner for his retirement as Professor of Greek at Edinburgh University. (privately printed) 7p.

'The Gaelic Movement' in Justin McCarthy (ed.) *Irish Literature* (New York) pp. 2908-2912.

DATI Journal, v.iv, pp.236-7, 606-15.

Address to St. Patrick's Club, Oxford, *IH*, 19 March 1904.

IAOS Annual Report, pp.215-24.

1905

Ireland in the New Century (popular edition with epilogue, London) xviii, 340p.

The Irish Agricultural Organisation Society and its Aims: to the Farmers of Ireland (Dublin) 4p.
DATI Journal, v.v, pp.216-32.
Memorandum on an Administrative Policy Supplementary to the Irish Land Acts (Dublin) 14p.

1906
DATI Journal, v.vi, pp.613-26.
DATI Journal, v.vii, pp.221-30, 625-34.
The Problem of Rural Life in the United States (Dublin) 20p.
Memorandum on Agricultural Organisation (Dublin) 27p.
Address to the Members of the Agriculture Board (Dublin) 3p.
'Some Aspects of the Irish Question', *International Quarterly*, v.12, pp.227-39.
Foreword to G. Boni, *Hibernica: Notes on Some Burial Places and Customs of Ancient Ireland*: translated from the Nuova Antologica (Dublin).
IAOS Annual Report, pp.133-6.

1907
Addresses Delivered at the Meetings of the Council of Agriculture during the First Vice-Presidency (1900-1907) (Dublin) 122p.
The Problem of Congestion in Ireland: Memorandum Submitted to the Royal Commission on Congestion, (Dublin) iii, 45p.
Presidential Address to the 14th Annual Meeting of the Association of Technical Instruction, 8 February (London) 14p.
IAOS Annual Report, pp.58-70.
Departmental Committee of Enquiry into the Provisions of the Agriculture and Technical Industries (Ireland) Act 1899. Cd. 3574, xviii, pp.8-38, 965-83.

1908
Address at Dervock, *IH*, 18 April.
'The Necessity for Agricultural Organisation', *IH*, 29 August.
Address to the Belfast Industrial Development Association, *IH*, 3 October.
The Neglect of Country Life: a Plea and a Policy (address at the formal opening of the Plunkett House, 11 November) *IH*, 14 November
The New Development in Agricultural Co-operation. Memorandum on Joint Action between the Agricultural Co-operative movements in England, Ireland and Scotland (Dublin) 10p.
Science and the Problem of Rural Life (Dublin) 8p., Address to the Agriculture Sub-Section of the British Association for the Advancement of Science (Dublin), *Report to the British Association for the Advancement of Science*, pp. 796-804; also reprinted in *IH*, 12 September.
Social Science for Country Life (Dublin) 15p.
Noblesse Oblige: an Irish Rendering (Dublin) 38p.
IAOS Annual Report, pp.21-7, 31-40, 43-5, 54-62.

1909
The Neglect of Country Life: a Plea and a Policy (Dublin) 16p.

A Country Life Institute: a Suggested Irish-American Contribution to Rural Progress (Dublin) 30p.

'Mr. Birrell's Irish Land Bill', *The Nineteenth Century and After*, v.65, pp.946-64; then reprinted as *The Unsettlement of the Irish Land Question* (Dublin) 50p.

'Agricultural Co-operative Awakening', *Spectator*, 11 September.

IAOS Annual Report, pp.78-81.

1910

Plain Talks to Irish Farmers (Dublin) 46p.; originally published in *IH*, 9, 16, 23, 30 July; 6, 13, 20, 27 August; 3 September.

'The Sociological Aspects of the Agrarian Revolution in Ireland', *Sociological Review*, v.iii, pp.185-96.

Report of House of Lords Thrift and Credit Banks Committee, House of Lords papers, v.ix, pp. 225-31, 242-5.

IAOS Annual Report, pp. 39-47, 70-5.

Five articles published in the *Outlook* (New York):
i   'Conservation and Rural Life: an Irish View of two Roosevelt Policies', 29 January;
ii 'The Neglected Farmer', 5 February;
iii 'The Human Factor in Rural Life', 12 February; ·
iv 'Better Farming, Better Business, Better Living', 19 February;
v   'Better Farming, Better Business, Better Living; Two Practical Suggestions', 26 February.

The Rural Life Problem of the United States: Notes of an Irish Observer (New York) xi, 174p. (articles reprinted and enlarged from the New York *Outlook*).

1911

Address to the Legislature of the State of Wisconsin on 'Co-operative Banking, Co-operative Credit and Allied Economic Subjects', *IH*, 8 April, 15 April.

Address to the North Wales section of the Agricultural Organisation Society, *IH*, 28 October.

Introduction to State Aid and Self-Help in Agricultural Development. A memorandum submitted by the Joint Board for Agricultural Organisation to the Development Commission (London).

The Crisis in Irish Rural Progress (London) 20p.

Memorandum upon the Relations between the Department and the IAOS (Dublin) 16p.

with Ellice Pilkington and G. W. Russell, *The United Irishwomen, their Place, Work and Ideals* (Dublin) vi, 50p.

IAOS Annual Report, pp.36-47.

Introductory notes to H. L. Pilkington, *Land Settlement for Soldiers* (London).

1912

IAOS Annual Report, pp. 44-53.

Foreword to S. F. Bullock, *Thomas Andrews, Shipbuilder* (Dublin).

Address to the Ulster Branch of the IAOS, *IH*, 13 April.

1913

'The American Agricultural Commission, its Origin, Scope and Purpose', *IH*, 3 May.

A Suggested Solution of the Rural Problem (Dublin) 32p., Address to the American Commission reprinted U.S. Senate Document 214, 63rd Congress, 1st Session: Agricultural Co-operation and Rural Credit in Europe, Information and Evidence, v.4, part 1, pp. 831-41.

Some Tendencies of Modern Medicine from a Lay Point of View (Battle Creek, Michigan) 31p.

IAOS Annual Report, pp.49-52.

Foreword to C. Holdenby, *Folk of the Furrow* (London).

Foreword to 'The Irish Question' in the *Round Table*, v.4, December.

1914

A Better Way: an Appeal to Ulster not to Desert Ireland (Dublin) 38p.

La nouva Irlanda (Turin); translation of *Ireland in the New Century*.

Address to the Co-operative Congress, Dublin, *IH*, 13 June.

Report of 46th Annual Co-operative Congress, Dublin, pp.30-1, 550-2.

'The Co-operative Reference Library, its Work and Aims', *Bulletin of the Co-operative Reference Library*, July.

'Ireland's Opportunity', *Bulletin of the Co-operative Reference Library*, November; also *IH*, 24 October.

IAOS Annual Report, pp.56-9.

1915

'McCarthy of Wisconsin', *The Nineteenth Century and After*,v.77, pp.1335-47.

'Catechism for Students of Agricultural Co-operation in Ireland', *IH*, 12 June.

'Continuous Cropping and Co-operation', *IH*, 26 June.

The Coming of Age of the Irish Agricultural Organisation Society (Dublin) pp.3-5, 6-17

'Report of the Departmental Committee on Food Production in Ireland, Minority Report', *DATI Journal*, v.xvi, pp.53-4.

1916

Memorandum upon the American Agricultural Organisation Society (New York) 23p.

IAOS Annual Report, pp.48-50.

Memorandum commenting on Balfour's proposals for an Anti-War League (Unpublished Ms PF BALF.A 19/1 and 19/2).

Confidential document presented to the Cabinet (on Anglo-American relations) (24 February) (copy in E. M. House papers, Yale University).

Memorandum on the Purpose, Scope and Function of a proposed American Press Bureau in London (23 March) (Unpublished Ms. PF APB 1).

Some Tendencies in Modern Medicine from a Lay Point of View (Dublin and Belfast) 31p.

1917

A Defence of the Convention (Dublin) 13p.

IAOS Annual Report, pp.48-51.

President's Address to the Annual General Meeting of the IAOS, *IH*, 29 December.

1918

Home Rule and Conscription (Dublin) 31p.

The Irish Reconstruction Association (Dublin), a letter to the press of 22 November, reprinted.

Report of the Proceedings of the Irish Convention, Cd.9019, 176p.

The Irish Convention: Confidential Report to H.M. the King by the Chairman (sine loco) iv, 154p.

1919

'Irish Misgovernment and the Essentials of a Settlement', *IS*, 1st series, supplement 8 November.

'A Message from Ireland to America', *IS*, 1st series, 13 December.

Dominion Self-Government: Sir Horace Plunkett's View (reprint of a letter to *The Times* of 15 April) (Dublin) 8p.

IAOS Annual Report, pp.934-6.

1920

Address to a banquet given in his honour in Dublin, 4 March; *IS*, 1st series, 13 March.

The Irish Situation in America, at Westminster and in Ireland (Dublin) 40p.; also published as a supplement to the *IS*, 1st series, 13 March.

'Vale Atque Ave', *IS*, 1st series, 19 June.

Irish Chaos: the British Cause and the Irish Cure (reprint of a letter to *The Times* of 2 June) (Dublin) 8p.

England's Irish Policy During and After the War (reprint of two letters to *The Times* of 8 November and 17 November) (Dublin) 11p.

1921

Oxford and the Rural Problem (Barnett House papers no.6, London).

'Ireland Today — Sir Horace Plunkett's Plan', *The Nation*, v.112, pp.738-9; also *US Congressional Record*, v.61, no.38, pp.1746-7.

'The Move Towards Irish Peace', *Saturday Review*, 2 July (unsigned, PD, 28 June 1921).

President's Address to the Annual General Meeting of the IAOS, *IH*, 2 April.

'The Message of the Farmers of Ireland: Agricultural Co-operation; its Origin, Achievement and Aim'. *The Survey* (New York) 26 November.

IAOS Annual Report, pp.42-50.

Report of the 53rd Annual Co-operative Congress, Scarborough, pp.442-4.

1922

Address to Emergency Meeting of the Dublin Chamber of Commerce, 25 April (concerning the restoration of law and order) (Unpublished Ms. PF) 5p.

Address to the Staff of the IAOS (Unpublished Ms. PF) 5p.
Agricultural Co-operation as a Factor in Ireland's Agricultural Policy (Dublin)
    8p.

1923

'The revival of the *Irish Statesman*', *IS*, 2nd series,15 September.
Ireland's own Agricultural Policy (Dublin) 27p; orginally published in five
    parts by the *IS*, 2nd series:
I.   'Better Farming, Better Business, Better Living', 24 November;
II. 'The Meaning and Importance of Better Business', 1 December;
III. 'Its Evolution in Ireland', 8 December;
IV. 'Its Rejection by the Old and its Hopes from the New Regime', 15
    December;
V. · 'An Appeal to One People and Two Governments', 22 December.
IAOS Annual Report, pp.41-3.
President's Letter to Annual General Meeting of the IAOS, *IH*, 26 May.
UAOS Annual Report, p.33.
'Farmers as Co-operative Organisations' (hearing before the Committee
    on Agriculture and Forestry, U.S. Senate, 67th Congress, 4th session
    relative to co-operative agricultural organisations, 16 January)
    (Washington D.C.).

1924

Memorandum on the Agricultural Situation and Outlook in the United
    States (Unpublished Ms. E. M. House papers, Yale University).
with K. Walter, *Agricultural Co-operation in its Application to the Industry,
    the Business and the Life of the Farmer in the British Empire* (London) 28p.
'Ireland's problems', in *These Eventful Years: the Twentieth Century in the
    Making* (New York) pp.514-24.
IAOS Annual Report, pp.42-5.
UAOS Annual Report, pp.31-2.
*Message to the Conference on Agricultural Co-operation in the British Empire
    from Sir Horace Plunkett* (London) 11p.

1925

Foreword to *Agricultural Co-operation in the British Empire* (London).
The Co-operative Reference Library (an address to a conference of special
    librarians, Oxford, September; unpublished Ms. PF).
The Evolution of Ireland's Agricultural Policy, a Retrospect and a Prospect
    (London; also Ms. in PF).
'The Agricultural Problem in South Africa'. *Journal of the Department of
    Agriculture of South Africa*, October.
Memorandum to the staff and employees of Peltons Colliery (Un-
    published Ms in E. M. House papers, Yale University).
UAOS Annual Report, pp.35-6.

1926

The Horace Plunkett Foundation: its Origin, Principles and Programme
    (London) 16p.

'Ireland: Agricultural Co-operation', *Encyclopaedia Brittanica*, 13th edition v.ii, pp.521-3.
'Co-operative Progress', *Commonweal*, 17 November.

1927
'Ireland's Economic Outlook', *Foreign Affairs*, v.5, pp.205-18.

1928
The Purpose of a Rural Life Organisation (address to a conference at Wadham College, Oxford, July) (Oxford) 7p.
'Co-operation as a Factor in the Economic, Social and Political Development of Rural India', supplement to the *Bombay Co-operative Quarterly*, September.
Address at the Annual General Meeting of the Scottish Agricultural Organisation Society in Edinburgh, March, *Report of the Scottish Agricultural Organisation Society Ltd.*, pp.39-40.
Introduction to Nagendranath Gangulee, *Problems of Rural India; being a Collection of Address Delivered on Various Occasions in India and in England by Nagendranath Gangulee* (Calcutta).

1930
The passing of the *Irish Statesman*, *IS*, 2nd series, 12 April.
'Professor T. A. Finlay, S. J.', in *A page of Irish History: Story of University College Dublin, 1883-1909* (Dublin) pp.246-57.

1931
'The Essentials of an Agricultural Policy', *Spectator* v.146, 4 April and 18 April.
Foreword to *Agricultural Co-operation in Ireland: a Survey by the Plunkett Foundation* (London).
Foreword to S. F. Bullock, *After Sixty Years* (London).
Foreword to W. A. Terpenning, *Village and Open Country Neighbourhoods*, (New York).

1932
Foreword to E. M. Hough, *The Co-operative Movement in India: its Relation to a Sound National Economy* (1st edition, London).

ADDITIONAL BIBLIOGRAPHY

AE (George W. Russell), *Co-operation and Nationality* (Dublin, 1912).

AE (George W. Russell), *The National Being* (Dublin, 1916).

R.A.Anderson, *With Horace Plunkett in Ireland* (London, 1935).

J.J.Auchmuty, *Lecky: a Biographical and Critical Essay* (Dublin, 1945).

J.C.Beckett, *The Anglo-Irish Tradition* (London, 1976).

George Berkeley, *The Querist* (Dublin and London, 1735-7).

Paul Bew, *C. S. Parnell* (Dublin, 1980).

George Birmingham (J.O.Hannay), *An Irishman Looks at his World* (London, 1919).

George Birmingham (J.O.Hannay), *Pleasant Places* (London, 1934).

Augustine Birrell, *Things Past Redress* (London, 1937).

Patrick Bolger, *The Irish Co-operative Movement, its History and Development* (Dublin, 1977).

M.J.Bonn, *Wandering Scholar* (London, 1949).

D.G.Boyce, *Nationalism in Ireland* (Dublin, 1982).

Andrew Boyle, *The Riddle of Erskine Childers* (London, 1977).

Sydney Brooks, *The New Ireland* (Dublin, 1907).

Sydney Brooks, *Aspects of the Irish Question* (Dublin, 1912).

Sydney Brooks, 'Sir Horace Plunkett and his Work', *Fortnightly Review*, new series, 91(1912) pp. 1011-21.

Terence Brown, *Ireland: a Social and Cultural History, 1922-79* (London,1981).

Patrick Buckland, *Irish Unionism* (vol. I) *The Anglo-Irish and the New Ireland, 1885-1922* (Dublin, 1972); (vol. II) *Ulster Unionism and the Origins of Northern Ireland, 1886-1922* (Dublin, 1973).

S.F.Bullock, *Thomas Andrews, Shipbuilder* (Dublin, 1912).

S.F.Bullock, *After Sixty Years* (London, 1931).

F.M.Carroll, *American Opinion and the Irish Question, 1910-1923: a Study in Opinion and Policy* (Dublin, 1978).

Erskine Childers, *The Framework of Home Rule* (London, 1911).

Michael Clune, Horace Plunkett: the Origins and Development of the Department of Agriculture and Technical Instruction and the Political Context, 1895-1907 (M.Ed. thesis, TCD, 1978).

Diarmuid Coffey, *Douglas Hyde* (Dublin, 1917).

Margaret Cole, *Robert Owen of New Lanark , 1771-1858* (London, 1953).

Michael Collins, *The Path to Freedom* (Dublin, 1922).

James Connolly, *Labour in Irish History* (Dublin, 1910).

James Connolly, *The Reconstruction of Ireland* (Dublin, 1917).

Lieut.-Gen. M. J. Costello, 'Farming Programme for Ireland', *Studies*, 41 (1952) pp.129-146.

E.T.Craig, *An Irish Commune: the History of Ralahine* (Dublin, c. 1920).

C. Cruise O'Brien (ed), *The Shaping of Modern Ireland* (London, 1970).

L.P.Curtis, *Coercion and Conciliation in Ireland, 1880-1892: a Study in Constructive Unionism* (Princeton, 1963).

George Dangerfield, *The Damnable Question: a Study in Anglo-Irish Relations* (London, 1976).

R.P.Davis, *Arthur Griffith and Non-Violent Sinn Féin* (Dublin, 1974).

Margaret Digby, *Horace Plunkett: an Anglo-American-Irishman* (Oxford, 1949).

Margaret Digby, *The Little Nut Tree* (Oxford, 1979).

Adam Duffin, *Thoughts and Facts for the Consideration of the Irish Convention* (Belfast, 1917) 20p.

Earl of Dunraven, *The Outlook in Ireland: the Case for Devolution and Conciliation* (Dublin, 1897).

Earl of Dunraven, *Past Times and Pastimes* (2 vols.) (London, 1922).

T.R. Dwyer, *Eamon de Valéra* (Dublin, 1980).

T.R. Dwyer, *Michael Collins and the Treaty: his Differences with de Valéra* (Cork, 1981).

T.R. Dwyer, *De Valéra's Darkest Hour, 1919-1932* (Cork, 1982).

John Eglinton (W.K. Magee), *Irish Literary Portraits* (London, 1935).

John Eglinton (W.K. Magee), *A Memoir of AE* (London, 1937).

Clayton S. Ellsworth, 'Theodore Roosevelt's Country Life Commission', *Agricultural History*, xxxiv (1960) pp.155-72.

Cyril Erlich, 'Sir Horace Plunkett and Agricultural Reform' in J. A. Goldstrom and L. A. Clarkson (eds.), *Irish Population, Economy and Society: Essays in Honour of the late K. H. Connell* (Oxford, 1981).

St. J.G. Ervine, *Sir Edward Carson and the Ulster Movement* (Dublin, 1915).

Darrell Figgis, *AE (George W.Russell), a Study of a Man and a Nation* (Dublin, 1916).

Elizabeth, Countess of Fingall, *Seventy Years Young: Memories as told to Pamela Hinkson* (London, 1937).

H.A.L. Fisher: *James Bryce, Viscount Bryce of Bechmont, OM*, (2 vols.) (London, 1927).

David Fitzpatrick, *Politics and Irish Life 1913-21: Provincial Experience of War and Revolution* (Dublin, 1977).

Moreton Frewen, *Melton Mowbray, and other Memories* (London, 1924).

A.L.H. Gailey, The Unionist Government's Policy towards Ireland, 1895-1905 (Ph.D. thesis Cambridge University, 1983).

A.L.H. Gailey, 'Unionist Rhetoric and Irish Local Government Reform, 1895-9', *Irish Historical Studies*, xxiv (1984) pp.55-68.

A.L.H. Gailey, 'Horace Plunkett and the Politics of the Non-Political', *Papers and Proceedings of the Society for Co-operative Studies in Ireland* , i (1985) pp.41-64.

Patrick Gallagher, *My Story, by Paddy the Cope* (Dungloe, undated).

O. St. J. Gogarty, *As I was Walking down Sackville Street: a Fantasy in Fact* (London, 1980).

J.W. Good, *Ulster and Ireland* (Dublin, 1919).

J.W. Good, *Irish Unionism* (Dublin, 1920).

A.P. Graves, *To Return to All That* (London, 1930).

Lady Gregory, 'Ireland, Real and Ideal, part ii', *The Nineteenth Century*, 44 (1898) pp.770-4.

Lady Gregory ed. *Ideals in Ireland* (London, 1901).

Lady Gregory's Journals (Daniel J. Murphy ed.) vol.I (Gerrards Cross) 1978.

Lady Gregory, Seventy Years: being the Autobiography of Lady Gregory (Gerrard's Cross, 1974).

Arthur Griffith, *The Resurrection of Hungary: a Parallel for Ireland* (Dublin, 1904).

S.L. Gwynn, *John Redmond's Last Years* (London, 1919).

Denis Gwynn, *The Life of John Redmond* (London, 1932).

M.B. Hanson, *Powder River Country: the Papers of J. Elmer Brock* (Kaycee, Wyoming, 1981).

D.W.Harkness, *The Restless Dominion: the Irish Free State and the British Commonwealth of Nations, 1921-31* (London, 1969).

Daniel Hoctor, *The Department's Story, a History of the Department of Agriculture* (Dublin, 1971).

Charles W. Holman, 'Sir Horace Plunkett's Co-operative Philosophy and Contribution to American Co-operation', in *American Co-operation 1937* (American Institute of Co-operation, Washington, D.C.) 1937 pp.5-19.

J.J. Horgan, *Parnell to Pearse* (Dublin, 1948).

Seán Hutton, 'Horace Plunkett agus Fótoghchán na Gaillimhe, 1901', *Studia Hibernica* 16 (1976) pp.158-74.

H.M. Hyde, *Carson* (London, 1953).

H.M. Hyde, *The Londonderrys* (London, 1979).

James Johnston, *Agricultural Co-operation in Northern Ireland: a History of the Ulster Agricultural Organisation Society Limited, the First Forty Years* (London, 1965).

Joseph Johnston, *Bishop Berkley's Querist in Historical Perspective* (Dundalk, 1970).

Thomas Jones, Whitehall Diary (K. Middlemas ed.) Vol. III *Ireland, 1918-1925* (London, 1971).

Carla Keating, Sir Horace Plunkett and Rural Reform, 1889-1914, (Ph.D. Thesis, University College Dublin, 1984).

Liam Kennedy, 'The Early Response of the Irish Catholic Clergy to the Co-operative Movement', *Irish Historical Studies*, xxi (1978) pp.55-74.

Kilteragh Visitors' Book (TCD Library)

J.G. Knapp, *An Appraisement of Agricultural Co-operation in Ireland* (Dublin, 1964).

J.G. Knapp, *The Rise of American Co-operative Enterprise: 1620-1920* (Danville, Illinois, 1969).

T.A. Larson, *History of Wyoming* (Lincoln, Nebraska, 1978).

Emily Lawless, *With the Wild Geese* (London, 1902).

Emily Lawless, *Ireland* (London, 1923).

W.E.H. Lecky, *A History of Ireland in the Eighteenth Century* (7 vols.) (London, 1892).

W.E.H. Lecky, *Clerical Influences, an Essay on Irish Sectarianism and English Government* (Dublin, 1911).

Joseph Lee, *The Modernisation of Irish Society, 1848-1918* (Dublin, 1973).

Anita Leslie, *Mr Frewen of England: a Victorian Adventurer* (London, 1966).

Shane Leslie, *The Irish Tangle for English Readers* (London, 1946).

R.J. Lucas, *Colonel Saunderson MP: a Memoir* (London, 1908).

Arthur Lynch, *Ireland, Vital Hour* (London, 1915).

Robert Lynd, *Ireland a Nation* (London, 1919).

F.S.L. Lyons, *The Irish Parliamentary Party, 1890-1910* (London, 1951).

F.S.L. Lyons, *John Dillon: a Biography* (London, 1968).

F.S.L. Lyons, *Charles Stewart Parnell* (London, 1977).

F.S.L. Lyons, *Culture and Anarchy in Ireland, 1890-1939* (Oxford, 1979).

E.E. Lysaght, *Sir Horace Plunkett and his Place in the Irish Nation* (Dublin, 1916).

M.J.F.McCarthy, *Five Years in Ireland, 1895-1900* (London, 1901).

M.J.F. McCarthy, *Priests and People in Ireland* (London, 1902).

R.B. McDowell, *The Irish Convention, 1917-18* (London, 1970).

M.N. McGeary, *Gifford Pinchot: Forester, Politician* (Princeton, 1960).

James McGurrin, *Bourke Cockran: a Free Lance in American Politics* (New York, 1948).

Edward MacLysaght, *Changing Times, Ireland since 1898 as seen by Edward MacLysaght* (Gerrards Cross, 1978).

P.J. Meghen, 'Sir Horace Plunkett as an Administrator', *Administration*, 14 (1966) pp. 227-45.

Rupert Metcalf, *England and Sir Horace Plunkett: an Essay in Agricultural Co-operation* (London, 1933).

James Meenan, *George O'Brien: a Biographical Memoir* (Dublin, 1980).

James Meenan and Desmond Clarke (eds.), *The Royal Dublin Society, 1731-1981* (Dublin, 1981).

W.L. Micks, *History of the Congested Districts Board* (Dublin, 1925).

Earl of Midleton, *Ireland, Dupe or Heroine* (London, 1932).

Earl of Midleton, *Records and Reactions, 1856-1939* (London, 1939).

J.C. Moody and G.C. Fite, *The Credit Union Movement: Origins and Development* (Lincoln, Nebraska, 1971).

T.W. Moody, *Davitt and Irish Revolution, 1846-82* (Oxford, 1982).

George Moore, *Hail and Farewell* (3 vols.) (London, 1911).

D.P. Moran, *The Philosophy of Irish Ireland* (Dublin, 1914).

A.E. Muskett (ed.), *A. A. McGuckian: a Memorial Volume* (Belfast, 1956).

W.G. Neely, *Kilcooley: Land and People in Tipperary* (Belfast, 1983).

George O'Brien, *The Four Green Fields* (Dublin, 1936).

J.V. O'Brien, *William O'Brien and the Course of Irish Politics, 1881-1918* (Berkeley, 1976).

William O'Brien, *An Olive Branch in Ireland and its History* (London, 1910).

William O'Brien, *The Irish Cause and the Irish Convention* (Dublin, 1917).

William O'Brien, *The Downfall of Parliamentarianism: a Retrospect for the Accounting Day* (Dublin, 1918).

Ulick O'Connor, *Celtic Dawn: a Portrait of the Irish Literary Renaissance* (London, 1984).

Cormac O'Gráda, 'The Beginnings of the Irish Creamery System, 1880-1914'. *Economic History Review,* 2nd series, xxx (1977) pp.284-305.

Standish O'Grady, *The Crisis in Ireland* (Dublin, 1882).

Standish O'Grady, *All Ireland* (Dublin, 1898).

Eunan O'Halpin, 'Historical Revision xx: H.E.Duke and the Irish Administration, 1916-18', *Irish Historical Studies,* xxii (1981) pp.362-76.

Eunan O'Halpin, 'Sir Warren Fisher and the Coalition, 1912-22'. *The Historical Journal,* 24,4 (1981) pp.907-27.

Seán O'Lúing, *Art O'Gríofa* (Dublin, 1953).

Michael O'Riordan, *Catholicity and Progress in Ireland* (London, 1905).

L.Paul-Dubois, *Contempory Ireland* (Dublin, 1908).

H.G. Philpott, *A History of the New Zealand Dairy Industry* (Wellington, 1937).

Gifford Pinchot, *The Fight for Conservation* (London, 1910).

Sir Horace Plunkett Centenary Handbook (Dublin, 1954).

'The Dismissal of Sir Horace Plunkett', *Spectator,* 27 April 1907.

'Sir Horace Plunkett and Mr. Birrell', *Spectator,* 12 June 1909.

'The Plunkett Scheme: its Reception and Prospects', *New Statesman,* 26 July 1919.

B.L. Reid, *The Man from New York* (New York, 1968).

Paul L. Rempe, 'Sir Horace Plunkett and Irish Politics, 1890-1914', *Eire — Ireland,* xiii (1978) pp.6-20.

C.C. Riddall, *Agricultural Co-operation in Ireland: the Story of a Struggle* (Dublin, 1950).

Henry Robinson, *Memories, Wise and Otherwise* (London, 1923).

Lennox Robinson, *Curtain Up: an Autobiography* (London, 1942).

Lennox Robinson, *Palette and Plough: a Pen-and-ink Drawing of Dermod O'Brien P.R.H.A.* (Dublin, 1948).

C.H. Rolleston, *Portrait of an Irishman: a Biographical Sketch of T.W. Rolleston* (London, 1939).

S. Rosenblum (ed.), *Against Home Rule: the Case for the Union* (London, 1912).

Theodore Roosevelt, *An Autobiography* (New York, 1924).

E. Rumpf and A.C. Hepburn, *Nationalism and Socialism in Twentieth Century Ireland* (Liverpool, 1977).

T.W. Russell, *Ireland and the Empire: a Review 1800-1900* (London, 1901).

E.F. Schumacher, *Small is Beautiful: a Study of Economics as if People Mattered* (London, 1974).

C. Seymour (ed.), *The Intimate Papers of Colonel House,* (4 vols.) (London, 1926).

G.B. Shaw, *The Matter with Ireland* (N. Greene and D. Laurence, eds.) (London, 1962).

G.O. Simms, *Tullow's Story: a Portrait of a County Dublin Parish* (Dublin, 1983).

Lionel Smith-Gordon and Cruise O'Brien, *Co-operation in Ireland* (Manchester, 1921).

Lionel Smith-Gordon and Laurence Staples, *Rural Reconstruction in Ireland: a Record of Co-operative Organisation* (London, 1917).

C.J.C. Street, *Ireland in 1921* (London, 1922).

A.T.Q. Stewart, *Edward Carson* (Dublin, 1981).

Henry Summerfield, *That Myriad Minded Man: a Biography of George William Russell 'AE'*, *1867-1935* (Gerrard's Cross, 1975).

Henry Summerfield (ed.), *Selections from the Contributions to the Irish Homestead by G. W. Russell — AE* (2 vols.) (Gerrard's Cross, 1978).

A.J.P. Taylor (ed.) *LLoyd George* (London, 1971).

John Turner, *Lloyd George's Secretariat* (Cambridge, 1980).

Katharine Tynan, 'Sir Horace Curzon Plunkett and his Work', *Fortnightly Review*, 74 (1903) pp.454-65.

T. de Vere White, *The Story of the Royal Dublin Society* (Tralee, 1956).

W.B. Wells, *John Redmond* (London, 1919).

W.B. Wells, *Irish Indiscretions* (Dublin, 1923).

W.B. Wells and N. Marlowe, *A History of the Irish Rebellion of 1916* (Dublin, 1916).

W.B. Wells and N.Marlowe, *The Irish Convention and Sinn Féin* (Dublin, 1918).

Thomas Wibberly, *Continuous Cropping and Tillage Dairy Farming for Small Farmers* (London, 1917).

Thomas Wibberly, *Farming on Factory Lines: Continuous Cropping for the Large Farmer* (London, 1917).

Burke Wilkinson, *The Zeal of the Convert* (Washington, 1976).

J.E.L. Wrench, *Struggle, 1914-1920* (London, 1935).

W.B. Yeats, *Autobiographies* (London, 1890).

Kenneth Young, *Arthur James Balfour* (London, 1963).

Calton Younger, *Arthur Griffith* (Dublin, 1981).

INDEX

275